MW00574035

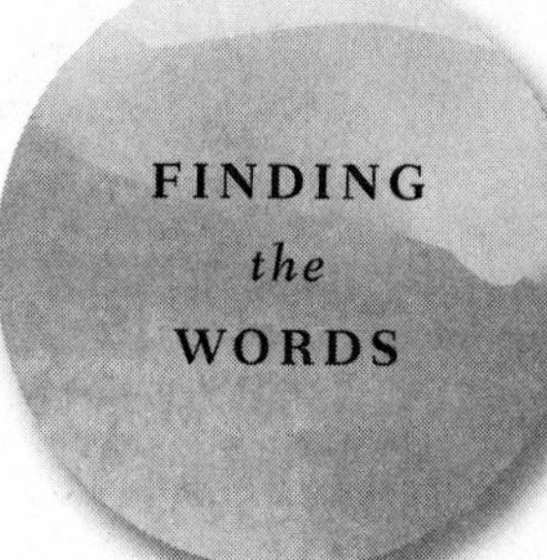
FINDING
the
WORDS

FINDING *the* WORDS

Working Through Profound Loss with Hope and Purpose

COLIN CAMPBELL

A TARCHERPERIGEE BOOK

An imprint of Penguin Random House LLC
penguinrandomhouse.com

Grateful acknowledgment is made to reprint the following:
"Ailey, Baldwin, Floyd, Killens and Mayfield (When Great Trees Fall)" from *I Shall Not Be Moved* by Maya Angelou, copyright © 1990 by Maya Angelou. Used by permission of Random House, an imprint and division of Penguin Random House LLC. All rights reserved.
"Sleep & Wake" from *Between Sleeping & Waking*, Lost Horse Press, copyright © 2020 by Albert Golbarth. Used by permission of the author.
"Geh bis an Deiner Sehnsucht Rand/Go to the Limits of Your Longing" from *Rilke's Book of Hours: Love Poems to God* by Rainer Maria Rilke, translated by Anita Barrows and Joanna Macy, translation copyright © 1996 by Anita Barrows and Joanna Macy. Used by permission of Riverhead Books, an imprint of Penguin Publishing Group, a division of Penguin Random House LLC. All rights reserved.

Most TarcherPerigee books are available at special quantity discounts for bulk purchase for sales promotions, premiums, fund-raising, and educational needs. Special books or book excerpts also can be created to fit specific needs. For details, write: SpecialMarkets@penguinrandomhouse.com.

Hardcover ISBN: 9780593421703
Ebook ISBN: 9780593421710

Printed in the United States of America
1st Printing

Book design by Lorie Pagnozzi

Give sorrow words. The grief that does not speak
Whispers the o'er-fraught heart, and bids it break.

—William Shakespeare, *Macbeth*

CONTENTS

A CRASH COURSE IN GRIEF

Sudden, Unexpected Catastrophic Loss

I always believed, deep in my heart, that my life would just keep getting better and better. It certainly felt that way as I moved through my thirties and forties watching my kids blossom and my marriage strengthen. I discovered my calling as a father and teacher, and each year I felt more confident with who I was and my place in the world. I didn't believe in god, or fate, or karma, but I did have an unshakable belief that whatever challenges I might face, "it will all work out in the end." That belief went hand in hand with the idea that "when one door closes, another opens," and "everything happens for a reason." I was sure any obstacles that I might encounter along the way would, with the right attitude, turn out to be opportunities.

And then, on June 12, 2019, at 10:45 p.m., all those sweet, naïve beliefs were shattered when a drunk driver crashed into my car and killed my two beautiful, charming, witty, talented, brilliant, and loving teenage children, Ruby and Hart. In an instant, my life would not ever "all work out in the end"; Ruby and Hart's deaths did not "happen for a reason"; and no more doors would ever open again for either of them.

My wife and I survived the crash. But our lives were destroyed. Our very identities were shattered. If I had to define myself, I was first and foremost Ruby and Hart's dad. Then Gail's husband, then a theater artist, a filmmaker, a teacher, a friend, a brother, a son, and so on. But all the other aspects of my identity were dwarfed by my role as Ruby and Hart's dad. Gail and I shared the parenting duties equally. We raised Ruby and Hart together as a team. Our days, like those of most parents, were filled with caretaking. We woke them up, made them breakfast, packed their lunches, drove them to school, made them dinner, helped them with homework, helped them navigate their social circles, took them to rehearsals, or Muay Thai, or to hang out with friends. And every night, we blew them a kiss and told them we loved them, and turned out their lights.

I worked from home for most of their lives, so I was the point person when it came to the kids' schedules. I coordinated most of the birthday parties and playdates, the doctor visits and dentist checkups. I was all in as a hands-on dad. And I loved it. I loved helping teach them to swim, ride bikes, climb trees, read, play cards, do pratfalls, and generally be ridiculous. And as they got older, my love for them only deepened.

So when they were killed, I was lost. Without them, all of life felt meaningless. I didn't want to be alive without Ruby and Hart. I felt like a scared little boy, all alone in a terrifyingly empty world. I didn't know how I would stay sane. Reality was literally too terrible to believe. I was untethered from life. For the first few months, I wasn't sure if I would be able to go on living without losing my mind. The enormity of their deaths was so awful it couldn't fit in my head.

I had plunged down into uncharted terror and I desperately wanted guidance. So even though it was hard for my traumatized mind to focus on words, I devoured books about coping with grief. I read the memoirs and the self-help books, books written by grief counselors and therapists, and by people who had lost children of their own. They all offered some kernels of insight, some useful piece of advice about grieving or finding purpose. But they all also, at some point, disappointed me. They presented grieving as this very mysterious and private process that I had to figure out on my own. They were short on specifics about what it means to mourn. What are we actually supposed to be doing? All the books went on and on about the importance of sharing my grief, but there wasn't a lot of guidance on how exactly to do that. How do I talk about my grief in a way that my family and friends can understand? How do I not scare them off with the intensity of my pain and rage? These books offered very few concrete examples of how I was supposed to get through the day-to-day agony of profound loss.

The first three years after Ruby and Hart's deaths were a brutal lesson in unwanted wisdom. In that time, I began to learn how to navigate my pain, lessen my suffering, combat my despair, access the love and support of my friends and family, and become even more connected to my wife. Most importantly, I learned how to hold close my thoughts, memories, and love of Ruby and Hart, without becoming completely overwhelmed by the pain and sadness of my grief.

I am not a therapist, psychiatrist, or licensed grief counselor. I don't have a PhD in behavioral sciences. But I have journeyed with an open heart to some of the scariest, cruelest, darkest places of human suffering, and I have come back with some hard-won truths about grief that I believe are worth sharing. I have also gained wisdom from talking with friends I've met in grief groups and from reading an inordinate number of grief books. By offering up both my raw experiences and the stories and thoughts of my fellow travelers, I hope to help others who are struggling with their own losses, and also open a window onto grief, a taboo subject that is often kept hidden away out of fear and, sometimes, even a sense of shame.

Grief Doesn't Have to Be a Mystery

The prevailing wisdom is that everyone's grief is unique, and each person processes their loss differently. Most therapists, grief experts, and books about grief all use the phrase "Everyone grieves in their own way." This can be a comforting thought in that it protects us from any sense of judgment. It implies that there is no "incorrect" way to grieve; there is nothing in particular that we should or shouldn't be doing as we mourn. And on a certain level, that makes sense to me. I certainly don't want someone judging my grieving or telling me how I should be mourning.

But there is a downside to saying we all grieve in our own unique way. It turns grieving into a mysterious process that we all must figure out on our own. It's a cop-out. The unspoken message is that we can't know or talk about grief because it is too big for us—too unknowable. But that is not true. We who have lost loved ones know a lot about grief. Those of us who are journeying through it often find that by talking to other grievers we discover many shared experiences and needs. There is a commonality to our struggles. Ultimately, I don't believe we all grieve in our own unique ways. Counterintuitive as it may sound, I believe the fundamental process of grieving is the same for all of us.

We each might *avoid* our grief in our own unique ways (through denial, compartmentalization, avoidance, distraction, drinking, drugs, exercise, isolation, misery, violence), but when it comes to actively grieving and processing our loss, we all need to give words to our pain, and that begins by talking about our grief and our dead loved ones *to other people*. We need others to bear witness to our loss. Most every society on earth has some form of public display of grief, some public ritual of mourning in which the griever shares their feelings of loss to their community. In order to process and integrate our incomprehensible loss, we need to share our pain, and have it be witnessed and acknowledged.

Grief Is a Communal Experience

The other problem with the idea that we all mourn in our own unique way is that it ignores the reality that grief is a communal activity. When someone dies, they are not just mourned by their parents, or their spouse, or their children, or their siblings. A death is like an earthquake. There is the epicenter of loss, but then the grief extends out in rings of devastation. It is so important that the people at the epicenter of that loss are connected with all the people who have been rocked by the same loss. They are on a journey together. Their grief is shared.

Prior to my own loss, I mistakenly thought of grief as some strange process in which the mourner sinks into solitary, overwhelming sadness for a while, until eventually they somehow manage to "snap out of it" and come back to life. I didn't understand that grieving is an active process that one does with other people, even though that act of sharing can often hurt. Grieving involves making difficult choices, over and over again. Grieving involves repeatedly leaning into the pain, in spite of our fears.

Talking about Grief

The need to articulate our feelings of loss is universal. And yet most people have no idea how to talk about grief, or what to say to the grieving. We don't know what words to use, because we rarely encounter any role models in our popular culture. In almost every case, films, television, and books depict people in grief as stoically choking back their tears and walking away to privately console themselves. Again and again, characters will be shown *avoiding* their pain, running away from opportunities to talk to other people about their loss. And as a result, people often assume that mourners *should* be left alone. So many of our friends and family have purposefully avoided talking to us about Ruby and Hart, because they were afraid of upsetting us. They worried that they might inadvertently trigger us, by reminding us of our loss. We had to explain to them all that they needn't worry, we were *already* triggered. We couldn't get more triggered. There was no moment in which we ever "forgot" that Ruby and Hart were dead.

There Are Words

By far, the most common phrase that gets offered up as condolence to people in grief is "There are no words." We encountered this unhelpful phrase over and over again. It was shocking how often people would say it, or email it, or write it on their condolence cards. Apparently, somewhere along the line, our culture teaches us that this is a benign, acceptable response to grief. I understand the idea behind it. It is saying that your loss is so overwhelming and tragic that no words are adequate to express my condolences. And for those who are frightened of saying the wrong words, it must seem like the safest of bets to excuse yourself from trying to say any words at all. Also, either subconsciously or by design, it acts as a perfect conversation killer. It immediately ends any chance of a dialogue about grief. It's telling the mourner that we can't really discuss their grief because there are no words that would be applicable. This empty phrase encapsulates all that is wrong in how our society handles grief. We need words to process our grief, and if the rest of the world is telling us, literally, "there are no words," then we are going to struggle and feel alone and abandoned in our pain.

The truth is, most of us don't know how to behave toward the grieving. Before I lost Ruby and Hart, I certainly didn't know. If the situation were reversed and a good friend of mine had lost a child or sibling or spouse, I am sure I would have said, "There are no words," and then hung back and waited for *them* to contact *me*, because I would have been too scared to reach out. And I am certain my fear would have caused us to drift apart. The problem is not with my friends but with our culture, which doesn't provide any guidance. It seems clear to me now that if mourners are able to reach out and tell their circle of friends and family what they need and which words are helpful and which are hurtful, these mourners might be better able to hold on to more of their community. In fact, by sharing their needs, they would be contributing to the larger education of our culture. They would be leading by example and helping to demystify grief in the process. This situation is, of course, unfair. The burden to reach out shouldn't fall on the shoulders of people grieving a terrible loss. We don't owe it to our community to educate them about grief. And yet, as challenging and unfair as it is, no one else can do it for us. And ultimately, I learned that the effort is worth it in the end, if it means we are able to get more support from the people in our lives.

In the following chapters, I give concrete examples of words that we used to get the help and support we so badly wanted. Gail and I often proactively reached out to friends and family and communicated our needs. We were clear and direct, and it almost always paid off. We were able to retain a loving community of supporters. None of our close relationships descended into bitter resentment. Some of our relationships changed and many others sadly faded in importance, but we lost no one to grief.

Delaying Grief

Many grief books will tell you that people grieve in their own time and that some people are just not ready to confront their loss. I disagree. I believe that everyone is ready to grieve. No one needs more time to get prepared to grieve. Or, rather, we *all* feel like we could use more time, but the reality is that grief is not something we control, and we gain nothing by trying to forestall it. The aching and the pain don't magically lessen over time if we're not processing our grief. Avoiding our grief for a few years doesn't then make the grieving any easier or more palatable. In fact, it can make it harder. It seems to me that we all might as well open ourselves up to the pain of our loss sooner rather than later. Ultimately, it will help us on our journey.

I know that no one wants to be told how or when to grieve. I risk alienating my readers by suggesting that everyone is ready to grieve now. But maybe a toothache is a helpful analogy. No one wants to go to the dentist to get a painful cavity filled. And yet the longer we wait, the worse it gets. And we all have to go to the dentist eventually—there is no way around it. So we might as well grab the first appointment available, no? There is a famous aphorism, sometimes attributed to Sigmund Freud, other times Anton Chekhov, that says "A person with a toothache can't fall in love." As long as we let the pain fester, we can't really focus on anything else. We can't be fully alive if we are busy trying to ignore our toothache, or our grief.

It may seem as though we can't bear the pain, but we can. After all, what's the worst that could happen to us? Facing our fears of grief can't possibly be more terrible than losing a person we love so deeply. And we've survived that. Ironically, avoiding our grief is what can actually hurt us the most.

Surviving Grief

The fact is, if you love someone, you will lose someone. Or they will lose you. Love and loss are inextricably linked. Grief is a universal human experience. We will all feel the pain of loss. We teach our children about love from the day they are born, and yet we keep death and grief shrouded in mystery.

In writing this book, I hope to remove some of that mystery. In one respect, what follows is an intimate journey of staggering loss. But I hope it's more than that. I hope that it can serve as a roadmap of our mourning, a guide to help others who are traveling the same journey I have traveled. I will share how Gail and I began the seemingly impossible task of processing the deaths of our beautiful children. Each month brought a new insight into grief, a new tool for surviving the pain, and a new way of honoring the lives of Ruby and Hart. Three years later, we have found a way not just to survive but to actively choose life. We continue to mourn and be rocked by waves of pain and aching, but we have also found a way to make room for other feelings such as joy, love, pride, and hope. We have found a way to think once more about a meaningful future and a life with purpose.

By offering detailed examples from our own grieving process, I don't mean to be preachy or to suggest that every griever needs to do exactly what we did. I merely hope to contribute to the conversation by offering our own experience of navigating profound loss.

Profound Loss

What do I mean when I use the term "profound loss"? It's a natural inclination to compare our own pain with that of others. It's hard not to think our own grief is so much more acute than anyone else's. But in this book, I don't want to be in the business of comparing loss or ranking people's grief. The distinction I am drawing here by using the term "profound loss" is not about anyone else's perception but your own. To my mind, a profound loss is when you lose someone who *you* feel is entwined intrinsically with your own identity. In other words, you define yourself partly in terms of this other person. As I mentioned earlier, my core sense of self is tied up primarily with being Ruby and Hart's dad. So to lose them is to suffer a catastrophic loss of my own identity. One of our central tasks as mourners is the very painful process of rebuilding our identity as we integrate our loss. We also need to redefine our relationship to everything and everyone in our lives, because each of our relationships changes after a profound loss. Parents who have lost children, people who have lost spouses, children who have lost parents or siblings—these are all profound losses. Some people's sense of self may be interwoven with a loving grandparent, or a particularly close cousin, or best friend, or fellow combat soldier, or first responder.

Whoever you have lost, I hope this book will speak to you. I believe the more honest and open conversations we can have about grief, the more we can come to understand this universal experience. If you are grieving, this book will not take away your pain. But hopefully, it will help you navigate your way through it and get the support you need from your community. I hope that the next time any of us encounter someone in mourning, we will avoid the phrase "There are no words," and instead be able to articulate our feelings and, in turn, make it easier for them to share their pain.

My Journey into Profound Grief

I always felt like I had a charmed life. I loved Gail and Ruby and Hart, and the family we had created. We loved spending time together, just the four of us. We loved our holiday adventures. Close-knit and kind, we supported each other. We protested for social justice together and played games together. Embracing our individual and collective strangeness made us feel special. That's not to say we didn't have our serious challenges along the way. Ruby struggled with depression and OCD and even suicidality. Hart struggled with preteen insecurities. I could get too controlling. I could lose my temper with Hart over his math homework and be too judgmental with Ruby about her time management. Gail struggled for a while with her own bout of depression. But I firmly believed that "it would all work out in the end."

And in fact, by January 2019, it felt like we had turned a corner. We had at last found the right medication for Ruby's depression, and thanks to the right treatment, her OCD was firmly under control. She had become an outspoken advocate for others living with mental illness. She was a true leader at her school, a bastion of kindness and wisdom. She was openly gay and proud of her sexuality, and her talent as an artist was blossoming. At last focused and productive, she was generating an astounding output of extraordinary artwork.

And Hart had grown from an anxious adolescent into a teenager of incredible kindness whose confidence outweighed his self-doubt. He brought laughter and joy everywhere he went. The source of nonstop hilarity and absurd humor, he was the true life of any party. And he had an extraordinarily high degree of emotional intelligence. Always at the ready to lend an ear or cheer people up, he had a deep understanding of other people's emotional needs. He made kindness cool. When I dropped him off at middle school each morning he would get out of the car and say, "I love you, Dad," not caring who would overhear. Even though most of his classmates would consider it a social faux pas, he was too full of affection to care.

Gail had also found the right medication and therapy, and her creative career had just jumped to a new level. In my career I had moved from the frustration of being a struggling independent filmmaker to the steadier and more satisfying role of a film and theater professor. And I was learning to be a better, more chill dad. I could see it paying off. We seemed to be growing even closer to each other as a family.

On June 8, 2019, while on a family vacation to Joshua Tree, we made an impulsive offer on a beautiful vacation home in the desert. Every year since the kids were babies, we would hike in Joshua Tree National Park, and we suddenly decided to throw our usual financial caution to the winds and buy a place of our own. We were all taken by surprise at our boldness. Hart captured it best when he said, "Are we really doing this?!" It felt to all four of us like we were entering a storybook period in our lives. We all started fantasizing about our wonderful future life, vacationing together in our favorite place.

And then, four days later, on June 12, on a trip back to inspect our new vacation home, our storybook life ended. At 10:45 p.m., our car was hit by a drunk driver going forty miles above the highway speed limit. This driver had a prior DUI. She had failed to appear at court for a subsequent ticket for driving with an open container of alcohol, and her license was suspended. That night, she was driving illegally, and drunk and high—no license, no insurance, and traveling at a recklessly high speed down a dark desert highway. Both Ruby and Hart were in the back seat, seat belts on. They were both killed instantly. One moment they were happily chatting away and in the next moment they were taken from us forever. We never saw the car coming.

The drunk driver T-boned us, hitting the rear passenger door. Ruby's door. At impact, my car was spun five hundred and forty degrees around. The drunk driver's engine was demolished and caught fire. Her car flipped, end over end, and landed back on its wheels, and didn't come to a stop for another one hundred fifty feet down the road. She never even touched the brakes. She slammed into us at full speed. Ninety miles an hour. Too drunk and stoned to even slow down. Gail and I were both briefly knocked unconscious. We came to, and found our children motionless in the back seat. They weren't breathing. Bystanders couldn't get a pulse. Gail and I staggered out of the car, in shock. We had no idea what had happened. A part of us knew they were dead, but we couldn't fully comprehend that reality. EMTs eventually arrived on the scene and performed CPR for some twenty minutes. For a moment, they detected a brief pulse from Hart, but then nothing. They never got a pulse from Ruby. They rushed both of them to the hospital, and later flew Hart by helicopter to a pediatric intensive care unit (PICU) nearby. The kind doctor there later told us he died from three life-ending injuries. My kids had no chance of survival in the back seat. They were officially pronounced dead the morning of June 13. But we say they died on June 12. They died on impact.

I was behind the wheel when we were hit. It was impossible for me to know that the distant headlights, far away on that dark desert road, were hurtling toward me at such an incredible speed. It was impossible for me to know that the drunk driver wasn't going to slow down one bit as she plowed toward us. Had I known, I never would have turned into the gas station. Had I turned two seconds earlier, or five seconds later, we would all be alive. I replay that night over and over in my mind. It's a terrible, excruciating burden.

I hope these details aren't too traumatizing to read. I include them for an important reason. Very early on, I learned to lean into the pain. I knew instinctively that if I shied away from the details of that night, I would be in danger of increasing my trauma. By actively facing down the worst night of my life, it helps me avoid some of the most egregious symptoms of post-traumatic stress disorder (PTSD): frequent nightmares, traumatic responses to cars and driving, and persistent anxiety. I also rely on detailed memories of that night to help me resist denial. Sometimes, when my life feels too surreal and unbelievable, I remember the events of the crash to remind myself that it is all true, and that I am not just having a terrible dream. It helps to ground me in reality. I find that the more I can stare at the horror with open eyes, and talk about it, the less of a hold it has on me. I am able to rob it of some of its power.

Leaning into Grief

This idea of leaning into my grief has helped me immensely. I find myself confronted on a daily, sometimes even hourly, basis with a stark decision: do I avoid thinking about Ruby and Hart and all that I have lost, or do I go ahead and open my aching heart to even more pain? Of course, I desperately want to avoid that pain. I'm always tempted to avoid looking at their pictures, or talking to their friends, or reminiscing with Gail about some sweet memory. I want to avoid, avoid, avoid. I want to protect myself because I've already suffered so much. But then I remind myself to take a breath and lean into the pain, because I don't want to hide from Ruby and Hart. I want to access all my memories of them. I want to look at their pictures, and feel the love we had for each other then, and the love I have for them now. I want to weep for them, for their loss, for their lives, which were stolen away. It seems to me that if I ever want to feel joy or happiness again, I have to embrace the pain. I don't get one without the other. So I lean into my grief. Not every time, mind you. I have learned that I need to pace myself and regularly recharge my batteries with some healthy self-care. Whatever loss you are surviving, this is the central challenge: how do we keep our hearts open to the pain, yet still allow ourselves to experience the joys of life as well? I'll explore this question of balance throughout the book and share what I have found to be helpful as I navigate life and my grief.

The Power of Sharing Words

I want to share one more detail from that terrible night. The compassionate PICU doctor who stood with us while we said goodbye to

Hart's lifeless body took us to a private room and had the courage to sit down with us. And in that awful moment, she did something wonderful. Dr. Janeth Chiaka Ejike said, "Tell me about your children." Even in my shock and anguish I knew how kind and smart that question was. It gave us a moment of *purpose* in our darkest hour. It gave us a loving task that honored Hart and Ruby and reminded us to think of them as they were when they were alive. Instead of wailing impotently, we got to share some beautiful thoughts about Hart and Ruby to this stranger who wanted to know about them. It is so strange how potent words can be in grief. How necessary. Right there, on the day of their deaths, this doctor taught me a valuable lesson about grieving, about finding the words, which I have never forgotten.

HOW TO USE THIS BOOK

Each chapter is organized around a central issue for people in grief: fear, pain, guilt, rage, and so on. I do not mean to imply in any way that these issues are sequential, or linear, or even distinct emotional states that I occupy one at a time. I did not progress from fear, to pain, and then on to denial, conquering each separate issue as I went. No. Not at all. I struggle with all these issues *every day*. They are all present with me all the time. Furthermore, they are all intertwined with each other. While the reader is welcome to jump straight to the chapter exploring the issue that is currently uppermost in their mind, the book is actually meant to be read sequentially. Some of the later ideas build on preceding ones.

In some respects, this book represents a radical approach to grief. The degree to which both Gail and I lean into our grief and pain may seem extreme or unusual. Very early on, we both adopted a very pro-active approach to our grieving. I believe it has served us well, but it may not be for everyone. I encourage you to embrace whatever parts of the book help you, and to ignore the parts that don't feel right for you. If you are grieving in a different way and it is working for you, please don't feel judged by me. The last thing we mourners need is to feel judged as we grieve.

I also want to acknowledge that some of the chapter headings are rather bleak. I'm offering an unvarnished look at profound grief. It's not an easy journey and there are no fixes for loss. I found that overly optimistic grief books that painted a rosy picture of loss were particularly frustrating to me. That said, I intend for this book to actually offer hope and a sense of purpose to those in grief. These bleakly titled chapters each offer concrete actions a person in grief can take to help them in their struggles.

I remember a particularly horrific night in which Gail and I fled from our very first grief group. It was only three weeks after the crash, and we just weren't ready to be in a circle of other people's pain. We staggered out into the parking lot and Gail doubled over as she wailed in raw agony, "What will we do? How will we live?" Those two questions seem central to grieving. What are we actually *doing* when we grieve? And how do we stay *in life* when so much of our heart doesn't want to live without the ones we've lost? This book describes what Gail and I did and how we stayed alive in the impossible aftermath of losing our two beloved children. I hope it offers some help and solace to others who are struggling with a loss of their own.

Taking Action in Grief, Journaling, and Rituals

At the end of each chapter, I provide some specific actions that you, the reader, can take on your journey through grief. It is my attempt to offer you something *to do* as you confront your own loss. I also include a number of journaling prompts. These prompts are not meant to be proscriptive; they are merely suggestions offered as help if you are feeling stuck. By no means am I proposing that you respond to all my journaling prompts! They are not meant to overwhelm, only to be a resource.

Beginning in Chapter Three, each chapter contains a specific mourning ritual that Gail and I created in the first year after our children were killed. I include these mourning rituals in the hopes that they spark your imagination and inspire you to create your own meaningful ceremonies to honor and celebrate the ones you've lost, and to honor your own grief.

CHAPTER ONE

Fear

The Terrors of Early Grief

After we kissed Hart goodbye for the last time in the PICU, the hospital put us in a cab and sent us home. It was an hour-long taxi ride of horror. Gail and I barely said a word, we were so overwhelmed with agony, confusion, and shock. Had we really just said goodbye forever to our two teenage children who were so brilliant and joyful and alive just a few hours ago? Our heads and our hearts could not process it. We were wrapped in denial. And then the cab pulled up to our home and suddenly we felt a new, terrible emotion: fear.

We were terrified to be home. At first, this feeling seemed to make no sense. Why would we be scared of our own house? The night before we had walked out of our picturesque front gate, framed by bright red and orange bougainvillea, full of excitement at the prospect of a spontaneous family trip out to our new desert home. And now, mere hours later, the prospect of walking back through that same gate was terrifying. We were filled with dread at the prospect of entering an empty, hollow home. A home that would forever be without Ruby and Hart.

Those first few days after the crash we had Gail's older sisters,

Betsy and Nina, take turns staying with us because we were too scared to be alone. When night fell, we became scared of the dark, scared to fall asleep, scared of the nightmares that would inevitably come. In my very first nightmare after the crash, I stood outside a Chinese restaurant, struggling in vain to find a dish on the menu that Ruby or Hart would like. I slowly realized the restaurant was empty and abandoned. As I stepped inside, I spotted Hart huddled beneath a table, terrified and alone. He couldn't see me. And at that moment I suddenly remembered that he and Ruby were dead. The image of him clutching the leg of the table, so scared to be dead, haunts me. I've had many dreams of Ruby and Hart over the past three years. Some of them are sweet; I've even gotten hugs and heard their laughter. But right in the middle of most of the dreams I suddenly remember, "Oh wait, no, you're both dead"—and my heart breaks anew.

Perpetual Panic and Desperate Searching

In those early days of grief at least a third of my mind was working on overdrive at all times, desperately trying to figure out a way to somehow rescue Ruby and Hart from death. It was as if, in my mind, I was stuck back in the car, replaying the moments before the crash, searching for some way to change the past and save them. As a result, I was perpetually on the cusp of full-blown panic, my mind and heart both racing. Every parental instinct was on high alert and in crisis, screaming, "You have got to save Ruby and Hart!" And yet there was nothing to be done.

A desperate need to "find" Ruby and Hart seized me. I scanned their computers for any shred of them in the form of essays or short stories. I desperately searched through all of Ruby's dozens of sketchbooks, devouring every drawing she ever made, trying to find *her.* I pored over all of Hart's text message threads, all of the videos his friends had made of him goofing around, trying to find *him* in the mix. It was almost as if I might be able to piece them back together if I only looked hard enough. And every moment I squandered meant that they were drifting further and further away, out of my grasp forever. That feeling of panic, and the desperate searching, both slowly faded as I chipped away at my denial.

Loneliness, Madness, and Meaninglessness

Novelist C. S. Lewis wrote, on the death of his wife, "No one ever told me that grief felt so like fear." Most people, when confronted with the death of someone close to them, are surprised to learn how terrifying early grief can be. We expect sadness and tears, but no one prepares us for just how frightening it can be. I think we mourners endure three essential fears: loneliness, madness, and meaninglessness.

Losing a loved one means that we endure a heartache that on some level will never end. We will always long for them, and the world will forever feel incomplete. The thought of living the rest of my life without ever seeing Ruby and Hart again feels terrifyingly lonely. There are moments every day in which I feel abandoned without them.

In the early days after the crash, Gail and I would fall into bouts of weeping that were terrifying in their intensity. Once I started, I wasn't sure I would ever stop crying. I felt out of control, with no hope of any consolation. My friend Eric captures the feeling well. After his daughter Ellie died of an overdose of fentanyl, "it was completely debilitating. It was like a dream, like a terrible hallucination. It was the biggest calamity, it was as if the earth had swallowed us up, it was as if my limbs had been torn from my body." Early grief feels timeless and bottomless. I thought it might drive me mad. Neurologist Dr. Lisa Shulman describes the disassociation that follows the severe emotional trauma of loss as being "a detachment from reality" and a "sense of incoherence" that makes us feel as if "we're going crazy."

This sense of being unhinged is exacerbated by a crisis of identity. If a significant portion of our own sense of self is built around our relationship to the person we have lost, then their death plunges us into a terrifying state of not knowing who we are anymore. Not only do we feel unmoored from reality and disconnected from our identity, but our very existence can seem meaningless after such a profound loss. All of my hopes and dreams were, in one way or another, connected to Ruby and Hart. They were my future. And now, without them, I felt I had no real purpose. It felt as though I had no reason to live.

The combination of loneliness, madness, and meaninglessness can be terrifying. It's no wonder I had the powerful urge to hide from my grief. Perhaps what makes grief even more frightening is the fact that grieving is the necessary but cruel process by which we banish our denial and come to accept the terrifying reality of our loss. There is such a strong urge to avoid engaging with our grief, and to instead foster our denial. It takes an incredible amount of bravery to willingly face our terrible new reality. It takes courage to grieve.

When Will This Get Better?

The thought that the rest of our lives would be this terrifying seemed literally unendurable. Gail and I would frequently ask our therapists and other mourners, "When will it stop being so awful? When will it ever get better?" They were all hard-pressed to answer, because in some sense, it never does. We will always ache and pine for the people we've lost. I wouldn't want it any other way. I don't imagine I will ever be done grieving. But the state of being in crisis, the acute fear and pain of early grief, does slowly pass. The constant panic and terror subside as we gradually process the reality of our loss. Remarkably, we slowly gain the ability to hold joy and happiness alongside our grief. Actively grieving allows us to move past helplessness and toward a place of reengagement with life.

Refusing to Be Afraid of Grief

Two days after the burial, I was in my living room looking up at four oversized photos of Ruby and Hart. These were the thirty-six-inch-by-twenty-four-inch prints mounted on foam core that our friend Yamara had made for the funeral service. We brought them home afterward and I taped them to our living room walls so that it would feel as though Ruby and Hart were still in our house. It was comforting to be able to look up into their smiling faces. Except this morning it wasn't. It was scary. I was seized by all the terrors of grief, and I looked away from their photos.

And in that moment, I had a powerful epiphany about grief. I realized that my fears had the potential to drive me away from my own children. I was in danger of running away from everything I had left of Ruby and Hart: my memories and thoughts of our lives together. Looking back up at the photos, I shouted out loud through tears, "I am not afraid of you!" I wanted Ruby and Hart's spirits to know that my love was strong enough to handle the pain. I would fight for our love to be felt in my heart, no matter how scary it was. My terror was not going to get in the way of loving my own children. In that moment I knew, in my bones, that I had to lean into my grief if I wanted to access every memory, every thought, every last ounce of my children's spirits.

The idea that I would not let my fear of grief hold me back from entering fully into the grieving process proved to be an essential realization. It colored almost all my decisions as I mourned Ruby and Hart. It also gave me strength. In my mind, it was the love we shared with each other that gave me my fortitude. So now, when I face down those same fears, it feels as if I am facing them down with Ruby and Hart by my side. Gail, Ruby, Hart, and I are doing it together. The four of us are grieving as a family. At least that's how it feels on the good days.

A Cautionary Tale

I had another reason for not letting my fears dictate my grieving process. Sadly, my mother-in-law served as a cautionary tale. Five years before Gail was born, her mother, Roz, lost a two-year-old child, Barbara, to pneumonia. In response to this terrifying, devastating loss, Roz decided that she needed to shield her two older daughters, Betsy and Nina, from her grief. While she and her husband and Betsy and Nina were out of the house, she had her brother go through their home and remove any and all evidence of Barbara's life. He got rid of her baby clothes, her pictures, her toys, and her crib. Afterward, no one in the family ever mentioned Barbara's name. It was as if the baby girl had never been. Roz believed it was the right way to deal with loss. It was partly a function of the times and partly, Gail believes, the way in which Roz tried to suppress her own grief.

When Gail was born five years later, she joined a family that was hiding a terrible, tragic secret. Gail didn't understand why her mom sometimes seemed so remote and depressed. It wasn't until Gail was seven that she first heard about Barbara, when her father explained why Roz periodically slipped off to the cemetery without a word.

When Ruby and Hart were still alive, Gail and I had talked about Roz's denial of Barbara's life and death. It seemed to us incomprehensible that she would attempt to erase all traces of her own daughter rather than publicly acknowledge her grief. Only now, I understood Roz in a whole new light. Her behavior made sense to me. I, too, wanted to flee from my grief. Part of me wanted to box away all of Ruby and Hart's photos, clothes, and toys, because it was agonizing to gaze at them now. But, of course, no one can escape from their own grief. Roz never for a moment forgot about Barbara. She undoubtedly felt the ache and pain of her loss every day. It was a burden she sadly chose to bear alone. By hiding Barbara's death, Roz also hid Barbara's life from the world. Gail and I knew we couldn't take that path. Having such a cautionary tale so close to home clarified how important it was for us to keep Ruby and Hart present in our lives.

A few days after I shouted "I am not afraid of you" in my living room, we called up Yamara and asked her to make four more foamcore prints of Ruby and Hart. We had those eight larger-than-life photos in our living room for the entire first year of our grieving. We had many more terrifying milestones ahead of us, but at least now we had a determination to face them, one at a time.

Saying Yes to Help (Saying Yes to Everything)

In the early days of my grief, my fears urged me to say no to everything. I didn't think I had the strength to see friends, or to go out into the world. I didn't want to face other people or do anything but cry. I wanted to hide away with Gail in our house of sadness and block out the rest of the world. But I knew that the urge to say no came from a place of fear, and I was determined not to be afraid of my grief. So in order to confront my terror, I overcompensated and said yes to everything. I made it a policy to accept *any* offer of help that came to me. This response was perhaps a little extreme, and not something everyone would want to try. And yet the clarity of saying yes to literally everything helped me in my early grief. I didn't have to think about it. If a friend suggested a walk, I said yes. If a friend offered a grief book, I read it. If someone offered to bring over food, I ate it. Gail and I together started seeing Ruby's OCD therapist. I started seeing my own therapist. I went skeet shooting. I tried out a fancy tea bar. I did grief yoga. I tried grief meditation. I started a grief journal. I went to a firing range and shot at targets with a Glock pistol. I met friends at the beach. I went to parks I had never been to before. I tried something new every week. I went to four different grief groups.

Every time I said yes, I really wanted to say no. No one wants to step out into the world and try new things after suffering a terrible loss. And I certainly didn't want to go to a grief group and share my pain. But I understood instinctually that I needed help. I didn't know how to grieve. No one had taught me anything about grief. I was lost and scared. And the stakes seemed incredibly high. It felt as though I were walking on the edge of a terrifying abyss, and I was willing to try anything to keep me from falling in.

Obviously, not everything I tried actually helped me. Grief yoga was frustrating. Grief meditation enraged me. (I didn't want to clear my mind of distressing thoughts, I wanted to think about Ruby and Hart!) Skeet shooting hurt my shoulder. But firing a pistol felt good.

Therapy felt good. Talking to friends felt good. The point is, I had no idea what might end up helping me in my journey through grief. By trying everything I could, I quickly weeded out what didn't work for me, and kept doing what did. Ultimately, it wasn't so much about finding enjoyable activities as it was about making the optimistic choice to push myself and trust that reengaging with life would eventually lead me back to meaning and purpose. It was aspirational.

Grief Groups

One of the most helpful things that Gail and I said yes to was joining a grief group. In the first week after the crash, we learned about Compassionate Friends, a national network that focuses on parents, grandparents, and siblings in mourning. We had two local chapters. Desperate for help, we joined both.

Each Compassionate Friends meeting begins the same way. We sit in a circle, with a box of tissues under every other chair. We go around the circle and say our name, the name of the child or sibling we lost, when they died, and how they died. Depending on how many people are in that circle, it can turn into a regular catalog of horror: overdoses, drunk drivers, suicides, blood clots, gunshots, drownings, aneurysms, medical malpractice, cancer, natural disasters, fatal accidents. It's an eye-opening array of death. But it's always the drug overdoses and the drunk drivers that kill the most kids. Those two categories alone take up three quarters or more of every grief circle I've ever been in.

Some people there are grieving a loss that occurred thirty years ago, while others are in fresh grief. As I mentioned, Gail and I attended our first meeting three weeks after the crash. We weren't quite ready to be in that circle of pain. We weren't yet ready to accept that these damaged human beings were our new community. But a month later we were. A month later we wanted to share with that circle and hear what others had to say about their struggles. We wanted to hear how they were surviving. We appreciated some of the participants' dark, dark humor. And there was comfort in the shared tears as well. We found solace in a community of people moving through a similar landscape of loss, and we developed close bonds of friendship with a number of them.

A few months later we also joined Our House, a Los Angeles–based organization that facilitates grief groups involving similar losses. Our group was exclusively parents who had lost children fourteen and older in a sudden, unexpected traumatic death that had occurred within the previous year. We all signed on to meet every other week for the next two years. This inspired structure meant that we had a great deal in common with the other eight grieving parents. Even though the time commitment was initially intimidating, going on the two-year journey together allowed us to form a powerful bond. Though our two-year commitment has ended, we remain in close contact and have regular reunions. My friend Lisa, whose son Hunter tragically died of an overdose of fentanyl, credits grief groups as one of the things that has helped her the most. "Being able to talk about the experience with people that understand the magnitude of the loss and the disorientation and the blaming. And then the shame. And the anger. That's been really helpful." Though Hunter died from his addiction, Lisa wanted to make it clear that he was so much more than that. "My son was creative, and loved to help people, and was talented. He had a very full life that happened to end too early."

Throughout this book I include insights and experiences of other grieving people. Each time, I share the name of their loved one and how they died. But Lisa is absolutely right, it's essential that we remember that all these beloved people are so much more than that. How they lived their lives, how they loved, is far more important than how they died.

Fear of Grieving

In one early Compassionate Friends meeting, a mother confessed that she carefully avoided even *thinking* about the daughter she had lost. Outside of grief group, she never mentioned her girl's name to anyone. She told us she didn't dare think about her daughter because she didn't know "what would happen." It was clear she was terrified that her grief would overwhelm her. I suppose she was scared she would either die or go mad. Her phrase "I don't know what would happen" stuck with me.

I wish I had spoken up and told her that I knew what would happen. If she allowed herself to think about her dead daughter, she would be convulsed with sobs. She would weep and feel desolate, despondent, and mad with grief and longing and aching. She would feel real genuine heartbreak, as though her heart were actually tearing apart. And while her weeping might feel like it would never end, it would end. Or at least, it would pause. Her body would give her a chance to breathe. And when her sobbing eventually stopped, she would probably feel raw, but a little better. She wouldn't be healed. She wouldn't have "gotten it all out." But she would have begun her journey of mourning. She would have started to discover how to find solace in the thoughts and memories of her beloved daughter instead of just pain and fear. And once she found the words to share her loss with the people in her life, she would have begun to grieve.

As David Kessler writes in *Finding Meaning: The Sixth Stage of Grief*, "Crying, just like everything else in this life, does end. If you can allow yourself to feel the pain in all of its depths and cry it out, you might feel very sad, but you would not be overwhelmed by it. Instead, that feeling will move through you and you will be done with it. I'm not saying that you'll never again feel pain over the death of your loved one. You will. But you gave that particular moment of pain its due. You didn't resist it and you won't have to keep reliving it."

There is no magic bullet here. Any progress we make in processing our loss is slow and incremental: for every ten steps forward, it's nine steps back. But it seems to me that each time we allow ourselves to think about our loved ones who have died, and endure the pain of that loss, we are giving ourselves opportunities to feel connected to them. We are making room for memories to come back to us. If we are not afraid of the painful feelings, we will have more access to the positive feelings. They go hand in hand now.

People Are Afraid of Mourners

Of course, it's not just the grievers who are afraid of their own grief. Everyone else is, too. Just as we were afraid to go through our front gate and step into our childless home, all of our friends and family were scared, too. I remember the night before the funeral, our friend Jesse came to our home to offer advice. Jesse's five-year-old son Gidi was killed in a boating accident three years earlier, in which she, her husband, and Gidi were all passengers. Jesse served as an invaluable guide to us in the earliest days of our grief. We told her we were concerned there might be a flood of strangers coming to our house to offer condolences, gawkers who just wanted to catch a glimpse of what catastrophic grief looked like. We didn't want our home filled with what Gail called "looky-loos." Jesse took our hands in hers and gently told us that no one wanted to come to a house with dead children. She assured us there would be no looky-loos. Anyone who had the courage to come into our home was only there out of love for us and for our children. It was a first lesson in how scared people might be of our grief, and the effort it took for them to even be with us.

Sharing Our Fears (Breakfasts with the Rabbi)

In the first few months after the crash, we had breakfast every Wednesday morning with our rabbi, Sharon Brous. We met each week at a French bistro and, over eggs and coffee, we shared the unfolding horror of our loss. Sharon sat with us in our grief. She overcame her own fears (this was the first time as a rabbi that she was called upon to counsel parents who had lost both their children) and asked us to share our struggles. We unloaded. We talked nonstop. We told Ruby and Hart stories, we described our aching and pain, we told her what it felt like to wake up every morning and weep, we shared our discoveries about grief, we complained about our friends and family who didn't get it, we complained about the annoying people in our grief groups, we shared our fears. Selfishly, we never asked her how she was doing or what was going on in her life. And she was okay with that. She paid close attention, asked good questions, and knew how to listen. She didn't try to fix our pain or cheer us up. She simply bore witness to our loss and accompanied us on our journey as best she could. We treasured those breakfasts. They were a gift to us, an opportunity to voice our early fears and be heard. Because they happened every week, they gave Sharon an opportunity to observe and reflect back to us how our grief was changing over time. Having a consistent witness allowed us to see that our grief was not static, and that we were, in fact, charting a course through this new landscape. Even though at times it felt like we were stuck, we were actually in movement. We were progressing through our grief.

Get Out of Bed Each Morning

Gail has a work colleague, Bob, whose son David died in a car crash many years ago. Gail was told that Bob preferred not to discuss his loss with colleagues, so Gail never asked him about it. But right after Ruby and Hart were killed, Gail was searching for any help she could find. She called Bob and asked about his experience of grieving his son. At first, Bob remained reticent, but Gail pressed him for any help he might offer her. He shared a simple piece of wisdom that has helped us both immensely in our grief: get out of bed each morning. He told Gail that no matter how tempted she was to stay in bed, no matter how unready she felt to meet the dawn, she would be better off standing up and starting her day.

I have read grief books that recommend staying in bed all day if that's how you feel. This advice is given in the spirit of encouraging you to take all the "me time" you need in your grief. I agree that we can be kind to ourselves and take a day off from our obligations when we are feeling underwater in our grief. But that is very different from spending the day in bed. Instead, I agree with Bob and would counsel anyone in grief to get out of bed every morning. We may feel overwhelmed with sadness, but staying beneath the sheets and marinating in that misery is not being kind to ourselves. Go ahead and cry. Weep, if that is where the morning takes you. But then get out of that bed.

Journaling My Grief

I'd never kept a journal before the crash. I think I had a snobbish notion that journaling was for wannabe artists or self-involved narcissists. And maybe a part of me was also afraid that if I tried my hand at it, my writing might wind up being disappointingly trite and embarrassing. It might expose a painful truth about my own intellectual limitations. But after the crash, I quickly realized that my old fears and preconceived notions didn't apply. A grief journal is not meant to be written "well" or showcase profound thoughts. Most of my journal entries are simply lists of what I did that day and some random feelings I had. No one would be interested in reading my journal entries. Sometimes I just write "fuck" a lot. Most of my entries are not articulate or inspired. But they help me organize my thoughts and feelings. They help pull me away from my formless sadness, and instead push me back toward life. Journaling helps me process the unimaginable.

The Value of Living an Examined Grief

My grief is so emotionally complicated and demanding that it's not easy to navigate. The more I explore and examine it, the more I am able to understand it, articulate it, and then process it. Which ultimately makes it less overwhelming and less unbearable. I've journaled about my grief, written a one-person play and a screenplay about it. I've talked to therapists, friends, family, and Gail about it. And I have written this book about it. Clearly, I feel a need to express myself in words. I might be an extreme example, but I suspect that even writing the occasional journal entry will be helpful for anyone navigating grief.

Numerous studies have confirmed the efficacy of journaling when it comes to processing grief or trauma. A leading proponent, Dr. James W. Pennebaker, has written several useful books, including *Writing to Heal: A Guided Journal for Recovering from Trauma and Emotional Upheaval* and *Opening Up by Writing It Down: How Expressive Writing Improves Health and Eases Emotional Pain.* Pennebaker argues that writing about troubling feelings and experiences can cause measurable biological changes that promote health and well-being. After citing numerous studies, he concludes, "Emotional writing is associated with general enhancement in immune function . . . better lung function . . . lower pain and disease severity . . . higher white blood cell counts . . . and less sleep disruption." Clearly, journaling about our grief can have measurable health benefits.

As mentioned earlier, at the end of each chapter, I provide a series of actions mourners can take as a part of their grieving process. After the actions, I then offer several possible journaling prompts. You can choose to respond to any prompt that speaks to you, or you can simply write whatever comes to your mind. Don't feel a need to respond to all the prompts! As you write, try not to judge or censor yourself. It's not easy to focus on our grief. It is almost guaranteed to initially bring up some pain, but in the long run it lessens our anguish. As Pennebaker points out, "Immediately after writing about traumatic topics, people often feel worse. . . . These effects are generally short term and last only for an hour or two . . . but the long-term effects are surely worth the momentary sadness. People who engage in expressive writing report feeling happier and less negative than before writing. Similarly, reports of depressive symptoms, rumination, and general anxiety tend to drop in the weeks and months after writing about emotional upheavals."

Journaling is particularly effective against our fears because, by voicing our own anxieties, by putting our darkest and scariest thoughts into words, we rob them of some of their terrible power. Emotional writing is a way of casting illumination into the shadows. Our inevitable feelings of guilt, shame, loneliness, and regret will feel less scary and overwhelming after we've written them down and shown them to the light of day.

Actions

- **Say yes to everything.** We don't know what is going to bring us support and solace until we try it. Our mind might tell us to say no. Fear, shame, exhaustion, and anxiety might urge us to withdraw from the world and reject offers of help or community. But taking actions and being in the world can play an essential part in our grieving process. Try saying yes.

- **Try something new each week.** Give yourself permission to have new experiences. It is hard to experience something novel without your loved one, but it is part of being alive.

- **Attend a grief group.** Get online and find a grief group near you. Some are generalized and some are for very specific losses. Try several to find one that works for you. No one wants to go to a grief group, and yet most who do keep going back. It is a safe space to share our experiences and find the words to express our pain. The others in that circle of loss understand what we are going through in a way that no one else can. As my friend Sharon said, "When you see people in the same city, in the same community, suffering like this, you feel you're not alone. You're not alone in the universe. It does help."

- **Find a therapist or grief counselor.** There is a freedom in talking to a therapist as opposed to a friend. They listen with no judgment and no personal relationship at stake. And good therapists have considerable wisdom when it comes to our issues of guilt, regret, shame, anger, and fear. Therapy doesn't have to be unaffordable. Many therapists work on a sliding scale; it doesn't hurt to ask. Check to see if your insurance covers counseling. Often a local university might offer low-cost or free counseling from their graduate students who are working under professional supervision. Community centers, hospitals, and places of worship sometimes offer free or heavily discounted counseling services. Your employer may have an employee assistance program that covers the cost of a limited number of sessions. Lastly, look online for nonprofit mental health networks or organizations. As my friend Eric says, "Anyone who has had a traumatic loss needs help. Professional help. For a while. It's just a given. It should be state-supplied. It should be part of the natural course—first you go to the cemetery and then you go to the therapist." (Important caveat—not all therapists are good. Some operate under the misconception that grief progresses in distinct stages, or that grief needs to be "resolved" according to a specific timetable, or that those in mourning are supposed to sever their emotional ties to the dead in order to move forward in life. If your therapist adheres to any of these ideas, please find a new one.)

- **Get out of bed every morning.** It's not easy to get out of bed. I never feel completely ready to begin another day without Ruby and Hart. But we're all better off facing our fears and starting the new day on our feet. Every chapter of this book has actions you can take in your grief. Some of them are about being kind to yourself, some are about honoring and remembering your loved one, and some are about building a community to support you. But all of them are going to provide more solace than staying in bed.

- **Begin a journal.** Ignore all the excuses and reasons not to that immediately leap to mind. Instead, just go ahead and start journaling anyway. I type my journal on my computer because my handwriting is slow and terrible. Gail journals by hand in Ruby's favorite brand of art notebook. It's yet another connection to our daughter. Inevitably, focusing in on our feelings surrounding grief and loss will bring some tears and anguish. It's not easy. Write through the pain. Journaling is an important way for us to process our grief and give it words. You don't need to journal every day and you don't need to journal for the rest of your life. Just journal when you need it.

Journaling Prompts

- Describe your fears. Put them down on paper even though they terrify you. Don't hold back.
- List all the brave actions you've taken so far in grief. Write about the strength that got you through the challenging things you've had to do: telling friends and family the terrible news, making the burial arrangements, planning the funeral service, and so on. Just getting out of bed and facing the world each day takes incredible courage.
- Describe the feelings you are having right now, no matter how inarticulate or repetitive it may sound. Your grief will feel different to you day to day and hour to hour. What does your grief feel like today? This hour?

CHAPTER TWO

Community

Not Alone

The morning after the funeral Gail and I woke up in our home that no longer felt like a home. "Just an empty building," as my friend James described his home after his wife Carolyn had died of cancer. We hadn't slept well. We had awful tasks ahead of us: taking Ruby's shattered computer to an IT company to see if any data could be retrieved, contacting health insurance and car insurance companies, getting hospital bills paid, contacting a lawyer, getting Gail to a surgeon to remove a piece of glass embedded in her lip from the crash, answering all those emails of shock and horror. But we didn't have the strength for any of it. After a while, we couldn't even read those emails, let alone answer them. Gail and I were simply reeling, in a fog of disbelief and pain. We had no appetite. Our family had to remind us to eat food and drink water. I remember hearing myself repeatedly emitting a sort of sigh mixed with a groan, and discovering that I was constantly rubbing my thumb and forefinger together in some kind of self-soothing compulsion.

And then, at sundown, people began appearing at our door bearing food, tables, chairs, and coolers. They were there to set up and prepare for Shiva, because in half an hour some one hundred fifty people would arrive. Our house and yard were about to be overrun.

Sitting Shiva

Gail is Jewish, and it was important to her that we raise our children as Jews. So shortly after Ruby was born, we joined our synagogue, Ikar. I insisted that if I was going to have to sit through sermons, the rabbi had better have something interesting to say, and Ikar's rabbi, Sharon Brous, inspired both of us with her fiery sermons on social justice, spiritual growth, and community. I had grown up in an atheist household, so my family culture had provided me no guidance on rituals surrounding death. Jews, on the other hand, have been developing and refining their mourning practices for millennia. So when it came time to mourn Ruby and Hart, I trusted in the wisdom of the Jewish tradition and did everything our rabbi suggested. Which is how I learned about sitting Shiva. Shiva taught me crucial lessons about the grieving process. It introduced me to the power of rituals and showed me how central it was to involve my community in my grief journey.

For the first seven nights after the funeral (excluding Friday night—you don't sit Shiva during Shabbat), Jewish mourners open their home to their community and "sit Shiva." In some ways Shiva resembles an extended Christian wake, but Shiva has a number of important practices and prohibitions that sets it apart. Typically, the mourner rends their garment at the burial (an action called *Kriah*), and then wears that same torn and unwashed shirt for all seven nights of Shiva. They are forbidden to groom themself. They are not allowed to shave or cut their hair. In fact, they are unable to even check their appearance, as all the mirrors in the house must be covered over with a cloth.

These rules made a lot of sense to me. I felt broken inside, and I wanted my outward appearance to reflect that. I wanted to shred my clothes and tell the world I was in agony. I didn't want to make myself presentable for anyone. Something as mundane as brushing my hair felt meaningless in the face of my catastrophic loss. Walking around disheveled in a torn and dirty shirt felt *right*.

Even though Shiva takes place at the mourners' home, they are not meant to act as the host. The mourners are under no social obligation to entertain or greet the people who come to their home. Traditionally, the mourners are supposed to sit on a simple low stool (hence the term "sitting Shiva") while their community brings the food, sets up the tables and chairs, and then cleans up afterward. In effect, the community hosts the event, so that there is no social burden on the grieving.

Traditionally, people are not allowed to speak to the mourner, unless the mourner speaks to them first. This allows the visitors to take their emotional cues from the mourner. If the mourner wants to laugh and tell funny stories about the deceased, the visitor can follow their lead. Likewise, if the mourner is weeping, or somber, the visitor can reflect that same emotional mood back. The mourner can simply sit in silence if that is what they prefer in the moment. Someone in fresh grief might behave very differently moment to moment, and they don't need someone else trying to change their emotions or strike a discordant tone. The rules of Shiva lend us that support.

Having our Ikar temple community show up for us and take care of us each night of Shiva was a powerful experience. No one was looking to be thanked or have their hard work even acknowledged by me or Gail. They just came to our house and quietly got the job done. I am now so grateful to them. At the time, in fresh grief, I found it very difficult to express gratitude for anything. It's hard to give thanks when you don't really want to be alive.

Sharing Our Pain and Our Love

For each of the six nights of Shiva we were expected to open our doors to a crowd of friends and family for prayers. At first, this rule felt like a punishment. Gail and I thought we just wanted to be left alone. We resented that our private space of grief was going to be invaded again and again each night. After a day of weeping, how could we face a crowd? And yet each night, when the appointed hour for Shiva came, and friends, family, and people from our synagogue filled our home, we discovered that we wanted this community to bear witness to our pain and loss.

Each night, after we said prayers, Sharon would turn to us and ask if we wanted to say some words to the assembled crowd. Often at Shiva the closest family members opt to stay silent, but our wise rabbi sensed that we needed to talk. Sharon encouraged us to speak each night. After sitting all day with our sadness, aching, shock, disbelief, and fear, we wanted to voice our feelings. We spent each day wrestling with our new reality, trying to make sense of the world of pain we now found ourselves in. When evening came it was a chance for us to share what we were going through with all the people who mattered most to us. That process of translating our grief into words and offering them to our community seems to me to be an essential part of the grieving process. The act of verbalizing our grief, and having it be witnessed by our community, was key to us moving toward acceptance of reality. I believe that Shiva lasts a full week because we needed so many nights of repeatedly publicly acknowledging Ruby and Hart's deaths in order to make some headway against our denial.

It was not just our pain that we shared. Shiva also gave us a platform to share Ruby and Hart stories. One night, Gail told the story of Angelique—one of the dozens of ridiculous characters Hart had created and performed for us. Angelique was a beautiful YouTube star who shared her makeup tips with an imaginary audience of millions. Hart, as Angelique, would strike a vogueish pose and drawl, "Hello, my fans! I know you all feel bad about yourselves because you can't be as beautiful and fabulous as me, so I'm going to show you the truth. I'm gonna get real with you. I'm gonna get vulnerable. I'm going to show you all how I look without any makeup on, so you can see the real me." Then he'd duck behind a wall and reappear wearing a full-headed, mascot-style pug mask, saying, "You see? Under all that makeup, this is who I really am." As Gail told this story, she held up the ridiculous dog mask and got a good laugh amid the tears. Later I heard her telling a friend, "I almost didn't tell that story, let alone pull out the pug head. It felt very weird doing prop comedy at my son's Shiva, but Angelique always made me and Ruby really crack up, and I wanted everyone to see how funny and absurd he was."

On another night, we read aloud the following very Ruby-esque document we found on her computer:

"Here Is a List of Things That Would Be Awesome to Know"

Romanian
Sword Fighting
Embroidery
Ballroom Dancing
Russian
Eskrima
JavaScript
How to Fly a Plane
Bagpipes
Mechanics
Animation
Etiquette
How to Drive a Boat
How to Pilot a Helicopter
Crochet
Lock Picking
Ice Skating
Nordic Runes
Gymnastics
Hockey
Magic!
Knot Tying
Scuba Diving
Archery
Writing
Avian Bone Structure
Braids
Lace Making
Stealth
Names of All the Countries
How to Clean Things
Manga Creation
Basic Medical Care
History
Norwegian
Arabic
Hang Gliding
Muay Thai
Drawing

What a sweet window into Ruby's singular brain. Some of the juxtapositions perfectly capture her duality as a nerdy craft girl/ bad-ass warrior: Lace Making and Stealth, Crochet and Lock Picking, Embroidery and Sword Fighting. And what is "How to Clean Things" doing on this list? And why does Magic get an exclamation point? Such a strange, beautiful mind.

Sharing these stories felt as though we were conjuring Ruby and Hart among us for a brief moment and allowing them to continue to give joy. We honored them as we all laughed at tales of their antics and escapades. Shiva felt important and *necessary*.

The Whole Community Mourns

It wasn't just Gail and I who needed to share stories. Our friends and family needed to speak as well. They, too, were steeped in a sense of powerlessness. They, too, felt passive in their grief and desperate for some way to show their love and support for Ruby and Hart, and for Gail and me. Shiva gave them an action. And it brought us all together. After Gail and I spoke, Sharon invited others to share stories. Ruby and Hart's teenage friends came forward in groups of twos or threes and spoke beautifully about our children. They shared sweet stories and funny stories, or simply shared their feelings of loss. I could see how important it was for each of them to say something publicly, even if it was only a few words.

It is easy to become overwhelmed in this moment. After all, there is so much to say, where does one even begin? How on earth can a few sentences ever suffice? How can we translate such a powerful emotion into mere words? I believe it is not so much the choice of words as simply the attempt. The *action* of speaking, of articulating one's feelings *to others* is actually what matters. No one who spoke at Shiva needed to be particularly eloquent or insightful. Just being honest was enough. Simply telling a story about Ruby and Hart was a way of communicating the depths of their love and loss.

My brother Christopher has said on a number of occasions that he is uncomfortable expressing grief in words. He felt unable to speak at the funeral and he struggled for what to say to me in my grief. He loved Ruby and Hart deeply and the depth of his love was precisely what held him back from speaking. By the fifth night of Shiva, I realized he had no plans to say anything aloud to the gathering. He was the only family member who had not spoken. By then, I appreciated the power of this ritual and I wanted him to take part in it.

I suggested that we could tell a story together, the two of us. It is one of my favorite Ruby and Hart stories. Years ago, we were all at my mother's cabin in the deep woods of Maine. Ruby and Hart were twelve and nine, and Christopher and I dared them to go out at night all by themselves, hike for a mile through the dark woods to a creepy Colonial-era graveyard, and do a grave rubbing by flashlight. We told them we'd give them each twenty bucks and they excitedly agreed. Ruby armed herself with a pointed stick for vampires and a magic potion to ward off werewolves. Hart held the flashlight and trusted in his big sister to protect them. They set off into the darkness, scared but thrilled. After about an hour passed, Christopher and I started to panic. What if they had gotten lost in the woods? What if they were shouting out for help and no one could hear them? We ran out after them but stayed in the shadows—we didn't want to cramp their style if it turned out they actually weren't lost.

Sure enough, about halfway to the cemetery, we spotted them in the distance, their flashlight bobbing toward us in the darkness. We separated and each found a hiding spot along the trail just as Ruby and Hart passed by, happily chatting away, unafraid of the dark and scary woods. From my hiding spot I howled like a wolf a few times, but they weren't particularly fazed. They kept up their banter as they continued down the road. My brother and I then secretly raced back to the house, taking a shortcut through the woods. We arrived just before the kids got there. Christopher and I were out of breath, red-faced and covered with sweat and brambles, but Ruby and Hart didn't even notice. They were too excited about their adventure, and proud of their successful grave rubbings, which they held aloft, triumphant.

Christopher and I told that story together, but in the end, he did most of the talking. He later told me with a grin that he realized if he didn't step up his game, I would steal all the best parts of the story. When push came to shove, he had no trouble finding the words. His hesitancy disappeared and he brought that story to life with loving details. Clearly, he had a need to share after all.

The Speechlessness of Trauma

In his studies on the neuroscience of trauma, Dr. Bessel van der Kolk found that when people relived their trauma, the left frontal lobe of their cortex, called Broca's area, was suppressed. This is our speech center. Trauma literally renders us speechless.

This inability to verbalize our feelings makes processing our grief that much more challenging. In order to emerge out from under our trauma, we need to use language. Articulating our pain and communicating our needs to our friends and family all become extraordinary challenges in this moment of inarticulateness. In grief it is harder than ever, and yet more important than ever, that we find our words.

The deaths of Ruby and Hart had rendered us all speechless with shock, horror, and anguish. Shiva brought us together and guided us toward language.

Lessons from the Mourner's Kaddish

Each night of Shiva our rabbi would say prayers and then Gail and I would recite the Jewish prayer of mourning, the Mourner's Kaddish, as the community looked on and said the occasional "amen" at specific moments. The Mourner's Kaddish is a short prayer that makes no mention of death or loss. It simply declares the greatness of God and wishes for an abundance of peace. The mourner is expected to recite this prayer every day for the first year after the death of a loved one, and then at specific holidays throughout the coming years. The mourner is forbidden from saying this prayer, however, unless there are at least nine other Jews bearing witness, creating a quorum of ten people in the room, or a minyan.

This rule is perhaps one of the most brilliant inspirations of Judaism when it comes to grieving. It requires the mourner to be surrounded by at least nine supportive people as they speak aloud their prayer of mourning. And they are required to search out these nine people on a regular basis as they journey through grief. Judaism declares it a mitzvah, or a blessing, to serve as a member of a minyan during the Mourner's Kaddish.

There were four essential lessons for me in the Mourner's Kaddish. The first was that we were asked to not turn away from our pain and loss. We would have to face that loss over and over again in that first year. Every week Gail and I attended an early-morning minyan and said the Mourner's Kaddish, and cried. Judaism asked us to repeatedly open our hearts to our loss. And we had to do so publicly, which was the second lesson. Having a community bear witness to our pain and grief was a key component to the Mourner's Kaddish. It could not be done alone, which meant we wept in front of other people. The ancient Jews who wrote the Torah understood that when we turn our attention to our grief, we should not be left on our own.

The third lesson was that grieving was active. We were tasked with performing rituals. Mourning was not just about feeling tremendous sadness, it was about taking action. We had to translate our pain into words and gestures. During the morning minyan service, several simple movements are built into the prayer. At certain words, the mourner must bow and raise their head. At one point they take three steps back, and then three steps forward. During the final stanza, the mourner customarily bows to the left, right, and center. It is not a lot of movement, but the important point is that our bodies are in motion. Properly performing the mourning service requires both taking physical action and vocalizing. Our voices have to be heard by the community in order for them to respond in the proper moments with their "amens."

The fourth lesson I received from the Mourner's Kaddish was that mourning involves celebrating life. The words of the prayer are not about pain or loss. The words are an uplifting celebration of the goodness of god and a wish for abundant peace and a good life. I interpreted this as a gentle directive to focus my thoughts on Ruby and Hart's lives, rather than their deaths. I was being encouraged to think about the beautiful memories I had of them, not just about the futures that were stolen from them. This was easier said than done. During the first months of grieving I was not ready to celebrate anything. But I understood it to be something I could reach for in the future. I could aim for the happy memories. I could aspire to not dwell in the tragedy.

God Is Love

As an atheist who spent a lot of time at temple with my Jewish wife and kids, I sometimes struggled with all the constant references to god. Those rabbis love to talk about god. In the Mourner's Kaddish alone, god is referenced thirteen times. It's hard when you just don't believe in an all-powerful deity. But I discovered a helpful trick. I replaced every reference to "God," and "He," and "Holy One" with the word "Love." It works incredibly well. Even some of the stranger references to god in the Bible (or Torah) turn out to have new beautiful meanings. Phrases such as "May He smite our enemies" translate into the charming idea "May Love smite our enemies." It's a nice visual: the most irritating people in my life suddenly becoming "lovestruck."

Sometimes, when I think the word "Love," I imagine it as a positive life-affirming force that courses through all beings. And sometimes I specifically imagine the love I shared with Ruby and Hart. Exalted and hallowed be Ruby and Hart's love. May Ruby and Hart's love be blessed forever and for all eternity. Blessed and praised, glorified, exalted and extolled, honored, adored and lauded be the name of Ruby and Hart's love. Amen.

The Last Day of Shiva

On the last day of Shiva, after the Mourner's Kaddish is recited, everyone accompanies the mourners on a walk around the block. It is a symbolic way of reintroducing the mourners back into the larger community. It may also be literally the first time the mourners have left their home in a week. It marks the passage from intense mourning to a new phase of grief.

It was a powerful experience to walk down our street with a crowd of people supporting us. We took up the whole road. It was a very public proclamation of grief. It was a community gathering together to stop traffic in the name of Ruby and Hart. And, once again, it was active. It demanded that we walk in our grief. The surest path out of despair is by transforming our pain and loss into physical action. Over and over again, I am struck by the power of this truth.

Not Knowing What to Say

Once Shiva had ended, and the ritual's structure was no longer there for our community, I found that our friends didn't know what to say to us. I was struck by just how often people were using the useless phrase "There are no words." When they came to visit us, they looked stricken and scared. They didn't know how to even greet us anymore. Typical salutations such as "How are you?" and "Great to see you" now seemed terribly inappropriate. Even worse for me, most of them were too scared to mention Ruby and Hart by name. They carefully avoided the topics of grief, or loss, or death. And they didn't dare mention their own kids for fear of upsetting us.

My friends were worried that if they said the wrong thing, they might cause us even more pain. And I think they were also scared by the possibility that we might break down and weep uncontrollably right in front of them. They had no idea what might possibly help us in our grief, and what words might accidentally "trigger" us. In their minds there were so many taboo subjects and emotional minefields that it made meaningful conversation impossible.

But Gail and I desperately wanted someone to talk to. We had learned from Shiva how important it was to share our feelings in order to process the powerful emotions that were coursing through us. We needed some way of removing their misconceptions and fears. We quickly developed what I called our "grief spiel."

Our Grief Spiel

We made it a practice of always pulling a new visitor aside and immediately delivering our grief spiel. The word "spiel" is Yiddish, meaning "a lengthy and extravagant speech or argument usually intended to persuade." In this case, we were persuading them of three important points. First, they needn't walk on eggshells around us. We explained to them that nothing they could say would trigger us. We were grappling with our pain and loss all day long, so mentioning the car crash, or death, or grief, or any other word or topic was not going to send us over the edge.

Second, we needed to talk about Ruby and Hart, and to hear people say their names aloud. It was actually upsetting and confusing when people *didn't* talk about Ruby and Hart. It felt bizarre and cruel when people would purposely avoid saying their names. In those first few months, how could we talk about anything else *but* Ruby and Hart?

Third, we told them that we also needed to talk about our pain and grief. We could talk about other subjects for a little while, but after say five or ten minutes, we needed our conversation to circle back to our loss. I described it as the emotional equivalent of being impaled on a spear. It would be bizarre to have a conversation with someone in which they didn't ask about the blade that's jutting out my back, or about the blood pouring down my chest.

My friends found our spiel extraordinarily helpful because it gave them ground rules that they could safely follow, and it also explicitly stated that not only were Ruby and Hart and our grief not going to be taboo subjects, but that we *needed* to talk about them. Our friends went from being terrified and tiptoeing around us to having actual conversations with us. Our spiel invited them to share Ruby and Hart stories and memories. And it made our friends into excellent listeners who asked helpful questions. We wanted people to ask us about our grief and how we were managing and processing this catastrophic loss. It was, after all, the only thing we were thinking about.

Altering the Grief Spiel

Early on, a lot of people didn't know what to say, so they fell back on sharing their own experiences of loss, as a way to connect to me. But since none of the people in my life had lost all their children in a car crash, their instances of loss felt upsettingly inappropriate. It was almost as if, by telling me their mother died last year, they were equating my unnatural loss of my children with the death of their elderly mother. I altered my spiel to include a sentence about not wanting to hear about different losses. My exact words were "I don't give a shit about your favorite cat who died, or your grandma who died, or your uncle who had a heart attack at sixty." I have a dark, blunt sense of humor, so this part of the spiel invariably got some much-needed laughs. But it was also effective. People stopped telling me about what it was like when their cousin died ten years ago. They stopped trying to relate to my pain, and instead just listened to me and bore witness. As time went on, I grew stronger and had more room for compassion. I dropped this part of my spiel when I was ready. Now I am able to talk compassionately to friends about all their losses and struggles.

Fear of Tears

It was about two weeks after the funeral when Gail and I realized friends would stifle their tears in our presence, and then discreetly sneak off to the bathroom to cry, hoping we wouldn't notice. The loss of Ruby and Hart was such a blow to our whole community that even just thinking about my family's loss and pain would send people to tears. They hid those tears because they knew that if they started crying in front of us, we would probably join in. They didn't want to add to our weeping. But they didn't understand that our relationship to crying had changed radically after the crash. Even though it hurt to cry, we welcomed it. It felt necessary. Crying jags had become a natural part of our day. In fact, if we went for too long without crying, we found ourselves spiraling down into a dark place of pent-up grief.

Rather than being upset by seeing friends and family cry, it actually gave us solace. It made our own tears feel more normal, like we were a part of a larger collective weeping for Ruby and Hart. It made us feel not so alone in our grief. We wanted the whole world to weep over the deaths of our children. So I altered my spiel to include the following: "I get a lot of solace crying with friends. I find it's a nice way to honor our love for Ruby and Hart. So don't be worried that you might cause me pain if you suddenly find yourself crying. It's okay. It actually feels good to cry."

One particularly close friend was always so bubbly and upbeat and talked so fast and cheerfully when she came to visit after the crash that it became hard for us to be around her. We found ourselves dreading her visits, even though we knew she loved Ruby and Hart deeply. We knew she was devastated and seeking therapy to help her in her grief. But around us, she was so buoyant that it was grating and exhausting.

Finally, I pulled her aside and told her that while I normally loved her effervescent and joyful spirit, right now it was too much for us. Her face fell as she told me that she needed to be relentlessly cheerful, otherwise she would fall apart and cry. I said I actually didn't mind crying, and she immediately burst into tears, and we wept together. Ever since then, it has always been good to see her and talk with her about Ruby and Hart, and to sometimes cry together.

Permission to Laugh

Gail and I like to make people laugh. So did Ruby and Hart. We were a family that appreciated a good joke. Gail, after all, has been a successful television comedy writer for the last twenty-five years. She and I both like to make inappropriate and crass comments. Hart loved a good sex joke, especially any use of the rejoinder "That's what she said." The dirtier the better. Ruby pretended to be the proper one in our family. She would react with shock and mock indignation. "Mom! Dad!" she would shout, going up in intonation at "Mom!" (in shock) and then going down in intonation with "Dad!" (moral indignation and disappointment). But Ruby was perhaps the most committed of all of us to the comic bit. She had a comic avatar named Sven who was a very shady Russian character. She would often turn into Sven on the phone and threaten us with her attack llama. At one point, she went so far as to create an elaborate fake website, called Sven's Rugs, devoted to selling overpriced rugs: https://svenrugs.wixsite.com/svenrugs. Sven's misspelled return policy is stated as "No Return or Refund. If you send Sven whiney email, letter, smoke signal, or messanger pidgeon about Sven's lack of such policy, no rug for you." On another page of the website, the return policy becomes "Sven not give refund. No retuns as well. Not come crying to Sven when Sven no give you discount. Sven has attack llama." On the website's FAQ page, she lists the Privacy Policy: "Sven respect's your privacy if you respect Sven's. Ex: You give Sven's location to authorities, Sven sends Jewish, Canadian, Russian, and Italian mafias after you. Sven has friends in high places. This makes Sven a target, but Sven can also make YOU target. Don't mess with Sven." It must have taken her hours to create this ridiculous website. And all just for a gag; just to make us laugh.

Part of how we as a family processed anything in life was through dark humor. Ruby and Hart's deaths didn't change that. If anything, our senses of humor got even darker. Sometimes a lot darker. I know some people have a hard time laughing after a profound loss. It can feel like a terrible betrayal. But Gail and I were making macabre jokes days after the crash. We needed to laugh in order to stay connected to our own identity, and deal with the incomprehensible reality we now found ourselves in.

Many of our friends were scared that any laughter on their part might be seen as offensive or insulting. It was important that we altered our grief spiel again to include the idea that laughter is okay, too. We needed to give people permission to follow our lead if we occasionally reacted with humor amid the horror of Ruby and Hart's deaths.

Humor as Avoidance

My friend Christopher's twenty-year-old son Charlie died in a freak skiing accident on a blue ski run in perfect conditions. Charlie's younger brother frequently employed dark, caustic humor as he navigated his way through grief. For example, when it came time for the painful process of choosing the inscription on the tombstone, he jokingly suggested "Exceptional human, mediocre skier." It was, as his father said, a solid joke. Very funny. But also very rough. Christopher struggled with how to respond. Was the joking getting in the way of grieving?

Several months later, his son shared the realization that he had been using humor to make the people around him feel more comfortable. But now he was tired of the constant joking. He had resolved to stop worrying about other people's comfort when it came to his own grief. He was going to stop making jokes and simply grieve on his own terms.

This resonated with me. I also sometimes find myself resorting to jokes in order to make others more comfortable with my catastrophic loss. But I don't want to be sidestepping my grief out of nervousness. So when is my humor a way of connecting to Ruby and Hart and our shared anarchic spirit, and when is it an avoidance of the discomfort? I think I just know in my gut. I think it comes down to understanding my own intention.

Developing Your Own Individual Grief Spiel

People in mourning can have strong opinions about how conversations ought to go. Certain pat phrases are infuriating to some mourners, while other mourners don't mind them at all. Some mourners want to use humor or even blunt, cynical sarcasm to face the horrors of their loss. Other mourners need conversations to be quiet and somber, and the sound of laughter feels cruelly disrespectful. Some mourners might want to talk about their faith while other mourners might take offense at uplifting spiritual beliefs. Some mourners might need to talk at length about the cause of death, while other mourners might feel a need to focus exclusively on happier memories.

As you work on your own grief spiel, it can help to think about what words or conversations upset you or left you feeling unsatisfied or resentful. Giving your friends and family guidance can be a way of nipping those unhelpful exchanges in the bud. Conversely, it can be equally useful to think about conversations you had in grief that went *well.* Notice which friends have a knack for asking the right questions, or treating your grief in a way that makes you feel seen and supported. Your grief spiel can be an opportunity to guide others toward that behavior.

Grieving is often treated as a taboo subject that is too sensitive to discuss openly. It can very quickly become the elephant in the room, which creates an atmosphere of shame and secrecy that further isolates those in mourning. Our grief spiels are a way of normalizing the experience and facilitating more helpful conversations.

Creating Bonds in Grief

As Gail and I attended grief groups and spoke to fellow mourners, we heard more and more stories of people who were going it alone, grieving without support. Many of these mourners had seen their community fail them, or simply fall away. Their bitterness acted as a warning to Gail and me. It was clear they were enduring another terrible loss on top of the death of their loved one. Shiva's communal rituals had shown us how important having the support of friends and family could be. I became committed to the idea of including as many friends and family as I could on my journey of grief. Even though I often felt too exhausted to socialize, I would fight the ever-present urge to withdraw, and instead I searched for ways to connect to my community.

One way in which we built up our grief support community was by asking friends to help with small tasks. Everyone who loves someone in grief is desperate for something *to do*, but it's often hard to know what will help people in mourning. Even though I am usually uncomfortable asking for help, I discovered that requesting small favors actually created a special connection between us and our friends. For example, by asking Yamara to help us get those foam-core photos made of Ruby and Hart, we built a bridge between us and created a new bond. Likewise, asking our friend Mark to take Ruby's shattered computer to a repair shop to extract files from her hard drive helped to include him in our postcrash life. Because Yamara and Mark had helped us in the early days of our grief, it made it that much easier for them to reach out later and check in on us. Once they had participated in our grief journey, even if only briefly, it gave them the authority to follow up with us and stay connected. It broke the ice.

It seems to me that most people who love someone who is grieving feel a certain amount of guilt. There is often the sense that they could have done more to help their grieving friend. And the more time that goes by without helping the griever, the worse these friends feel, and the harder it becomes for them to reach out. The bonds between friends are tested in such an excruciating way by grief. Asking for help, or accepting help that is offered, are ways of strengthening those grief bonds with our community. Take as many people as you can with you on this terrible journey by making it easier for them to accompany you in your darkest moments.

In some ways our community expanded after Ruby and Hart were killed. We connected with others in mourning, through our grief groups and friends of friends who had lost someone dear. People we didn't know from our temple accompanied us on this journey. They showed up for minyan services. They organized a meal train along with Hart's school, Campbell Hall. They signed up volunteers to bring us meals every night for the first three months after the crash. Strangers reached out to us, touched by our story. People who didn't know us, but who knew Ruby and Hart, connected with us and told us stories.

A Grief Spiel for Work

Returning to work can help us return to the flow of life. Work can give us meaning and purpose at a time when we may need it more than ever. Work can provide us with supportive colleagues. But work can also pose serious challenges to someone in fresh grief. Just like our friends and family, our work colleagues might not know what to say to us. They might avoid us or gossip behind our backs. We may feel even more alone than when we were at home. The question becomes, how do we honor our grief while at work? How do we integrate our new identity, as someone in bereavement, with our previous occupation?

When Gail and I both returned to work about three months after the crash, we decided we needed to develop some sort of grief spiel for our work colleagues. Gail works in film and television as a writer and director. She returned to work in August on the television show *Black-ish*. Gail was very nervous that her colleagues would think she was broken and no longer "herself." She was scared people would look away when they saw her, and whisper to each other behind her back about the car crash. She felt it was important that she give everyone her grief spiel at the very first meeting. She wanted to tell them all herself what had happened to Ruby and Hart so there would be no secretive tiptoeing around the subject. She came prepared. She wrote out exactly what she wanted to say. She knew she was ultimately going to improvise her speech, but it helped her to have it all written out in case she felt lost in the moment. She bought all new makeup because she wanted to look polished and not "like a ghost."

It was the start of the new season and the entire cast and crew of *Black-ish* gathered to say hello and share stories about what they had all accomplished over the summer break. There was lots of applause for how well the show did the previous season, and new writers were introduced, and then the writer in charge of the show said that Gail would like to say a few words. It got very quiet. She told them how Ruby and Hart were killed. And she told them she would be coming in part time and that they didn't need to worry about her if she wasn't there on certain days. She told them that she liked hearing Ruby and Hart's names and, since most of them had met the kids when they had visited her at work over the years, that she would appreciate any Ruby and Hart stories they might want to tell her. She told them they didn't need to be scared of her or her grief. She put a couple of jokes into her speech, just to reassure people that she was still herself, and still a woman capable of being funny. In reality, she didn't feel like herself. She had real concerns that she might never again be able to make jokes about families. But it was a leap of faith that if she told people to treat her like herself, one day she might actually feel like herself, or at least a version of herself that could still find humor and joy in creating a family comedy for television.

As she spoke, people nodded encouragement to her, and afterward they all applauded. She felt supported and loved. And in the end, she was gradually able to reconnect to her sense of humor and, once again, cherish opportunities to work with children on family comedies.

A few months later, Gail was scheduled to work with a group of colleagues who she didn't know nearly as well as the *Blackish* team. She was hired to direct a second episode of the television show *Grace and Frankie*. This time, she decided to email her grief spiel ahead of time, to make it easier on everyone.

Hello Beautiful and Talented Cast and Crew,

I'm so excited to be coming back to work with you all!

Before we all meet again tomorrow, I'd like to give you a heads-up about a terrible tragedy my husband and I suffered almost eight months ago. On a family road trip our two teenagers, Ruby and Hart, were killed when a drunk driver hit our car. Colin and I are somehow managing and surviving, largely in part to our amazing family, friends, and incredibly supportive work environments, which particularly includes you all for hiring me at a moment when, as you can imagine, some people are a little afraid of me. (There is no need to be, it's just another part of a very understandable response to overwhelming grief.) The truth, however, is that returning to this wonderful, life-affirming, funny, emotional workspace is the perfect balm for me and is also a great solace.

I find that sending an email ahead of time is a good way to share such excruciating news—it gives people time to react on their own, rather than having to navigate the first rush of hearing it from me in real time. I also want to let you know that it's totally okay to ask about my kids or how Colin and I are doing, and I may talk about them if it comes up organically in our days together. Their memory and their ever-presence is something that I'm choosing to weave into my life, as opposed to compartmentalizing. And telling stories about Ruby and Hart and our family is too wonderful to give up anyway. And that goes for hearing stories about your kids and family, too. I love it. Also, laughing and crying is all cool with me. No worries on that front.

Also, I've been finding great comfort in my faith: my rabbi and my synagogue community have been huge sources of support. If you're a person of faith, I hope yours helps you move through grief and pain as well. However, if your worldview includes the belief that my tragedy is part of God's plan, or that my children are in a better place, please don't share that with me. It will only upset me. I believe their deaths were senseless and random, and that there's no better place for them than here on earth with me. I hope you understand.

Okay, that's it. Wanted to let you know. Have a good night and I'll see you tomorrow.

Many thanks, and with great gratitude and love,
Gail

By emailing her spiel ahead of time, Gail was able to put her co-workers at ease, let them understand that she planned on talking about Ruby and Hart, and gave them permission to do so as well. She also gave them permission to joke and laugh, and preemptively stopped them from sharing their religious faith with her. Many of her co-workers emailed back their profound thanks. Her email broke the ice, gave some ground rules, and prevented grief from becoming a taboo subject.

When Gail got to work the next day, the first meeting with everyone went well for her. The effort and awkwardness of sending that grief spiel email paid off. That meeting could have gone terribly awry. Imagine how painful it would have been for Gail if she had been greeted by people saying, "There are no words." Or, even worse, if everyone had completely avoided all talk of Ruby and Hart for the entire day, because they were all too scared to remind Gail of her loss. Either way, Gail would have come home furious and hurt, feeling alone and abandoned. Instead, she received the kind of support and compassion that she needed.

Everyone's workplace dynamics are different. Each mourner has to figure out for themself what to say to their work colleagues, as well as how and when to say it. If it is a new work colleague, maybe you don't want the first thing they find out about you to be that you are grieving the death of a close friend or loved one. Maybe you would rather have individual conversations than send a group email. However you choose to handle your situation, I would encourage you to find ways of acknowledging your grief while at work. Finding opportunities to honor your loss and integrate your grief into all parts of your life will give you strength and stability.

Grieving with a Partner

There is a common misconception that profound grief drives couples apart. The death of a child, in particular, is thought to cause "most" unions to dissolve. There is a widely cited figure of eighty to ninety percent of all marriages ending in divorce after the loss of a child. Numerous people, including other grieving parents, have shared some version of these dire statistics with me. Setting aside the question of why people would feel compelled to tell me this ominous prediction in the first place—after all, how is that supposed to help me as my wife and I grieve?—it is important to clarify that those statistics are untrue. A high divorce rate among grieving parents is a myth.

As Stephanie Frogge explains in an online article for Tragedy Assistance Program for Survivors (TAPS), "Like many myths, nestled inside is a tiny kernel of information that snowballed into its current, unrecognizable form. One of the earliest books on grief and loss, groundbreaking at the time, was *The Bereaved Parent* by Harriet Schiff, published in 1977. It was the first of its kind, and bereaved parents everywhere found solace in the words of a woman who was also on the grief journey following the death of her ten-year-old son. Schiff was not a mental health professional but a former reporter, able to articulate the perspective of a bereaved parent.

"In the book's chapter titled 'Bereavement and Marriage,' Schiff writes, 'In fact, some studies estimate that as high as 90% of all bereaved couples are in serious marital difficulty within months after the death of their child.' Schiff doesn't cite her sources, and subsequent analyses of the bereavement research of that time do not clearly indicate where that opinion might have originated. Yet somehow this relatively innocuous statement about marital strain became a divorce 'fact.' People began to perpetuate the notion that ninety percent of all marriages end in divorce following the death of a child."

The reality is that divorce rates among grieving parents are lower than the national average. Two extensive studies conducted by Compassionate Friends, in 1999 and again in 2006, found that parental divorce rates after the death of a child were between twelve percent and sixteen percent, compared to a national average closer to fifty percent. And of those who did get divorced, less than half of them reported that the death of their child had contributed to the dissolution of the union. In fact, twenty-five percent of respondents felt that their marriages had strengthened in the aftermath of their loss. This makes sense to me. Gail and I certainly feel closer and more inseparable now. A friend once asked me if we fight a lot and I replied, "What would we fight about—who did the dishes? Our kids died. In comparison, nothing else matters."

Gail and I found ourselves on remarkably similar tracks as we mourned. At random moments we would discover that we were thinking about the exact same thing or experiencing the same emotional turmoil. But then, when we did find ourselves out of sync, that was okay, too. Sometimes it was actually helpful to be in contrasting rhythms. If I was feeling despair it helped to have her in a more optimistic state of mind, and vice versa. I think much is made of couples grieving differently when, in fact, it's not always a strain on their union. As my friend Jesse put it, "We're different people. In general, we handle emotions differently, so I don't know why we would handle grief the same."

My friend Gretchen grieves very differently from her husband Russ, and at first it *was* difficult for her. She had expectations that he would want to talk about their son Dana and their grief as much as she did, but he did not. "Russ is not as willing to delve into some of the history and some of the emotion and tears and stories. The difficult stuff. It brings up tears for him." But Gretchen discovered that when they were on long road trips, he was suddenly able to have those grief conversations that she needed. "I guess it is a safe place for him to have his tears on these long drives when we are on vacation. That's how it's always been for us, even when Dana was living. On road trips was when we got into our best conversations. It's the landscape—the wide open, the uninterrupted space." So now she looks forward to those car rides. And in the meantime, she has become comfortable relying on friends and fellow mourners to have the additional conversations about grief that she craves.

My friends Jen and James also approach grief very differently. As Jen describes it, "James gets a lot of support from being public. I have had to be comfortable with him wanting to be public. And he has to understand that I have my limit with that. I really want my privacy." But they respect their differences and, in fact, are grateful for their opposite energies. They feel they complement each other. According to James, their shared grief over the death of their son Luke has created a remarkable bond. "No one can touch what we have. No one can understand—nobody, not our therapists, our siblings—no one else. We are the closest we are ever going to get to another person."

Sex and Grieving

Sexual intimacy is another challenge grievers have to struggle with. When do we resume sexual activity? And how can we juggle arousal and grief? Let's face it, there is nothing sexy about loss. It can be hard to get back into a rhythm with a partner who may also be grieving.

When is the right time to even bring the subject up? After the crash Gail's torso had a series of vivid and disturbing bruises. Every night as she undressed for bed, I would, out of concern, chart the course of their healing. About a month after the crash, I found my gaze suddenly shifting from concern to erotic appreciation, which felt confusing and wrong to me. It felt like a betrayal of my grief. So instead, whenever she took her clothes off, I would look away. After a few nights of this, she caught on and confronted me, concerned that maybe I could no longer stand the sight of her body. She was scared that we might never have sex again. It is so easy to misread each other's cues in grief. Luckily, we were able to talk about our mixed emotions and guilt. We decided that having sex again was not a betrayal of Ruby and Hart, and that it was something we both wanted, just as soon as we could manage it emotionally. A few nights later something clicked, and we dove into bed with a ferocity that felt primal.

Making love that first time was an important step, but it's still not easy. As Gail puts it, "It's really hard to want to have sex. We are exhausted at night from a day spent managing our grief, we wake up depressed, and if we don't really hurry it along, we start to have intrusive thoughts. So when it happens it's intense, but there is very little romance or foreplay. It's more animalistic. It's a good release and relief, but it's hard to get your head in the game." It takes a conscious effort to prevent those intrusive, grief-oriented thoughts from entering our minds. In the early days we consciously labeled sex as "self-care." It might not have been the most erotic label, but it helped us to frame it as a healthy, necessary part of our grieving. It was a way of giving ourselves permission to have sex again.

If you are grieving the loss of your partner, this is all obviously much more complicated and fraught. But ultimately all of us grievers will have to find our own way back to our sexuality. If sexual desire played an important role in our identity before our loss, it is likely important to us to reconnect to it in some form or other.

Pulling Friends and Family Closer

It has taken my friend Gretchen a long time to reconnect to certain members of her community. Three years ago, Gretchen lost her son Dana to an accidental overdose at age twenty. A lethal combination of prescribed Xanax and unprescribed oxycodone caused him to stop breathing. Her pain and the circumstances of Dana's death led her to withdraw. "Our sidewalk is a place where people run and ride and walk—it's a busy place. So when Dana died, I didn't go in the front yard to garden anymore. It was just too hard. There were too many people with too many questions and condolences. I didn't want it to be, 'Oh, there's the woman who lost her son,' or 'There's the house where Dana lived.' Blech! I hated the negative attention. But recently, it shifted, and now I am comforted by the fact that people knew Dana. And the neighbors knew the wonderful Dana. They didn't know the addict. So there was a shift in the past few months to where I am just glad that he was known and loved by friends and families here. And I realize now it's not actually negative attention, it's love and support. And now I can appreciate it rather than fear the comment or question about Dana. Now I garden in the front yard. I wish I could have brought it on sooner, but I guess it comes when it comes."

As the scientist and journalist Stephan Klein writes in his book *The Science of Happiness*, "Both clinical and neurobiological experiments show [that] it's loneliness, more than any other factor, that causes stress. It's a burden on both mind and body. It results in restlessness, confusion in thought and feeling (caused by stress hormones), and a weakening of the immune system. In isolation, people become sad and sick." We are already grief-sick, why add on the stress of loneliness by isolating ourselves?

I don't mean to imply that it is easy to reach out to friends while we are in mourning. It's not. Most days I feel like I don't have the emotional bandwidth to talk to anyone, let alone reach out to them first. It can be hard to ask for help when we are in such pain. And even harder if those requests go unanswered or are rebuffed. I have had to learn that some friends and family are limited in their ability to engage in my grief. No matter how many times I tell them what I need, they just aren't able to accompany me in the way that I would wish. I have learned to try to accept those limitations. Instead of turning bitter and resentful, I try to take whatever I can get from each relationship. I try my best to stay open to anyone who has any love to offer me, Gail, Ruby, or Hart. Gail and I make sure to hold some memorial gatherings each year that are open to everyone who might come, no matter how limited their grief capabilities are.

Wisdom from Hart Campbell

My son Hart has left us with a beautiful piece of wisdom when it comes to reaching out to our community for help. When he turned thirteen, as part of his Bar Mitzvah (a Bar Mitzvah is kind of the Jewish equivalent of confirmation), he had to deliver a short sermon on a section of the Torah. Because his birthday was at the end of March, his section (or parsha) was Leviticus 12:1–15:33, also called Tazriah-Metzorah. This segment of the Bible is known to be particularly challenging to understand, as it goes into great detail on how to treat people afflicted with a bizarre skin disease, called tzaraat, which doesn't quite line up with any illness known to modern humans. In his sermon, Hart expanded the concept of tzaraat to include emotional illness. I have included an excerpt below from his sermon. If you replace "illness" and "sickness" with "grief" and "loss," Hart offers us grievers some inspiring wisdom.

> *What seems strange to me is that a person suffering from tzaraat must go out into the community and shout repeatedly, "Unclean, unclean!" At first, this commandment seems extremely cruel. Why must someone who suffers announce their disease in such a public way? It would make them feel self-conscious and more isolated. Wouldn't it be better to warn others quietly and privately? Seems like the person who made this rule doesn't understand what it feels like to be afflicted. And what even is tzaraat, anyways? A disease that can affect humans, houses, and clothes? This sounds like some really weird sci-fi stuff.*
>
> *Maybe we can get some help sorting this out from Cantor Ellen Dreskin. She writes, "Today, both physical and spiritual wounds or sores can create a metaphorical tzaraat, clogging our pores, scarring us, thickening our skins, deadening our emotions, and making it difficult for god's light to be revealed. Debilitating illness, guilt, weakness, anxiety, or depression can cause one to withdraw, to separate from friends and community—we feel ill, tarnished, weakened, confused and unworthy."*
>
> *I like Cantor Dreskin's interpretation of tzaraat. If we're thinking of tzaraat as an emotional disease, like anxiety, I think*

there's a big benefit to announcing your illness. People who are sick are often ashamed of their sickness. When we're anxious, we don't want to let others know because we're scared of them seeing us in a weak, bad light. We're afraid people won't want to be around us because they won't want to be dragged down by our anxieties and negativity. These fears make us secretive, which makes us not want to open up to our community to get help because we're ashamed.

The truth is that we as a society are suffering from an epidemic of anxiety. The National Institute of Mental Health reports that 38% of teenage girls and 26% of teenage boys either suffer from anxiety or have an anxiety disorder. And it's not just kids. In this room of three hundred people, one in every four have or will struggle with anxiety. Add in the political climate and the fact that most of us here are Jewish, I'd say it's more like one in three. We're all carrying around more bad feelings than ever, and most of us feel the need to keep it secret.

If we listen to this parsha and announce our struggles, whether they are physical or mental, we give our community a chance to support us and help us. Others who are suffering secretly may also come forward because they can understand it's okay to open up. So really, talking about illness helps the whole community, not just the afflicted.

When I first read this parsha, it seemed irrelevant for today's times. However, by digging deeper, I found some really spiritual truths in it. Everyone has his or her own version of tzaraat, whether it's anxiety or some other mental issue. So, the next time you are struggling or suffering, think about what I've said and consider opening up because it will make you feel better and it might help others, too. And that's definitely easier than running through the streets shouting, "Unclean! Unclean!"

Shabbat shalom!

Hart was thinking about his sister Ruby when he wrote this sermon. She struggled with OCD, and he saw firsthand how she suffered from the shame and secrecy surrounding her mental illness. Then he witnessed her recovery after she opened up and got help. His sermon was a beautiful gesture of love to his big sister. And now it is an offering of love to all of us who struggle with grief. Thank you, Harty, my wise, brave boy. I love you so.

Actions

- **Create your own "grief spiel."** Make a short guide to your grief needs that will put your anxious friends and family at ease, enabling them to give you the support you need. Be sure to modify your grief spiel as your needs inevitably change.
- **Preemptively reach out to friends and family.** Don't wait for friends and family to reach out to you. (Otherwise, there is the distinct possibility that many of them will keep "giving you space" forever). Be preemptive. Call them and ask for some small favor.
- **Find out which friends and family are comfortable sitting with you in grief.** Share what you are going through with them. Find a way of talking about your grief process.
- **Talk to people who have suffered a similar loss.** People who are struggling with similar losses have a lot in common. My sister-in-law, Nina, reached out to a woman who had also lost a nephew. Not only could they share their grief, but they also talked about the challenges of supporting a sister whose children have

died. They bonded over shared feelings of worry, guilt, and helplessness. It helped them both.

Journaling Prompts

- Practice writing out your grief spiel. What do you want people to know about how you prefer to talk about your loss? Be honest and keep it short. Chances are, your community is nervous to talk to you, because they don't want to remind you of the death of your loved one. How can you reassure them and guide them toward a more meaningful conversation?

- What are some of the frustrating responses you have gotten to your grief? What are some words or phrases that you find offensive or upsetting? What are words you might find helpful?

- How has your community already begun to honor your loved one? What are some other things they could do that might help you honor their memory?

- In the midst of your emptiness and loneliness, when are you able to feel the love and support of your community?

- Think about all the people in your far-flung community of friends and family and neighbors (include any friends from your distant past or any casual acquaintances who may have reached out to you after your loss). Who might be best suited to sit with you in your grief? Who might be a good listener? Who might be able to share stories of your loved one? Who can you go to for self-care? Or for a laugh? Who might you cry with? Who might be game to experience something new with you?

- It's hard to see friends whose lives have not been wracked by loss and grief. Write about your complicated feelings of resentment, envy, and anger. Don't judge your negative feelings.

CHAPTER THREE

Ritual

To Mourn Is Human

Fifty thousand years ago, in a cave in Qafzeh, in what is now Israel, early humans conducted burial rites for their dead. The bodies were anointed with ochre paint and buried in caskets, along with burial trinkets and food. An elaborate feast was held to mourn the dead. Funeral rites are one of the oldest cultural practices we have evidence of, predating even the earliest cave paintings. For as long as we have been human, we have felt the need to publicly mourn our dead in the form of some sort of ritual.

The Purpose of Mourning Rituals

Mourning rituals serve three main purposes. One, they memorialize the dead by speaking aloud the name of the deceased and paying tribute to their life. Two, they physicalize our loss, turning our pain into action by translating our grief into a concrete physical task that we must perform. Three, they demand that the community bear witness to the loss and grief. In a public ritual we must be seen and heard by the people in our life. Our pain is shared and validated.

Mourning rituals reveal that while our loved one is dead, they have not disappeared from the living. A part of them is still here within us and everyone who was ever touched by them.

Performing rituals of mourning can give us purpose and direction at a time when we lack both. Like stepping-stones or signposts, they guide us through the sorrow and loss. They pull our community to us and provide a structure in which our people can support us. Rituals of mourning take us out of our passive role as helpless victim, and instead call us to action. Every religion on earth holds rituals of mourning in order to help the grieving.

Jewish Rituals of Mourning

Confronted with having to mourn my children, I was grateful to be able to lean on our rabbi and the Jewish traditions of my wife's family. I figured the Jews had five thousand years to get this all worked out, so I embraced their rituals and trusted in their wisdom. After all, the rituals of Shiva gave me great solace and direction. But Shiva only lasts one week. Once the last day of Shiva had ended, Gail and I were plunged back into undifferentiated grief. Luckily, there was another signpost for us to aim for on our journey: marking the end of Shloshim.

Shloshim

Jews designate the first thirty days after the funeral as the period of Shloshim. During the rest of this first month, some of the rules of Shiva are relaxed, but other rules remain in place. Mourners are still not allowed to cut their hair or beards. And they are not allowed to listen to live music.

I was initially confused by this rule about live music. It didn't make a lot of sense to me. But then, seventeen days after the funeral, I went to see the play *Indecent*, by Paula Vogel. It's a terrific exploration of Yiddish theater in New York in the 1940s. It has a lesbian Jewish central character and contains powerful scenes about the Holocaust. I knew Ruby would have loved it, and so I went partly in her honor. But it was a mistake. It was painful seeing people performing live on stage. The passionate actors were so full of *life* that it was very hard for me to watch. I suddenly understood the edict against listening to live music. Music, theater, dance, and sports are all exuberant expressions of life, and people in fresh mourning might not be ready to experience them. I wished I had waited for at least thirty days before going to see the play. Once again, I was shown the wisdom of these seemingly odd ancient rules of mourning.

What was most helpful to me personally about Shloshim was the idea that we would be marking the end of it with a public ritual. Planning this ritual was a way of organizing our days in early grief. It helped give us direction and purpose.

Ritual: Marking the End of Shloshim

Thirty days after the funeral, in mid-July, we held a ceremony to mark the end of Shloshim. It is an important milestone in Jewish mourning, but there is no set ritual proscribed. Aside from saying certain prayers, mourners can mark the day however they wish. It had been twenty-three days since we last gathered our community together to honor Ruby and Hart. Gail and I realized that the end of Shloshim was a new opportunity to pull our community together, and, by extension, help hold us up. We took some of the lessons we learned from Shiva and crafted our own meaningful ceremony.

First, we had to decide where to hold it. We knew that the location had to have some meaning for our family. And we also knew that wherever we chose would from now on hold new meaning for us. It would become a special place to connect with Ruby and Hart's spirits. Our ceremony would sanctify the space.

The Los Angeles Arboretum

Gail and I decided to dedicate two trees at the Los Angeles Arboretum and hold the ceremony beneath them. We chose the LA Arboretum because we as a family had spent dozens of afternoons there over the years and had countless memories of wandering around the park. Ruby and Hart used to climb the trees in the bamboo forest and happily spend hours scrambling around the tangled branches of an amazing climbing tree in the African section. We'd stay at the park till closing, then head to dinner. While we waited for a table at the nearby Din Tai Fung restaurant, we would play cards. And after dinner we'd go to Yogurtland for dessert. We loved our outings to the park.

The last time we went was only a month before they were killed. I remember in the car ride home that night we had an absurd conversation about how dangerous the peacocks at the park could be. Peacocks were originally imported to the property from India back in 1879 and they have since flourished. The park now numbers over two hundred peafowl. Although strikingly beautiful, these birds are also known to be violent and belligerent. Many high-end black cars in the parking lot have been horribly scarred by angry peacocks who have viciously attacked their own reflections in the shiny dark paint.

Ruby googled "people killed by peacocks" and regaled us with a gruesome story of an owner being pecked to death. Ruby and Hart wondered how many peacocks it would take to kill me, and we all laughed as I described how I would fend off a swarm of angry peacocks by grabbing one by the neck and swinging it around to bludgeon the rest of its vicious peacock friends. I imagined I would take out about a hundred of the creatures before being overrun. Hart laughed and marveled that we were probably the only family in the world having such an absurd conversation. We all four felt so proudly in sync that night.

Gail and I went searching through the arboretum for two trees to dedicate to the kids. We went to the most remote corner of the park, looking for a tranquil, private spot. We found a stand of Engelmann oaks, beautiful trees that were each over seventy years old. On a hunch, we wandered into the middle of the stand and came upon two trees in a little clearing. High above us, their branches magically intertwined, as if the two trees had their arms around each other. At that moment, we spotted a large family of coyotes lope past and disappear into the surrounding woods. Gail and I took it as a sign that this spot was wild and untamed: it was the perfect place to hold the end of Shloshim. The park expedited the tree dedication process so we were able to get their names on the plaques in time for the ceremony. We invited a close group of our friends, and Ruby and Hart's friends. We formed a circle around the two trees. Our rabbi, Sharon, had everyone put their hands on someone who had their hands on someone whose hands were on us, and on the outer edge of the circle people placed their hands on Ruby and Hart's trees—linking all of us. We stood for a moment just listening to the sounds of the trees, the sounds of nature. We felt an incredible energy—a light, a life force—emanating from our circle of people holding so much love between us. Sharon gave a beautiful sermon.

She spoke about spiritual disorientation and what it means to have your whole world turned upside down so that you don't even know which way is north. And how when such a thing happens to pilots, the aviation manuals warn that our instincts may be off, so we must look to the control panel and trust our instruments. Even when they seem wrong, the instruments will help guide us back to solid ground. Sharon suggested that in this first month of acute grief Gail and I had come to trust the instrument panel of the Jewish tradition, through burial and Shiva, in minyan and now in Shloshim. She spoke about the idea that there needed to be containers created to hold the grief, again and again. Then a guitarist accompanied our friend Rebecca as she sang a song of aching loss. We shared stories about Ruby and Hart. We all wept. It was a beautiful, magical tribute.

But we also needed to share our pain and suffering. Gail talked about how a part of us wanted to hold the ceremony at the crash site, in the midst of the smoke and fire and twisted steel and broken glass. We wanted to share the horror and shock, too. Our rage at the terrible violence of their deaths is also part of the story.

It was difficult to get to those two trees. The arboretum was about a thirty-minute drive east of the city. And once you arrived, it took another twenty minutes to walk to the top of the hill. The fact that it took such an effort to get there is part of what made the ceremony so powerful. We asked people to make a pilgrimage to a site that now feels special to our community. Many of Ruby and Hart's friends continue to make the pilgrimage to those two trees when they feel the need to be closer to them, or to mark an important anniversary. By performing our ritual, we sanctified a beautiful space and tied it forever to Ruby and Hart's spirits.

The ceremony was a gift to our community and to us, but it was also emotionally exhausting. It took its toll on us. Gail and I opened our hearts to a lot of pain that night. But we had learned that our path through grief involved leaning into the pain. That night was another powerful experience that furthered my understanding of mourning rituals. I began to learn how to grieve with my community.

A Need for More Rituals

Many of our friends were not familiar with all these Jewish rituals of mourning. They marveled at how much time was spent in public mourning. They felt the power of coming to our house night after night for Shiva. They were moved by the ceremony to mark the end of Shloshim. Some complained that their own family or religious traditions of mourning simply stopped after the funeral service, or the wake. In their tradition, mourners were expected to get all their public grieving out at one gathering and that was it. Our friends all recognized the importance of having these communal rituals of mourning. Sharon was right. I, too, had come to rely on them to get me through my days.

But after the end of Shloshim, Judaism held no more rituals for the next eleven months, until the unveiling of their headstones. In terms of formal markers, or signposts for us on our journey of grief, there were no more. Sharon acknowledged it as a failing. It was clear to Gail and me that we were going to need more rituals in order to get us through the days and months to come. We were going to have to take the lessons we learned from Shiva and the end of Shloshim and build our own meaningful ceremonies in order to give us something to *do* in the face of our grief.

Turning Grief into Action

Studies of trauma survivors have repeatedly shown that those who were able to take some form of action, really any action at all, during their traumatic event were much more likely to have fewer and less severe symptoms of PTSD. As Dr. Bessel van der Kolk writes in his book *The Body Keeps the Score*, "Being able to move and *do* something to protect oneself is a critical factor in determining whether or not a horrible experience will leave long-lasting scars" (his emphasis). We who have suffered a profound loss are enduring our own trauma, and the more mourning rituals we can create in response, the more empowered we will feel.

Creating Powerful Mourning Rituals

As we began to think about designing more rituals to honor Ruby and Hart in the months ahead, I made a list of lessons I learned from the Mourner's Kaddish, Shiva, and Shloshim:

1. Don't mourn alone. Involve the community. They need to mourn, too, and we need our grief to be witnessed.
2. Put our feelings into words. Verbalize our grief. Over and over again. It doesn't matter if it seems repetitive, boring, or trite, grief needs to be shared. Repeatedly articulating the reality of our situation helps us combat denial.
3. Talk about the person who has died. Share stories about them with our community. Receive stories about them from our community.

4. Our role in these rituals is not to be a host. We don't need to be entertaining or take care of the people who are there to support us. We don't need to dress up or look our best or "pull ourselves together" for them. It's okay to be broken in public.

5. Have a physical component to our ritual. Have an action that needs to be performed by everyone present.

6. Grieving takes us outside the bounds of normal social interactions. Typical day-to-day rules of politeness don't apply because grief takes precedence over social niceties. We can go ahead and ask for what we need.

7. One, or two, or three ritual gatherings might not be enough. We might need many signposts to guide us. We might need many stepping-stones on our journey through grief.

Why Do We Have to Create Our Own Rituals?

It might seem counterintuitive or unfair that we are the ones who have to create these rituals ourselves. Aren't we burdened enough already with our grief? Why is it our job to design rituals and invite others to join them? Why can't someone else take care of this stuff? Unfortunately, no one else can design these rituals for us. Only the people at the epicenter of the earthquake of loss can be in charge. Only we know what sort of ritual will feel right. Besides, the power of a ritual lies in the action of performing it. We cannot be passive participants. The more we are involved in leading or organizing these rituals, the more we will get out of them.

I don't think it is accidental that there are no fixed parameters in Jewish custom for marking the end of Shloshim. I think it's actually unstructured by design. It forces us mourners to create a ceremony that is meaningful to us. It introduces us to the idea that we can construct our own rituals, and in a way, it invites us to keep on inventing more ceremonies in the future.

Mourning Rituals Don't Actually Make Us More Sad

Some people might imagine that performing these additional rituals would make me sadder and more depressed. After all, these activities remind me of my loss. It is certainly true that performing these rites will often bring tears to my eyes and aching in my heart. But by making myself available to the pain of my loss, I am also allowing myself to remember the good times I had. After performing one of these rituals, I find myself able to dwell more in the good memories of when Ruby and Hart were alive, and I become less fixated on the circumstances of their deaths. I become engaged in the story of their lives, rather than focusing on all the years that were stolen from them. These rituals actually lead me away from depression and despair. They help me process my loss and live more fully in the present. In short, they wind up making me feel less sad and more invested in my current life.

Some people might worry that if we spend too much time thinking about our loss, we will get stuck in the past. These people will encourage us to try not to think about the death of our loved one. They become nervous when we want to hold yet another ceremony, build yet another shrine. But the exact opposite is true. Mourners who try to "stop thinking" about their loss are the ones who are stuck in the past, unable to find a way to hold their memories and pain with them as they move forward in life. My friend Shirley's son Jon was shot and killed three years ago. She and her daughters created an ofrenda, or altar, in their living room, with photos of Jon, along with his soccer shirts, his hats, his rosary, a statue of his favorite saint the Virgin Mary, flowers, a glass of water that Shirley always keeps filled, and a candle she always keeps lit. Her relatives did not approve. Having it always so prominent in the living room seemed too painful to them. And besides, Shirley wasn't raised Catholic, so it felt wrong to them. "But I just tell them, first of all, it's my house. Second of all, it's something that makes me feel good to do. Even though it's a sad thing, it just makes me feel good. They thought I was just going to do it for a short while, like a memento, but no, my son is going to be remembered for my whole life."

Mourners need to integrate their loss in order to lead full lives. How on earth are we supposed to just "not think" about the death of a child, parent, sibling, spouse, or friend? That is absurd. Of course we are going to mourn them for the rest of our lives. That doesn't mean we can't go on to lead a full, rich life that can hold joy and delight and wonder. But in order to have all those good feelings, we also need to allow ourselves to feel the pain as well. We can't have one without the other.

Grief leaves us feeling out of control and powerless. We couldn't prevent our loved one from dying. Taking action by planning and carrying out rituals to honor the deceased is a way to give agency back to ourselves. Rituals are a way of giving structure and organization to the days, months, and years ahead.

Public Rituals

Public rituals allow our grief to be witnessed. They allow us to connect with our community and create sanctified spaces in which to mourn the dead. People who are on the periphery of the earthquake that is Ruby and Hart's deaths are often at a loss as to how to mourn their passing. They think about Ruby and Hart and feel weighted down by sadness and impotency. Providing a ritual is a way to help them as well as myself. And the most powerful rituals are ones in which the community of mourners gets to speak aloud about the dead. The incredible gift that I receive from such sharing is that I often learn something new about Ruby and Hart. People share stories that only they know, and these stories create "new" memories for me. These gifts are priceless.

We have had large crowds come to our public rituals, and I get solace in seeing so many faces in support of Gail and me. We are blessed with an expansive community of caring people, largely because Ruby and Hart were so beloved. But I know that some people in mourning don't have such a big community to draw on. Having large crowds is not necessary in order to perform public rituals. Sometimes a small intimate gathering of a handful of witnesses can be even more powerful than a big unwieldy crowd.

If, however, you feel like you have no one in your life who would support you in a mourning ritual, I encourage you to connect with a local grief group. Seek out other mourners and find community there. Don't grieve alone.

Private Rituals of Mourning

Public rituals take a lot of work and are not something I would want to organize more than a few times a year. But I need help navigating my grief on a daily basis. This is where private rituals can come into play. Private rituals are an active way for us to regularly commune with our loved ones. They are a way of weaving our grieving into our life. Here are a few actions I take that I consider to be my private rituals of mourning.

- On many days I wear some of Ruby's favorite T-shirts.
- Many evenings I wear some of Hart's pajamas.
- On tough days I wear a remembrance bracelet that Hart's friends made that reads "Hart & Ruby—Gone But Never Forgotten." These bracelets were sold to raise money for the Trevor Project, an organization that helps combat suicide among LGBTQ youth. We know Ruby and Hart would approve.
- When I travel, I buy an enamel pin from a local gift shop because that's what Ruby would have done. Just recently, I went to a Van Gogh exhibit and bought a pin of his sunflowers and added it to her collection.
- Every time Gail and I drink wine or a cocktail, we clink glasses and toast Ruby and Hart.
- Every time I jump in the ocean, I think about Ruby and Hart.
- Every time I eat a spicy chip or Cheeto, I dedicate it to Hart.
- Every time I hear "Hotel California," I dedicate it to Ruby.
- At night, as I pass by their old rooms, I blow them each a kiss goodnight.

- In the mornings, as I pass by their rooms, I wish them a good morning.
- Occasionally, I write them letters.
- I drink my morning cup of tea out of a mug they gave me as a present.
- I wear a custom baseball cap they were going to give me on Father's Day (they were killed four days before the holiday).
- When I buy plants for my garden, I always buy them in pairs—one for Ruby and one for Hart.
- I visit their graves and place a rock on each of their tombstones.
- I visit their two trees in the arboretum.

These private rituals are a way of connecting to my dead children. They give me an opportunity to take actions and physically express my love for them. They give me a moment to stop and think about Ruby and Hart and honor the place they will forever hold in my heart.

My friend Gretchen has a powerful private grief ritual. When she is driving in her car around her neighborhood, she talks to her son Dana. "I talk about memories, and sometimes I talk about current things that are happening, like an update. Sometimes I apologize. I talk to him about the sorrow and the sadness that he's not here. And sometimes I have to pull over because it gets too much, and I don't want to be behind the wheel when I get so emotional. I am in Los Alamitos and Long Beach, where Dana lived his life and spent so much time with me in my car before he got his license. We had a lot of conversations in the car. Now I am constantly driving by the many places that hold either memories of sad times or happy times. Whether it's the ocean or golf course or his school or picking him up when he locked his keys in the car. All those memories are all over my daily drive routine and I guess that's why I talk to him in the car."

My friend Jesse's family has a beautiful ongoing ritual to honor her son Gidi. "The week he died was the week of his fifth birthday, so we had already ordered all the supplies for his party. And one of the things we were going to do was a treasure hunt for jewels, little plastic jewels hidden around the house and yard. So we had a huge bowl of plastic jewels. Those jewels still live at his place at the kitchen table, and we make art out of them: hearts, and sunshines, and if it's raining, little umbrellas. And if it's a holiday, you know, maybe a menorah, or a New Year's Eve design. We take those jewels and turn them into things and it's constantly changing and shifting. And our friends or family who come over know they can always make art at Gidi's place with his jewels."

My friends Jen and James have a daily ritual that they perform in Luke's bedroom. A year after Luke died, they converted the space into a Zen meditation room. James explains, "The transformation of that room was very hard. It felt very, very lonely. Over a year had gone by and you can't bear to part with anything, but we had gotten to the point where it was an unbearable experience to go inside his room."

So James took out the bed and they filled Luke's shelves with books on grief, meditation, and philosophy. They added a plant and put cushions on the floor. "We wanted it to be sacred but continue to be Luke's space. Every morning I go in there and I do yoga and meditation and light candles and incense. And every night we do meditation in there together."

My mother developed a sweet private ritual every day for the first year after the crash. It was hard for her to talk about Ruby and Hart with me and to express the pain of her loss in words. But she wanted to connect to both me and the memories of her grandchildren. So every day she would search through her vast collection of photographs of Ruby and Hart, and she would carefully choose one that she thought might help me on that particular day. She would then take a photo of it with her phone and text it to me. It was a simple, wordless connection. Similarly, our friend Dave takes a photograph of a flower and texts it to Gail and me almost every day for the past three years. It is a wordless expression of love and support. It's his way of telling us he is thinking about us and about Ruby and Hart.

Tattoos

Occupying a space somewhere in between public and private, tattoos are a common way to commemorate our lost loved ones. Tattoos give us private moments of connection, while also serving as public proclamations of our loss. They can spark conversations with others about our loved ones and our grief. My friends Irwin and Sharon both got their first tattoos in their seventies, after their son Russell was killed by a reckless driver who was high on drugs. They each have tattoos of Babar the Elephant, which was Russell's favorite character. As Sharon says, "It is a constant reminder of him. Every time I look at it, I think it's Russell. Why do I have a tattoo? It's because of him. Part of my life inside of me." My friend Eric has a giant tattoo of his daughter Ellie's name across his forearm. My friend James has tattoos of his son Luke's art all over his body. Gail has Ruby and Hart's names, rendered in her own handwriting, tattooed on the inside of her wrists. I have two pieces of Ruby's art on my forearms. They are two wolves. One reminds me of Hart and the other of Ruby. I like looking at them every day. I like that they are inked on my body. And when people ask about them, it gives me another opportunity to talk about Ruby and Hart.

Mourning Rituals as Transgressive Rebellions

My friend Lindsey lost her older sister Casey when they were both teenagers, and one of the central mourning rituals Lindsey and her family perform is inspiringly transgressive. Growing up, Lindsey and Casey spent hours together drawing their favorite characters from *The Lion King*, and Casey's bedroom walls were covered with her versions of Simba. Casey had just gotten her driver's license and was thrilled to finally have a dedicated parking spot at her school. She only got to use it once, however, because on the second morning of the new school year, she died of a rare heart condition. After she died, Lindsey and her parents, using Casey's drawings as a reference, painted an enormous Simba mural on her parking spot. It was a beautiful memorial to Casey and a place for students to gather and remember her. A few months later, the school, in cold bureaucratic efficiency, painted over the mural. The school said that if they allowed one student to paint their parking spot, all the students would start painting their spots and they "clearly" couldn't allow that to happen. The following year, around the anniversary of Casey's death, Lindsey and her parents hopped the school fence after hours and repainted the mural. Which the school then painted back over. Thus began a yearly tradition in which Lindsey and her parents illegally broke onto the school grounds and "defaced" Casey's old parking spot anew with Simba the Lion in all his glory. Lindsey confided, "It's so out of character for my family because we're such rule followers. I think there's something rebellious that makes it feel really good. We go in the evening when the gate is closed and we're rebelling against the world and it's a small act, but it feels really big."

My friends Jen and James also have a transgressive ritual in honor of their son Luke. Close by their home is a footbridge over the Los Angeles River that Luke loved. His girlfriend had shot several videos of him skateboarding across that bridge. Now Jen and James feel Luke's presence there, amid the rushing water and birds, so they essentially took it over. They replaced the official city park's sign with one that reads "Luke's Crossing" along with a quote from Luke, "Time Never Stands Still." A friend designed a skateboard with Luke's handle, "Axel Lives," and James permanently fastened it to the bridge with ten locks. "I always used to talk to Luke about subversive art and guerrilla art. I know how to install stuff that is hard to take off." James also permanently attached three plaques dedicated to Luke. And now the bridge is strewn with dozens of memorial locks in honor of Luke. Two are dedicated to Ruby and Hart.

These transgressive acts remind me of the last night of Shiva when we all strode around the neighborhood, blocking traffic in the name of Ruby and Hart. Mourning publicly can feel defiant and transgressive. I want to break some rules in their honor! It feels as though the universe has betrayed our trust by allowing our loved ones to die, and mourning rituals give us a chance to fight back a little. We refuse to let the world paint over our loved ones as if they never existed. Even though Casey's school tries to blot out her mural with black paint each year, they never truly succeed. According to Lindsey, the faint outline of Simba is always visible, just beneath the surface.

How Many Rituals Are Enough?

When I ask other mourners about their rituals of mourning, some become defensive or look away as they guiltily murmur something along the lines of "I guess I did do something like a ritual after they died, but I only did it once," or "Yeah, I should probably be doing more rituals."

I think it's important to remember that mourning rituals are for the living, not the dead. They only serve a purpose in so far as we need them. For a while after the crash, Gail and I saw Ruby's OCD therapist, Dr. Jonathan Grayson. As he often told us, "should" doesn't belong in the conversation. Whenever we started talking to him about our guilt and all the things we *should* be doing, he told us to "stop 'should-ing' all over the place." Instead of saying "should," he suggested we ask ourselves, "Will it benefit me?" According to Grayson, "'Should' is the authority figure wagging their finger at us."

I believe you only need to perform more rituals if that is what you think will benefit you. So far, I personally have found rituals necessary to navigate my loss. But I don't imagine needing so many rituals forever. I don't mean to condemn any of us to a life of endless mourning rituals. Rituals are simply a tool, never an obligation.

Embracing Rituals of Mourning

In addition to the rituals that I outline in this book, you may also find inspiration from mourning rituals of your own cultural or ethnic background. Chances are your religion or your family or cultural tradition already has some rituals for mourning the dead. I suggest that you find out about them and embrace them. Examples are a vigil, a memorial service, a wake or a repast, a ritual washing of the body for Muslims; a Homegoing for African American Christians; thirteen days of mourning for Hindus; services on the third, seventh, forty-ninth, and hundredth day after the funeral for Vietnamese Buddhists; and so on.

Our modern society treats grief as a private activity, meant to be hidden from public view and not discussed. Yet historically, this is an aberration. For most of human existence we've held public rituals to honor and celebrate those we have lost to death.

In his classic treatise, *Western Attitudes toward Death: From the Middle Ages to the Present*, Philippe Ariès describes a gradual move from death being a very public ritual in the Middle Ages, involving neighbors, friends, family, food, and games, to the very private event that it is in today's modern society. Grief in the premodern era was open, emotionally unrestrained, and highly visible. He writes that prior to World War I, "the death of each person was a public event that moved, literally and figuratively, society as a whole. It was not only an individual who was disappearing, but society itself that had been wounded and that had to be healed."

In contrast, our contemporary culture emphasizes control of one's emotions, in which any lamentation occurs quietly, behind closed doors. "The beginning of the twentieth century saw the completion of the psychological mechanism that removed death from society, eliminated its character of public ceremony, and made it a private act. At first this act was reserved for intimates, but eventually even the family was excluded as the hospitalization of the terminally ill became widespread." Ariès continues, "There is a conviction that the public demonstration of mourning, as well as its too-insistent or too-long private expression, is inherently morbid. Weeping is synonymous with hysteria. Mourning is a malady."

By taking grieving out of the public sphere and turning it into a private illness, we have isolated people in mourning and stripped them of the rituals and community support they need to process their loss. As a society we have become uncomfortable talking about death. As a result, grief has become more mysterious and frightening.

I hope you are able to defy societal pressure and gather your community, no matter how big or small, and create meaningful public and private rituals to help you on your journey through grief. Please share those rituals with me at findingthewords.com. I would love to borrow some of your choices. I have a lot more anniversaries and holidays in my future. I could use some fresh ideas.

Actions

- **Find ways of sharing your feelings, no matter how trite or "unoriginal."** We don't need to be poets to share our words about our grief. We just need to share our truths. Write a eulogy (even if the funeral has passed). Speak at the funeral. Speak at the memorial. Speak to your friends.

- **Take advantage of any rituals of mourning your religion, culture, or family has.** Be an active participant in those rituals. Shape them to best honor your loved one.

- **Create a public mourning ritual of your own that will hold meaning for you.** Pick an important upcoming anniversary that will be hard for you: their birthday, the day of their death, your anniversary, Mother's Day, Father's Day, Valentine's Day, Christmas, and so on. Choose a location that is special to you or to your loved one. Invite supportive people from your life and from the life of your loved one. Give everyone a simple physical task. Ask people to share their words.

- **Create several private mourning rituals of your own.** Give yourself physical actions that somehow honor the memory of your loved one, or that open up space in your day to think about and connect with your loved one's memory.

- **Define your sacred spaces.** Think about the places you shared with your loved one. What are some of the locations where you found the most joy together? Consider making pilgrimages to those spots. Use them to connect with your memories and your loved one's spirit. What physical gesture can you make in each spot in honor of your loved one? For example, you might place a special stone, take a hike, have a picnic, jump in the water (if it is a lake or river or ocean), pour out their favorite beverage, eat their favorite snack, sing them a song, talk to them, and so on.

Journaling Prompts

- Brainstorm places that hold meaning for you and your loved one. What memories does each evoke?

- What are your associations with the word "ritual"? What are some rituals that have meaning for you personally? What rituals of mourning did you grow up with or experience as an adult? Are there elements of any of them that you might borrow in order to create your own?

- If your loved one were in charge of creating a memorial or a mourning ritual for themself, what do you imagine they would come up with?

- If the funeral has already passed and you weren't able to speak at it, write a eulogy now for your loved one. Share it with people you love.

- How do you feel about my idea that we mourners need our grief to be witnessed? Do you feel you need the people in your life to acknowledge your pain? How would you want them to do that? Do people sometimes acknowledge your pain in ways that you find grating or upsetting? Who in your community does it just right? Can you articulate what the difference is for you (it's not always so obvious or clear)?

- Write a letter to your loved one. What do you want to say to them right now?

- What does your grief feel like today?

CHAPTER FOUR

Pain

The House in Joshua Tree

The week before the crash, the four of us spent a wonderful weekend in Joshua Tree, a sweet small town in the high desert of the Mojave, about two and a half hours east of Los Angeles. We had such a terrific time that, on an impulse, we made an offer on a vacation home there. We realized that all four of us loved scrambling on the incredible rock formations of Joshua Tree National Park. We had gone there many times over the years, and the thought of owning a getaway home near the park was suddenly thrilling.

We were driving back to Joshua Tree the night of the crash because I had lined up meetings with contractors to see about building a pool and an extension on the house so that Ruby and Hart could have their own kids' bungalow where Hart could videogame and Ruby could have her own painting studio with views of the iconic rocks. It was going to be the vacation home of our dreams. The morning after the crash, I called the real estate agent and canceled the sale. Obviously. We assumed that we would never go back there again. How could we? It would be too painful.

And yet buying that house was one of the last things we did as a family. Joshua Tree held countless wonderful memories for us. How could we turn our backs on it now, when we needed those sweet memories more than ever? Three days later, I called the agent back up and told him we wanted the house after all. We realized our vacation home could now become a grief retreat for us, another place where we could feel especially connected to Ruby and Hart.

The problem was, in order to get to the house, we had to drive right past the crash site. There was no other way to get there. We would have to brave all the terrible traumatic memories of that night if we hoped to get to our desert sanctuary. It felt like the perfect metaphor for the grieving process: if we want to access all the sweet memories and feelings we shared with our loved one, we have to face the full pain of our loss.

Leaning into the Pain

As we moved through the first months of early grief, Gail and I were continually confronted by the pain of everything we had lost. Everywhere we looked, we were reminded of Ruby and Hart's agonizing absence. Every morning there was no one to greet and make breakfast for; every evening there was no one to kiss goodnight. Every spot in our house held their memories. So did every corner in the neighborhood. All our favorite restaurants and parks and beaches were suddenly hard to visit. Even our friends and family reminded us of our kids. Everywhere we turned, we were struck by the pain of our loss. A part of us wanted to retreat to our bed and shut the whole world out. A part of us wanted to die, rather than face the agony of our grief.

Our instincts tell us to run from pain. But what if, in the case of grief, our instincts are wrong? After all, the reason it hurts so badly is because we love them so much. The pain is from love. If we look at it that way, the pain can be understood not as a bad thing, but as a beautiful tribute. The love and the pain are now forever entwined. We can't have one without the other. If we run from the pain, we'll also be running from the love we shared. And what if, instead of simply enduring the pain of our loss, we actually seek it out? What if we *lean into the pain*, in order to bring ourselves closer to our loved ones?

The first time going back to Joshua Tree was terrifying. It took us two months to build up the courage. I had to ask my brother-in-law to drive. I was shaking, my whole body clenched, as he drove us. Gail warned us that at any moment she might need us to turn around and go back home. We drove in terrible silence. As we approached the site of the crash and prepared to pull to the side of the road, a large truck ahead of us suddenly hit its brakes and swerved to the right, almost cutting us off. John had to veer into the next lane just as traffic was whizzing past. His knuckles were white as he clenched the steering wheel. His arms were sore for days afterward.

There was a small shrine by the side of the road, put up by a local teenager. It was a wooden cross painted light blue that said "Beautiful Angels 06-12-19." We got out and stared at it. It was beautiful and awful. A gesture of love on the side of a hot, grimy highway, traffic racing past in the blaring desert sun. Is this really where our kids died?

Once we finally made it to the house, we weren't exactly relieved. It was hard standing where, only a few months earlier, we had stood with Ruby and Hart, full of so much hope for the future. But then we went for a hike in the rocks above our property and we felt the kids' presence. It was almost as if we could see them up ahead, scrambling over the boulders. They had never had the chance to climb these specific rocks, and yet it felt to me as though all four of us had been there before. Climbing over those rocks allowed us to connect with Ruby and Hart, if only for a few moments.

That first visit to the Joshua Tree house was hard. But we knew we had to get through that first time in order to slowly acclimate to the pain. Gail and I have since been back to the house in the desert many times. It did, indeed, become a sanctuary. It is a sacred place to us, where we feel extra connected to the kids. And every time we go, we drive past the crash site. I blow them kisses, and I ache for them, and sometimes I cry. But I am grateful that we were able to incorporate both the house and the site of the crash into the fabric of our lives. I am glad we ignored the impulse to never go back there again.

Every one of my connections to Ruby and Hart causes me some pain. I pay a price every time I look at a photo, or hear a favorite song, or recall a memory, or spend time with their friends. But it seems to me that over time, I am able to access more of the joy and feel less of the pain. It feels a little like exposure therapy. Ruby struggled with an obsessive-compulsive disorder (OCD). The primary therapeutic process used to treat OCD is to gradually expose the patient to their worst fears. The idea is to have the patient slowly become more and more comfortable tolerating their own distress. Over time, the patient essentially grows less fearful of their own fears. By repeatedly exposing myself to the emotional pain of my grief, I have grown less fearful of it.

It's often said that time heals all wounds. I think that's bullshit. But my relationship to the pain of this wound has definitely changed. A wise friend of ours suggested that maybe grief starts out as a terrible weight that presses down on us, but then, as we slowly process our loss, the pain shifts, slides down off our shoulders, and becomes something that moves alongside us. The pain never goes away, but it becomes more bearable. It accompanies us, just as the memories of Ruby and Hart will always accompany us. The pain and love go hand in hand. To quote C. S. Lewis, "The pain I feel now is the happiness I had before. That's the deal."

David Kessler writes in *Finding Meaning: The Sixth Stage of Grief*, "The word 'bereaved' has its origins in the Old English words *deprived of*, *seized*, and *robbed*. That is exactly how it feels when your loved one has been taken from you—as excruciating as if your arm had been ripped from your body. You've been robbed of what is dearest to you. The pain you feel is proportionate to the love you had. The deeper you loved, the deeper the pain. But you will find that love exists on the other side of the pain. It's actually the other face *of* pain."

Pain is a natural, necessary part of grieving. Normally, the body shrinks away from hurt because it is a signal that something should stop—stop touching that hot pan, stop stepping on that sharp spike, and so on. But in grief, the hurt is productive and necessary. It is a beautiful sign that our heart is working. We are processing a profound loss and mourning a loved one.

The Dangers of Avoiding Our Pain

Experiencing the pain of loss is a necessary part of the grieving process. It can't be sidestepped, or rushed past, or skipped over. There is, of course, a temptation to avoid it altogether, to numb ourselves with alcohol or drugs. My friend Eric stayed drunk for the first year and a half after Ellie died. "I drank myself almost to death. It wasn't a matter of trying to feel good, I was trying to feel nothing. And it worked. The time itself was a black hole. I don't remember much. I certainly didn't get any better. It hurt me. *Not* talking about my grief set me back." By the time he finally got sober and was ready to feel the pain and grieve, he had "such a high wall—this reinforced, half-mile-thick concrete bunker around my heart and emotions that I had built brick by brick to protect my soul and brain and everything else from feeling this agonizing pain. So later on, when I tried to access my feelings, I really struggled." Sadly, when we numb our feelings of pain, we are also numbing all our other emotions. As Brené Brown shares in her TED Talk "The Power of Vulnerability," "You cannot selectively numb. So, when we numb those [hard feelings], we numb joy, we numb gratitude, we numb happiness. And then we are miserable." Eric now regrets that he could have spent that first year and a half grieving and talking about his daughter, rather than avoiding the terrible pain.

Sonali Deraniyagala, in her memoir of loss, *Wave*, describes years spent in a haze of alcohol after the loss of her husband and two children in a tsunami. For five full years, she isolated herself from almost everyone in her past life, overwhelmed by her grief. By the time she finally talked with her children's friends, they had grown up and were out of sync with her grieving. A lot of opportunities for communal support had been lost to her. As Dr. J. William Worden writes in his *Grief Counseling and Grief Therapy: A Handbook for the Mental Health Practitioner*, "If [processing the pain of grief] is not adequately addressed, therapy may be needed later on, at which point it can be more difficult for the person to go back and work through the pain he or she has been avoiding. This is very often a more complex and difficult experience than dealing with it at the time of the loss. Also, it can be complicated by the presence of a less supportive social system than would have been available at the time of the loss."

In her book on grief, *Bearing the Unbearable*, Dr. Joanne Cacciatore recounts several harrowing personal histories of people who paid a terrible price for avoiding their grief. There are tales of addiction, abuse, and violence. Dr. Cacciatore writes, "Repressed grief ravages individuals and dismantles families; its tragic effects seep like groundwater into communities and societies. And the emotional economics of grief denied its rightful place are grim." Dr. Cacciatore's book, with its emphasis on the importance of facing the pain of grief, was a touchstone for Gail and me in our early grief. We ordered copies for everyone in our family and insisted they all read it. It was a way for us to communicate to them that we intended to talk openly about Ruby and Hart and about our grief. We weren't going to shy away from the pain, and we hoped they would join us on this difficult journey.

Masculinity and Grieving

Many men, and some women for that matter, were raised with the idea that it is best not to talk about our feelings. It is seen as a weakness to share our pain. Many of us were given the idea that when struggling with a powerful emotion like grief, strong people simply "handle it." In other words, they don't whine to others about their problems or their pain because they are tough enough to take care of those things on their own. What they mean by "handling it" is that they forcibly compartmentalize those upsetting emotions and then bottle them up and lock them away. They avoid their grief by pushing it out of their mind and "getting on with their lives." They try to stuff down their grief and hope that over time it just goes away. But of course, it doesn't go anywhere. No one can successfully stifle grief. Instead, it comes out in other, sometimes subtle, self-destructive ways: high-functioning depression, isolation, inability to connect to others, anger issues, alienation. No one can "get on with life" without first dealing with their loss.

But even if these men wanted to share their feelings, they might be hard-pressed to find a willing listener among their male friends. After the crash, Gail had a wide and diverse group of women she could reach out to for emotional support, but my circle of close male friends was much smaller by comparison. Over the years I had neglected a lot of my friendships, since I preferred the company of my wife and kids. And I think I am not alone in that. I think it is fairly common for American men to have drastically fewer emotionally open friendships than women. After the crash, I consciously tried to expand my circle of guy friends. I said yes to any of them who reached out. I said yes when I really just wanted to be left alone. I knew instinctually that I needed a change.

Having a planned activity with these men seemed helpful to me. We weren't meeting just to talk, we were meeting to take the dogs for a walk, or go to the batting cages, or to the shooting range, and so on. The talking happened in and around the activity. I had some good grief talks in diners and coffee shops, but some of my best talks with other men were either in the car or on hikes. I think it's easier to open up when both of us are facing forward, rather than across from each other over a table. I remember reading somewhere that it is often easiest to have meaningful talks with teenagers while driving for that very same reason. Maybe we're all still teenagers at heart, struggling to talk about the hard subjects.

Sharing one's grief is an act of bravery. Wading straight into the pain of loss is much more difficult and courageous than staying silent and pretending to be unaffected. The easiest thing to do is act tough and independent; the much harder choice is to stand before others and allow yourself to feel the pain. And ask for their help.

Pain versus Suffering

In her book on grief, *It's OK That You're Not OK*, Megan Devine makes a useful distinction between pain and suffering. In her model, the pain of loss is an unavoidable and healthy part of the mourning process. Suffering, on the other hand, is the unhelpful torment that often accompanies our grieving. In the suffering column, she includes when people judge our grieving, when people dismiss our pain, when we don't eat well or sleep well, when we spend time with toxic people, or when we punish ourselves with feelings of guilt. She writes, "Whenever possible, choosing to avoid those 'things that don't help' decreases your suffering, making you more available to tend to your own pain."

Another way of looking at it is to think of pain as our body's biological response to harm, whereas suffering is our purely psychological response. Our degree of suffering depends on how we choose to interpret and respond to that harm. In other words, we can make things a lot worse for ourselves if we're not careful. As the Japanese novelist Haruki Murakami writes, "Pain is inevitable. Suffering is optional."

I find myself thinking often about this distinction between pain and suffering. I try to be mindful of it as I mourn. For example, to my mind, weeping while looking at a photo of Ruby is healthy pain, but allowing my mind to spiral into regret at all the moments I could have been a better dad to her while she was alive feels like unhelpful suffering. Guilt and regret are natural and inevitable, but I don't need to dwell on those thoughts. I don't need to confuse being open to the pain of my loss with being open to the endless suffering of regret. I can let those thoughts of self-judgment occur but then pass on by. I know Ruby and Hart wouldn't want me to suffer. They loved me so sweetly. I can imagine them putting their hands on my shoulders and urging me to be kind to myself as I grieve. I owe them that.

Crying Is Not Suffering

Crying is part of the productive pain of grief. I never actually want to cry, but like exercise, I always feel better afterward, even if it hurts while I'm doing it. Crying doesn't magically heal me. I never "cry it all out" and feel done with my grief. But it definitely helps me. Sometimes it feels akin to the need to vomit when I am ill. The longer I fight the urge, the worse it gets. Once I give in and finally throw up, I feel a little better. I find that if I go for too long without crying, I descend into a dark place. It is almost as if my spirit is ill and the world has turned sour. It's always a little scary to let go and cry; there is always the fear that I might never stop. But the sobbing always subsides. Afterward, my spirit lifts a little and I feel more able to engage with the world.

Masculinity and Tears

I think men in general have a hard time crying. We're not used to making ourselves so vulnerable to the sway of our emotions. All our lives we've received the message that "real men" don't cry. We are expected to suck it up and stifle such signs of weakness. Even though

I know intellectually that such messaging is absurd, I can still find it hard to shed tears.

In the past, I would sometimes tear up at weddings, or an emotional moment in a movie, but I never really cried. I hadn't wept since I was a small child. Now I cry a little almost every day. And every week or so I genuinely weep. But I still mostly do it in private. I find it hard to cry in front of other people; it makes me feel self-conscious. I think we'd all be better off if everyone wept more openly.

On the second night of Shiva, Sharon shared a Hassidic idea that our bodies are full of water: "We are bones, muscle, blood, and then filled head to toe with water. There's no empty space inside us. So when something new happens, whether it's grief or joy, tears pour out as a way of making room for us to assimilate this new reality. Otherwise, it wouldn't *fit* inside our bodies—there would be no place for it to go. We don't want to make space to accommodate this new set of truths, this terrible grief, but we must. And so it's critical that we let the tears flow, not apologize for them or stifle them, because creating space for our grief is an act of love and grace."

Our tears are sacred.

Self-Care versus Suffering

It is hard to take care of ourselves while we mourn. After a profound loss, even a basic level of self-care can seem pointless. Why bother to shower, brush our teeth, or eat three meals a day? Why not stay in bed and try in vain to fill our empty void with sugar, pills, or alcohol? It can seem like a betrayal of our grief if we exercise or take care of ourselves. It can feel as though we are being unfaithful to our loved one if we allow ourselves to laugh or feel a moment of pleasure.

I put all these self-punishing thoughts into the category of needless suffering. Treating myself poorly does not honor the memories of Ruby and Hart. In fact, it directly interferes with my ability to grieve. Grief places terrible stress on the body and mind. It can block our appetites, disrupt our sleep, cause us to grind our teeth. Grief sickness can also compromise our immune system and leave us vulnerable to infections and viruses. Grief exhausts us. Now more than ever, we need to stay healthy. We need all the emotional strength and resilience we can muster in order to face the pain of our loss.

It's never easy to avoid being lazy and eating poorly, but we need to care for ourselves. Especially when it comes to drugs and alcohol. I was shocked by the amount of THC gummies and hard liquor that friends gifted us in the early days of our grief. It was enough to keep Gail and me stoned and drunk for months on end. But of course, getting drunk or high would just be us trying to avoid the pain of our loss. It wouldn't help us grieve at all. Gail and I are careful with how frequently we drink. As victims of trauma we know we're more prone to addiction.

Do Not Ever Drink and Drive

I can't mention alcohol and not say something about drunk driving. More than ten thousand Americans are killed every year in drunk driving crashes. I won't call them accidents, because they're not. They are the result of someone deliberately choosing to drive drunk. Ten thousand completely preventable deaths every year. Now, with Uber and Lyft, there is no excuse for it. Don't ever drive to a bar or a party if you plan to drink alcohol. Period. And don't ever get into a car with someone who is drunk behind the wheel. And if you are at a party and see someone who is drunk, please take away their keys. You can tell them that Ruby and Hart told you to.

Seeking Solace versus Healing from the Pain

Many people use the word "healing" in relation to grief and loss. The idea is that through the grieving process our wounds gradually heal. But I don't believe that accurately captures what is going on. Loss is a wound that never heals. The hole in my heart will never close over. I will always ache for Ruby and Hart. But if healing isn't the right word, how would I describe the moments when I feel some measure of peace or relief as I mourn? If I am trying to move away from suffering, what word do I use to describe what I am trying to move *toward*? What am I seeking as I travel through this journey of grief?

I was in synagogue when I found a possible answer. It was during the services for Yom Kippur, the holiest day in the Jewish calendar. I looked down at my siddur, or prayer book, and saw a prayer that wished for solace for those in mourning. It was Isaiah 57:18: "I will guide them and mete out solace to them, and to the mourners among them." I grabbed hold of the word "solace." It made sense to me. Solace doesn't promise ease or comfort; it doesn't imply a process of healing that might eventually be complete. I could get behind seeking solace. To my mind, it didn't suggest that I was trying to get past my pain or escape my pain. It felt like solace meant finding a way to live with the pain without being tortured by it. Solace felt like the opposite of anguish, or torment, or suffering. I could ache for Ruby and Hart, but at the same time, I could also look out over the vast Pacific Ocean and feel some solace within.

Nature Gives Solace amid the Pain

I find great solace staring out at the endless ocean, or across a wide expanse of desert, or up at the night sky. There is something about the enormity and timelessness of nature that helps me put life and death into a larger context. I know another griever who derives great solace contemplating ancient redwood trees for the same reason. Thinking about water and rocks and plants that were here long before us and will still be here long after us can be helpful as we process our grief.

My friend Steve tries to go swimming in the ocean every single day. "It feels very good spiritually; I find being in nature easier than being in civilization. I just find greater peace in nature." Steve's wife Linda fought a long, hard battle against a terminal disease. And then, a year after she died, Steve and his two children, Rebecca and Michael, were taking a walk when they were suddenly struck by an airborne car driven by a woman who was high and out of control. Steve was gravely injured and his two children were both tragically killed. "When I am in the ocean, before I turn to come back to shore, I speak to my wife Linda and my children Rebecca and Michael, and then to people I have lost recently. I give a prayer to them, and I thank them for being a part of my life. I let them know they are not forgotten, and that they live on in the acts and memories of their loved ones. But I am the only one who hears this, other than maybe the dolphins and fish."

It Takes Courage to Face Our Pain

I know many mourners who get angry when people say they are heroes for just getting through their day. These mourners shrug off the compliment with the blunt response: "What choice do I have?" The idea here is that we all have no choice but to go on living, so to call us heroic is superfluous and possibly even patronizing. But I disagree. We do have choices as mourners. And by making the daunting choice to lean into our pain and embrace the work of actively mourning, we are taking the heroic path. We are consciously facing down our pain and despair. I recently saw Bill Irwin perform a solo show titled *On Beckett*, about his favorite playwright, Samuel Beckett. Irwin described Beckett's bleak characters as personally inspiring because they courageously "go toe to toe with despair." The path of mourning that I am suggesting in this book asks for a lot of courage. It asks us to look our own despair straight in the eyes. But I believe that courage has its rewards.

Where Do We Find Our Courage?

I am not sure exactly where I personally find the courage to face the pain of my loss. It feels like maybe it comes from Ruby and Hart and the love we shared. I don't believe in god or an afterlife, but I do still feel them inside me. They helped shape me into the person I am. I carry Ruby and Hart with me, and I do lean on the love they felt for me to get through the harder days. I imagine them rooting for me, spurring me on to have the best life I can manage in their absence. I also find courage from Gail, and the love we have for each other. Grieving can make me feel excruciatingly alone. No one can take away my pain or heal me. And yet this terrible loss is something Gail and I share. We mourn together. She is extraordinarily brave and strong. The fierceness of her love is inspiring. She gives me courage.

Does the Pain Ever Lessen?

The short answer is, yes, sort of. Over time, the waves of overwhelming pain become less frequent. More importantly, our relationship to the pain changes. I think it becomes both softer and less unwelcome. But I think, paradoxically, the pain only becomes more bearable if we are willing to engage with it precisely when it feels unbearable. My friend Christopher offers the following insight: "Grief is a cruel, tyrannical ruler that demands total subjugation, and it is only by completely abasing ourselves before it, bowing down and groveling and saying, 'Yes, I will submit completely for the rest of my life,' only by totally, earnestly giving in to grief, only then will this tyrant lighten up and actually allow us some happiness. But we can't fake it! We can't just go through the motions all the while winking because we know we're going to feel better later. No. We have to fully commit to the certainty that we will never feel better and never 'heal,' in order to actually feel better and heal."

Predicting the Pain

Sometimes I am blindsided by the pain of my grief. It hits me seemingly out of the blue and takes me by surprise. But most of the time, I can see it coming. Knowing when it's coming can help me navigate the aching. Here is a partial list of the things that are bound to set me off:

Airports, family gatherings, playgrounds, the beach, traveling, the desert, back-to-school events, movie theaters, every time I get behind the wheel, every time I make a left-hand turn, driving on the freeway at night, seeing someone who is drunk or high, the Fortnite video game, horror movies, ABBA songs, blue hair, blond children, happy families, older teenagers hanging out, ice cream stores, any references to safety or being protected, cemeteries, hugs, goofy faces, playing with a small dog, playing cards, wild mushrooms, painting, young actors, hot Cheetos, vegetarian dishes, Chinese food, peacocks, bad jokes, swimming in the ocean, winter, spring, summer, fall, photos and videos of Ruby and Hart.

I don't avoid any of these things. In fact, I seek most of them out on a regular basis. But they always take a toll. What's on your list?

The Pain of Grief Comes in Waves

It's also helpful for me to know that the pain comes in waves. So even as I become engulfed in the hurt and feel like it's too much to bear, I can take some comfort in knowing that this tide of emotions will eventually ebb. I won't ever stay in a state of acute pain for very long.

When Ruby was struggling with OCD, she found herself occasionally overwhelmed by her obsessive thoughts and compulsions. At times it felt to her like she was drowning in her mental illness, with no end in sight. With help, she gradually learned to stay calm during her OCD flare-ups and trust that they would each eventually pass. No one stays in crisis forever. Your body will naturally let you off the hook after a while. She learned to trust in that. At the start of eleventh grade, she wrote a personal essay for her English class titled "Ocean." It is an insightful and inspiring piece about learning to breathe through a wave of intense discomfort. It was published posthumously in *Psychology Today Online*, where it continues to reverberate and inspire hope in others. I offer it here as a helpful tool for all of us who must navigate the waves of grief.

Ocean, a Personal Essay by Ruby Campbell

My feet smack the hot sand as I run forward, sea breeze whipping at my hair. The day is hot and the sun is bright, not a cloud in the sky. The loose sand below my pounding feet changes form, transitioning from a soft, dry powder to a densely packed, damp surface. The water pulls at my feet as I slow my pace, reaching a standstill in front of the cresting waves. They're peaking high today, the larger breakers somewhere around twelve feet high. They're some of the biggest I've ever seen.

I begin to walk again, luxuriating in the feeling of the water reach my ankles, my calves, my knees, until the waves are at my waist. In front of me are the monsters, the twelve footers, the massive walls of water that slam the sand with a fury. I continue forward, until I'm almost at the breakers. The thrill of anticipation and adrenaline spikes inside me and I dive forward, slicing through the water as the first of the larger waves rumbles towards me. I duck under it, feeling my head submerge for the first time and feeling the rush of the cool water around me. I come up on the other side and push forward.

Now the water is colder and I can sense the danger in the air. I can feel a lull in the waves as the water pulls back, so I swim forwards.

I am almost through the breakers, then I see a wave approaching. It's far away, but already is a bump several feet high.

It's going to be massive.

The wave has grown, and now is an immovable wall of water descending towards me. In this sense, the ocean and my anxiety are one and the same. Waves of water and emotion come crashing towards me, unstoppable. And so I do my best. I take a deep breath in preparation, and I dive to the ocean floor, digging my fingers into the sand and waiting for the wave to pass above me. Most of the time, it works, but every now and then the wave is too powerful. It rips me away from the sand, dragging me across the ground and flipping me around and around. I tumble through the foam, unable to tell which way is up. When the world is nothing but darkness swirling around me there is nothing I can do but curl up and hold my breath.

Waves come in sets of three, this I know, so the second I resurface, gasping for air, I'm on the lookout, scanning the sea for the next one. This one is larger than the first, more terrible, so I dive down again, desperately clutching at the sea floor. This wave pulls me up again, leaving no pretenses as to who is in charge. I'm whirled around and slammed against the hard-packed sand, mind and body battered. I'm under for longer this time, and I wonder what is more constricting: the water around me or the white of hospital walls.

Finally, I come up for air once again, strengthened by the oxygen rushing through my lungs. I wonder, will the next wave come? It feels both inevitable and impossible at the same time. If (when) it hits me, will I go under again? Will I struggle for air against the ancient rage of the sea?

Or will I swim fast and strong, slicing through the last wave to the place beyond the breakers? Will I float on my back under the summer sun and listen to the waves crash in the distance? This would be a peaceful life, a good life, and I will only have to brave one more wave.

I see it approaching, slowly building, and so I swim forward to meet it, the taste of salt on my tongue.

I find the idea of taking grief one wave at a time to be so helpful. And the idea of bravely swimming out to meet that wave is truly inspiring. I taught Ruby how to swim in the ocean. I taught her how to dive into and under the incoming waves to avoid getting rolled. She took that knowledge and found an insight about how to face the struggles of life. And in turn, my daughter taught me to lean into my grief. Now I follow her brave example. I love her so.

I know the specific day at the beach she is describing in her essay. It was at my forty-ninth birthday celebration. Every year in early September, I would throw what I called my Beach Birthday Bash. And this leads naturally to the first mourning ritual that Gail and I created after the end of Shloshim.

Ritual: My Birthday Beach Memorial

My fiftieth birthday came almost exactly three months after their deaths. I was in no mood to "celebrate" anything. I was halfway through life, and Ruby and Hart's deaths felt as though they had just rendered the first half meaningless and the upcoming second half pointless. But my birthdays in the past were always a highlight for our whole family. Each year, we hosted a huge party at the beach. I would invite my friends, Gail's friends, and Ruby and Hart's friends. I would insist on getting individual sandwich orders from everyone, and then I would place a huge order at our favorite Italian deli, Bay Cities. Gail offered to organize it, but I always wanted to host my own party. We took over a swath of the Santa Monica beach and we'd stay till the sun went down. All four of us loved swimming in the ocean, and at some point we'd all slip away from the other guests and swim out past the breakers together, like a little family of dolphins.

Now, even contemplating a birthday beach party overwhelmed me with pain. The thought of seeing all my friends, or worse, seeing all Ruby and Hart's friends gathering at the beach seemed unendurable. But I had been grieving for three months, and by now I realized how important and helpful it was to embrace opportunities to create mourning rituals. I changed my birthday bash to a Beach Memorial instead. No birthday song or presents, just a gathering to celebrate Ruby and Hart. I wanted to have some ritual component, some action for everyone to perform. My friend Mark suggested that everyone could bring a stone and we could all spell out "Ruby & Hart" in the sand. I thought that was a beautiful idea.

Gail and my sister-in-law Betsy were concerned that I was in no shape to host such a large gathering. They anxiously suggested that I keep the gathering small and skip the individual sandwich orders this year. One friend offered to take over the invitations. Another friend arranged a possible quick exit for Gail and me, in case we were overwhelmed by the pain of it all. These were good, smart precautions, but I *wanted* to take the lead and organize the event myself. It gave me a sense of continuity, a connection to my life before the crash. And taking on such an organizational role gave me agency. I was able to translate my grief into action. The gathering wound up being twice as large as my usual birthday parties. It felt so good to be surrounded by so many friends there on the beach that day. And the rock ceremony was magical. Each person brought a stone they had carefully selected for

Ruby and Hart. East Coast relatives mailed us their specially chosen rocks.

When it came time to arrange them on the sand, people wanted guidance. How big should each letter be? In what order would people put down their stones? Who would place all the extra rocks that were sent from our relatives on the East Coast? In that moment, I suddenly realized that it would be much more meaningful for everyone if there was no direction from me. If every person had to decide for themself where to put their rock, it would make each gesture more special and hold more meaning. Instead of being told what to do, each participant would be a part of the larger collective, together creating an ephemeral monument to Ruby and Hart. And magically, each letter they formed was just the right size, and spaced apart by just the right amount. And we ran out of rocks just as we finished the "t" of "Hart." When it was done, everyone stepped back into a large circle and stood in silence. Some wept, some held hands. It was a powerful moment, an unforgettable ritual that we all had created on our own. And then we all leapt into the ocean as we shouted out loud, "Ruby and Hart!" We stayed for hours on that beach. We went toe to toe with despair and came away feeling stronger. And more loved.

We built a thing of beauty and gave it over to the ocean, which eventually washed it away. In doing so, we consecrated a site in the name of Ruby and Hart. It felt to me like my kids were there with us, conjured by our collective love. That particular stretch of the Santa Monica beach is now a special, sacred place for me, a place where I can feel their presence more strongly. On a day that might have been nothing but misery for me—my first birthday without them—I instead was able to feel some solace and precious connection even as I ached and wept for them.

Embracing the Pain

I believe I am able to stay close to so many of my friends, and I am able to remain creatively productive, because I have not shied away from the pain of my loss. More importantly, my marriage to Gail has remained strong, honest, and loving, despite our catastrophic loss, largely due to our shared practice of leaning into the pain. I also think embracing the pain has enabled us, on a daily basis, to think about and take solace in the love we shared with Ruby and Hart.

It may be that you feel your loss is less catastrophic and therefore you don't need to lean so far into the pain and grief. Perhaps it feels better to compartmentalize your grief or ignore it for long stretches of time. It may seem as though you are functioning just fine in life without talking about your loss. But what price are you paying for your neglect of the pain? What relationships are suffering because of your avoidance of the heavy lifting of grieving? What creative projects are you shortchanging because you have blocked out such an important emotional need? In order to avoid the pain of grief, are you numbing yourself with unhealthy levels of drugs or alcohol? What anger issues are going unchecked? Sadly, there is always a price paid for trying to ignore grief.

Leaning Too Far into the Pain

Of course, any healthy habit can be taken too far. I have found that it is possible to lean so far into grief that I step outside the flow of life. I can become so desperate to make every moment an honoring of Ruby and Hart that I miss out on my own life. At times, my relentless pursuit of grief can feel like self-punishment.

During the early days of the COVID-19 pandemic, many of our friends confessed that they were sitting around watching too many movies on the couch. Gail and I suddenly realized we hadn't watched any movies at all. We hadn't read any books for pleasure, just grief books. Even our walks were dedicated to Ruby and Hart's memories. Our days were spent focused on grief work—either journaling about our loss, writing thank-you cards to people who honored our kids, planning the next mourning ritual, going to grief groups, or going to therapy. We had allowed our days to be so full of grief that there wasn't room for much of anything else.

Ruby's OCD therapist, Dr. Grayson, actually mandated that we watch an hour of television each night. We watched *Schitt's Creek* and *Tiger King* through all of April and May. We laughed and didn't feel too guilty. We wished we could have been watching with Ruby and Hart, but we found a way to enjoy it anyway. We had been so austere and self-punishing that we had needed a doctor to prescribe television for us, just to get us to lighten up.

Part of what had driven me to be so single-minded in my grieving were my residual feelings of parental responsibility and guilt. At times I feel as though I have to take care of my kids' memories non-stop, or else I am somehow failing them. I work myself up into parental overdrive. But Ruby and Hart are dead, and I need to accept that reality and let go of the anxieties and guilt of parenthood. The truth is, Ruby and Hart don't need me anymore. I need to grieve, but Ruby and Hart don't actually need me to grieve. In other words, I don't need to feel a guilty obligation to grieve so hard. I can try to learn to let go of that self-judgment. I can be kinder to myself as I grieve. And I can allow myself to open up more to the life that is happening around me.

Confusing Pain for Love

The reason we are in such pain is because our love was—is—so deep. In that sense, our pain is a reflection of our love. But that does not mean that pain equals love. We who love don't need to be in constant agony to prove it. We are not condemned to expressing our love for those we have lost solely by the degree to which we are in pain. Absolutely not. Our love is more truly found in the joy we feel as we think about the beautiful life we shared with them. We can tap into our love as we remember all the good times, and even the struggles we had together; they were all part of the life we shared and the beautiful everlasting bond we forged.

Paradoxically, we lean into the pain of our grief precisely so that we can then be able to let that pain go and access the joyful memories instead. The idea here is not to wear our pain as some kind of badge of honor or proof of our love. Being in pain is not the goal of grieving; quite the opposite. Our loved ones don't want us writhing in pain; they want us to hold on to all the joy they gave us in life. But of course, like all things about grieving, it's easier said than done. Janine Kwoh writes in *Welcome to the Grief Club*, "The pain of their death is not the only bond you have left. Joy also connects you to them through the happiness they brought to your life when they were alive. . . . Joy is not at odds with our grief, but rather an essential part of our healing. Joy gives us a bit of relief when it hurts too much to keep going; it provides fuel to keep living. Joy reminds us what we're living for."

Actions

- **Gradually expose yourself to some of the things that remind you of your loss, even if it's painful.** Spend time with their photos and belongings. Read what they wrote. Watch their videos. Eat at their favorite restaurants. Listen to their favorite music. Spend time with their friends. Do the things you are scared to do. One at a time.
- **Allow yourself to remember.** In fresh grief, it's hard to remember much. Shock and denial make it difficult to recall what they looked like or how they sounded. But gradually, the memories return. They are always painful at first, as we ache for what we've lost. Breathe through the pain and let yourself remember and feel some of the joy.
- **Allow yourself to tell stories about your loved one.** Even though it hurts at first, the rewards are always greater than the pain. It's part of what we need to do as mourners.
- **Allow yourself to take healthy breaks from your mourning.** Your grief is not going anywhere. It will be there for you when you are ready to return to it. Allow yourself to feel pleasure and enjoyment. Embrace some distractions.
- **Stop doing something that causes you suffering.** Identify the behaviors that lead you to suffer unnecessarily as you mourn. How are you punishing yourself? In what ways do you harm your mind or body? What interactions with other people leave you feeling bad about yourself? Try to change those behaviors and interactions. Try to let go of the self-punishing thoughts. Try to be kind to yourself as you mourn.
- **Take care of your mind and body.** Develop an exercise regimen that you can maintain. Practice good sleep hygiene. Improve your diet. Eat less sugar. Reduce or eliminate your alcohol or drug intake.

- **Spend more time in nature.** Take a walk on the beach, a hike in the desert, a climb in the mountains, a swim in the lake, a bike ride through the park.

Journaling Prompts

- What are the things you are avoiding because you are scared of the pain they might cause you? What places or parts of your life have you closed off to yourself out of fear? What would happen if you actually went to those "forbidden" places? Would your feelings evolve if you kept going there over and over again?
- Explore what it means to you to separate the healthy pain of grief from the burden of unnecessary suffering. What are some examples of things that cause you pain but keep you engaged with your grief? What are some examples of things that take you away from grieving by making you suffer instead? Are there actions you could take to lessen your suffering? Can you change or eliminate toxic interactions with unhelpful people?
- Write down happy memories of your loved one, even though it may make you cry.
- How could you be kinder to yourself? What pleasures could you treat yourself to?
- Write a letter to your loved one telling them about a new experience you had.

CHAPTER FIVE

Denial

Amortizing the Pain

At first, denial protected me. In the early days of grief, I couldn't fully process the loss; it was literally too monumental to be believed, too painful to be endured. Of course, intellectually, I understood that Ruby and Hart were killed. I saw their dead bodies, and I was there when we buried them. But there was, and honestly still is, a part of me that somehow expects to see them walk in the front door someday. It is almost as if, in the far back of my mind and heart, I assume that at some point I will tell Ruby and Hart all about this awful experience I am having. I always told them about what was happening in my life, so why would this be any different? A large part of how we process any experience is by sharing it with the people we love the most. Am I really having these experiences if I can't tell them to Ruby and Hart? Is any of this really happening?

The denial of early grief is a strange, liminal experience. Mourners will often say, "I can't believe they're gone." And we mean it literally. We cannot believe it. It is unreal. This is denial protecting us. Denial allows us to amortize the pain and stretch it out over months and years, so our minds don't seize up and implode. Elisabeth Kübler-Ross and David Kessler write, in *On Grief and Grieving*, "Denial and shock help us cope and make survival possible. Denial helps us to pace our feelings of grief. There is a grace in denial. It is nature's way of letting in only as much as we can handle."

Denial Is Not Our Friend

But in the long run, denial is not our friend, because denial keeps us from real life. It traps us in a past that no longer exists. I don't want to live in that liminal space where I am sitting around waiting for Ruby and Hart to come back home. Because they aren't coming home.

One of the problems with denial is that it limits our existence by insisting that we block off huge swaths of our lives. Denial urges us to avoid all the people and places and things that remind us of our loved ones, because they all also remind us that our loved ones are gone. So denial urges me to close Ruby and Hart's bedroom doors and never go inside. Denial pushes me to avoid looking at their photos, and to avoid thinking about all our happy memories. Denial urges me to avoid all our favorite places in a vain attempt at keeping reality at bay. If I take a hike in Griffith Park, or Joshua Tree National Park, or the Los Angeles Arboretum, or Huntington Gardens, I will inevitably be flooded with memories of Ruby and Hart. And I will also be flooded with grief, loss, and aching. So denial urges me to stay home. In the short term that may feel safer. But of course, in the long run, it means missing out on all that life has to offer. And it means hiding from everything that reminds me of Ruby and Hart. I know I can't do that.

Ultimately, I need to confront my denial. I have to say goodbye to Ruby and Hart. Over and over again.

A Jewish Burial

I want to mention one last Jewish ritual of mourning—the actual burial practice we observed—because I think it holds important clues about confronting denial. It is the Jewish custom to gather the mourners and their community by the side of the open grave and have them all witness the lowering of the coffin. After some prayers are spoken, the central mourners step forward and cast the first three handfuls of soil upon the casket. Or, more accurately, the concrete burial vaults that encase their caskets. The sound of the dirt hitting the vault is stark and brutal. It is an unforgettable sound, a rasping percussive blow against any comforting wisp of denial that you might be clinging to.

The central mourners then take a front-row seat and watch as each person in their community comes forward and, one at a time, throws three more shovelfuls of dirt. The entire community literally buries your loved one. We do it with our bare hands. There is no euphemism here. It is physical, visceral, and undeniable. At first look it seems cruel: why make the mourners witness everyone throwing dirt on the casket? Why make them endure the prolonged agony of such a stark practice? Shouldn't they be shielded from as much pain as possible on this of all days? And yet there is no shielding us from the pain of loss. It's our reality. Death can be such a hard thing to accept, especially a sudden, unexpected death. It seems to me Jewish burial customs are designed to help us combat that denial. It was a tough-love kickoff to what has been a long battle for me against my denial.

When everyone had finished, our community formed two lines leading away from the grave all the way to our car. Gail and I and both our families then walked through this gauntlet of love and support. We encountered our community not as the earlier undifferentiated crowd of the funeral service, but now as individuals. Each person had their own place in the line. And as I walked through, I made eye contact with every one of them. Our rabbi likens it to having rails of support: they are there to catch us if we fall. It is also a powerful moment in which we meet, eye-to-eye, with our community for the first time on the other side of loss. These are the people who are here for us now, and we will need to forge a new relationship to them because we are no longer the people we once were.

A Shattered Identity

When Ruby and Hart were killed, I no longer understood who I was. I had thought of myself first and foremost as a dad to two wonderful kids. It informed every aspect of my identity. All my hopes and dreams for my future were intertwined with their futures. I took for granted that they would always be with me for holidays and vacations for the rest of my life. I looked forward to helping raise their children. Toys and books from my childhood were carefully stored in the attic in the hopes that one day I might share them with grandchildren.

And now, the life I had is over. My old identity is gone. So who am I now? Mourners are all faced with a version of this crisis. How are you still a spouse if your spouse is gone? How are you a sibling if your sibling is gone? How are you a child if your parent is gone? I have become a man with two dead kids. That is my reality. I can't deny it. I need to reorganize my identity and define how I plan to live as the father of children who were killed on June 12, 2019. This is part of the work of grieving.

What makes this grief work so hard is that we don't want to do it.

We desperately don't want to integrate this loss into our identity. We want to still have the future we used to have. We want to keep moving forward in *that* life. Our heart resists the work of change that we must do. This resistance makes our grief work even more difficult and exhausting.

Facing Down Denial and Rebuilding Our Identity

I need to take my shattered identity and put it back together, piece by piece—but different. I have a new relationship to everyone in my life. I used to walk into my local Jersey Mike's sandwich shop and the person behind the counter knew my order by heart—two turkey sandwiches, one with American cheese and lettuce, the other with Swiss cheese, lettuce, and tomato. Sandwiches for me and Hart. Now I only get one sandwich and I ache for Hart and everything he and I have lost. I get together with friends who have kids, and our dynamic has changed. There is pain, loss, and yearning everywhere I turn. This is true for all of us in grief. If you lost a spouse, how do you now fit in with all those other couples you were both friends with? Do you still get invited to their dinner parties? If you lost a sibling, how do you now function in a family with a gaping hole? If you lost your closest friend, or a soldier who fought by your side, how do you relate to all the people who can't fathom your grief? We need to redefine our relationships to everyone and everything in our lives in order to put our identity back together in this new reality.

Denial urges me to avoid this process of reintegration. And denial is tempting. It sounds like it might be nice, imagining that Ruby and Hart are still alive. But it's not. Because it is not true, and I can't actually trick myself into believing that it is. So instead, it feels awful and unsatisfying. I can't wish them back to life.

"But That's Not What Happened"

Sometimes I become fixated on trying to change the past in my mind. I get stuck in a loop thinking about what I might have done to avoid being hit by the drunk driver. I replay the events of that night over and over again, imagining the thousands of tiny changes I could have made that would have put my car on a different path. It is almost as if my brain can trick itself into believing that if I concentrate hard enough and put my mind to it, I might actually be able to change what really happened. If I just try hard enough, I might be able to figure out a way to keep Ruby and Hart alive.

Ruby's OCD therapist, Dr. Grayson, once interrupted me in one of these obsessive loops of denial by firmly stating, "But that's not what happened." In the moment, it felt like a brutal slap in the face. But it worked. It pulled me out of the endless coil of "what ifs" and returned me to the reality that we *were* hit by the drunk driver, and Ruby and Hart *were* killed.

All of us mourners can find ourselves trapped in these obsessive thoughts. What if we went to the hospital sooner, what if we had gotten a second opinion, what if we hadn't let her go to that party, what if we had taken him to rehab one more time, what if we had just not gotten into that damn car, or plane, or boat, or ski lift, what if, what if, what if? Sometimes now, when I catch myself slipping into yet another brutal and futile cycle of "what ifs," I think to myself, "But that's not what happened," and it helps me. It helps me step out of denial and back into reality.

Dwelling in the Fantasy

Dr. Grayson has a stark but compelling definition of denial. "I would say that denial takes place any time I compare reality to a fantasy world. And in the case of loss, the statement of fantasy is 'life would be better if they were still here.' And the reason it's a fantasy is because that could never happen. Everyone, no matter how psychologically aware they are, is going to start their loss in denial. Because that is an unavoidable thought. I don't just get to get rid of denial by decision. To move from denial to acceptance involves mourning. It's a process. It takes time. It involves the change of giving up the fantasy. And giving up the fantasy is always a loss." At first, his definition of denial struck me as too extreme. Of course I will always believe that life would be better if Ruby and Hart were still here. How could I ever *not* think that? But, on the other hand, if I am going through my day constantly comparing my current life with a fantasy world of my choosing, I am only going to be dragging myself down. Reality will never beat fantasy. I think the journey is to slowly dwell less and less in that moment of comparison.

Dr. Grayson goes on to say, "The truth is that acceptance sucks. In the short run acceptance means I am going to agree to live the second-best life. Acceptance only has one thing going for it initially: we don't have a choice. We can't bring them back. So moving to acceptance is moving to that. Obviously, I will still think about the ones I've lost, I will still be sad, I'll still miss them, but what I move to is that, on a day-to-day basis, I also enjoy life in the present."

Now, when I find myself suddenly, desperately, wishing that Ruby and Hart were still alive, I let myself ache for them, but then I try to let the wishing pass. I try not to dwell in comparison. I try to accept this life I am living.

Separating Grief from Trauma

The first few months after his son Charlie died, my friend Christopher spent a lot of time replaying in his mind the events that led up to the fatal accident. He leaned into the pain of it in his desire to face his loss and not avoid his grief. But as he replayed those events, he focused on all the thousands of "what ifs." Over and over, he thought about all the moments leading up to the accident, trying to pin down where it went so wrong, the thing he could've changed, the decision that would have led to a different outcome. Instead of leaning into the pain of his loss, he was leaning into the trauma and, in the process, he was retraumatizing himself. It wasn't until he realized he needed to separate his grief from his trauma that he was able to grieve without becoming overwhelmed by the suffering. He also found that doing eye movement desensitization and reprocessing (EMDR) was extremely helpful in getting him out of the traumatic loop of "what ifs." It allowed him to stop obsessing over the manner of Charlie's death and instead focus on appreciating Charlie's life. EMDR treatment has had a lot of success in treating PTSD by using the biological processes involved in rapid eye movement (REM) sleep to help patients quickly process and integrate traumatic events.

The day after the crash, I wrote out everything I could remember of that night. I described every awful detail. It was my way of desensitizing myself to the trauma. It helped me let go of some of the horror of that night. Once I wrote it all out, I didn't have to think about it so much. By writing out every detail, I didn't need to then keep searching through that night for "answers." Because, of course, there are no answers. If you are grieving a sudden, unexpected loss, you are also coping with trauma. I hope you are able to find ways of letting go of that trauma, whether it's through therapy, meditation, journaling, or EMDR. I hope your trauma doesn't send you into loops of denial.

My friend Gretchen has found similar relief in journaling about her trauma. "Writing down—venting—the sad, angry and traumatic times that we had with Dana has helped a lot, because then I don't send it around and around in my head. I know I have it written down and I am not going to forget it. The trauma has its place on the paper as opposed to me just rethinking it. Because with kids that die of a drug-related death it's probably true for most parents that you are left with the chaos as the most recent part of their life. So getting that out and on the page has allowed me to bring up the good memories and happier times."

Every "First" Is a Struggle

It's clearly not helpful to wall off parts of my life in an attempt to hold on to my old identity. I need to do the work of reintegrating my entire existence to this new, awful reality. And each step hurts. The reason the year of "firsts" is so painful—the first Christmas without them, the first Mother's Day, their first birthdays, and so on—is because that is when we typically do the bulk of this grief work. Every "first" we experience is an instance of us redefining our relationships. At each integration, we are acknowledging that our loved one is gone from this part of our life, too. In a way, it feels like we are saying goodbye to them over and over again. It's heartbreaking.

Every "first" after a loss can make us feel as though we are "re-grieving." The experience can send us right back to the scary emotions of fresh grief. But it is helpful to me to know that each subsequent time will be a little easier. I knew that it would be terrifying to get behind the wheel again, or to drive again at night. I knew I would be flooded with terrible thoughts and a fresh wave of aching. But I also knew that delaying doing so would just make it all the harder. I started driving a few days after the funeral. And I drove at night for the first time again at some point in the first month.

Each step back into the world, each interaction with the people in our life is a heroic act of grief work on the road to accepting reality. The choice to take these painful steps is ours to make. As the psychiatrist and Holocaust survivor Viktor Frankl wrote, "Everything can be taken from a man but one thing: the last of the human freedoms—to choose one's attitude in any given set of circumstances, to choose one's own way."

Becoming an Active Protagonist in Our Grief

In thinking about actively choosing how we respond to our loss, I am reminded of a screenwriting lesson I often impart to my students. It concerns the importance of creating an active protagonist, rather than a passive one, for the simple reason that an audience will care more about a character who makes choices and takes actions in their own life. A passive protagonist is a central character who merely reacts to life's challenges but takes no actions on their own. Although there are some notable exceptions, in general a passive character is not compelling to an audience because they are not engaged with the struggle of life, they are simply beaten down by it. As Robert McKee writes in his *STORY*, "True character can only be expressed through choice in dilemma. How a person chooses to act under pressure is who he is—the greater the pressure, the truer and deeper the choice to the character."

We in mourning are facing the greatest of pressures. We are grappling hand-to-hand with the reality of loss and mortality. There is no greater dilemma. And the choices we make now have never been more important to our lives. Ruby and Hart's deaths had turned me into a passive protagonist. The night of the crash, I was unable to save them. And afterward, I became helpless and hopeless in the face of my overwhelming grief. For a while, I was simply a passive receiver of the terrible, unbearable pain of their loss. Performing rituals, reaching out to friends, and choosing to beat back denial are all ways of making my grief active. Instead of passively ruminating alone in my sadness, I am choosing to look directly into the abyss of my loss and take action.

Not all the time, mind you. We can't walk around confronting mortality in every moment; that would be exhausting. And it would also feel like self-punishment. Sometimes I need to be able to just lick an ice cream cone, for example, without also taking in the enormity of my loss. I find that the practice of confronting denial is most helpful when it encourages me to be more fully in life and to take emotional risks in order to experience all that life has to offer.

Rainer Maria Rilke writes:

> *Let everything happen to you: beauty and terror.*
> *Just keep going. No feeling is final.*
> *Don't let yourself lose me.*
> *Nearby is the country they call life.*
> *You will know it by its seriousness.*
> *Take my hand.*

This translation by Anita Barrows and Joanna Macy made an impact on me as I grieved, particularly the line "Just keep going. No feeling is final." The idea of persevering with the knowledge that my grief will inevitably feel different over time was comforting to me. My friend Thomas Bartscherer pointed out that the translators took some poetic license with the text. A more literal translation might be "One must simply go. No feeling is furthest." I find the idea that "No feeling is furthest" is also compelling. To my mind, it's saying that no feeling is so far away that it is unreachable, even in our grief. Feelings of love and joy are still within our grasp. We must simply keep going to get there.

The Importance of Continuity

Another important reason for us to reconnect with the people, places, and things of the life we led before our loss is this notion of continuity. I was first introduced to continuity in the context of grief by my therapist. He saw me struggling to process my loss and he noted that it seemed helpful to me when I took actions that fostered a sense of continuity with my past.

We have suffered a terrible schism in our lives. For us, time will forever be divided into the Before and the After. This violent rupture can cause us to feel disconnected from our own identity. Grief can leave us feeling unmoored and adrift in the After. Denial can compound the schism by encouraging us to blot out our past and to run from everything and everyone that reminds us of what we have lost. In order to rebuild our identity, we need to be able to feel connections with the person we once were. We need a sense of continuity in our lives in order to bridge the chasm and find direction again in our lives. One way in which I connected to my past was to return to the community of Hart's school.

Ritual: The Hart Campbell Kindness Award

About two months after the crash, I suddenly felt a powerful urge to speak to the students at Hart's school, Campbell Hall. Some of his friends had created red memorial bracelets that said "Hart & Ruby—Gone But Never Forgotten," and they were selling them in order to raise money for the Trevor Project, a nonprofit organization dedicated to preventing suicide among LGBTQ youth. Ruby was a lesbian who had struggled with suicidal ideation. Hart was a fierce defender of his sister and they both actively fought against homophobia, speaking out against homophobic slurs and marching for equal rights and gay marriage. So the Trevor Project seemed like an excellent charity that would honor both Ruby and Hart.

But I suddenly had a bad feeling as the fall term approached. These friends of Hart's were sweet and sincere, and several of them were also LGBTQ. I had anxious visions of these ninth graders being targeted by cruel older students at the school as they sold the Hart and Ruby bracelets. I felt a need to give a talk to the whole school as a sort of preemptive strike in the name of kindness. I wanted to protect them.

Fear, however, was urging me to stay far away from the school. The thought of stepping back onto campus and seeing all those youthful faces was terrifying. Talking to all those kids about Hart and Ruby would be leaning far into the pain and I wasn't sure I could do it. Just as I was struggling with these thoughts, my sister-in-law

Betsy proposed the idea of giving an annual prize to someone at Campbell Hall, in Hart's name. Gail and I loved it. We all decided it should be a prize for acts of kindness. Hart was an extraordinarily kind young man. And he made kindness seem cool. Shortly after the funeral, a fellow student posted the following on Instagram:

> *One day I was alone crying at lunch and Hart and a few others walked by. He sat down next to me, not saying a word. Just knowing someone was there was so comforting. After five minutes of this silence, he said "do you want to talk about it or get your mind off of it?" He didn't pressure me into telling him a word, and God it felt so good to know someone cared. I said I wanted to get my mind off of it, and so for a few minutes he told me funny stories and jokes. Once he knew I was okay, he went back to his friends. He saved my life that day. I only wish I could have saved his, and Ruby's. I have never known someone as kind and caring as him.*

Betsy came up with the idea of making it a cash prize, and offered to fund it. Betsy had a history of making twenty-dollar bets with Hart and then winding up getting repeatedly fleeced by him. And then there was a memorable time when she was babysitting Hart and her one job was to get him to school on time. But that morning Hart said he didn't feel well, so Betsy tested him by offering him *four hundred* dollars if he would go to school. At first, Hart didn't take the bait, but after lunch he was feeling better, and he slyly asked if Betsy's offer was still on the table. Betsy said that half the school day was over, so now she was only offering two hundred dollars. But the deal was that he had to swear he would never tell us. He took the deal and stayed true to his word. I didn't find out about this crazy bad-parenting deal until the second night of Shiva when Betsy finally confessed. In honor of her and Hart's outrageous pact we decided it should be a four-hundred-dollar cash prize for kindness. The winning kid would get two hundred dollars to pocket and squander as they saw fit, and another two hundred to give to the charity of their choice. Together we created the Hart Campbell Kindness Award.

At first, the school felt uncomfortable giving a cash award for kindness. It felt antithetical to them. Campbell Hall's headmaster told me that you can't reward compassion with money. They felt that people should be kind for kindness's sake. Instead, they wanted to create a Paper Tree of Kindness. Every benevolent act would get written on a paper leaf and added to the branches of the paper tree. When the tree was filled with leaves, the school would plant an honorary tree on the campus. But I thought, "What teenager cares about some tree getting planted on campus?" Big deal. That ritual seemed doomed to neglect after the first year. I wanted to create an annual tradition that would go on for years and years. I wanted kids to be doing acts of kindness in Hart's name for centuries! And I thought cold hard cash would make sure that it would happen. Plus, I liked that it felt "wrong." Campbell Hall's headmaster was correct, you're not supposed to reward kindness with cash. It was as though we were breaking some unspoken rule, and that felt good to us. Hart enjoyed breaking rules and being a little transgressive, and he would appreciate the gesture. Besides, I didn't want some lame paper tree for my boy.

I gave a speech to the entire high school community in which I talked about Hart and about bullying and I introduced the Kindness Award. It was a powerful assembly for everyone. I got a standing ovation and a lot of love from the students. My fears about bullies were misplaced. These kids were generous and grieving. Campbell Hall held grief circles over the summer for students and faculty. The school honored both Hart and the grief of the whole community. They set up a special box in the school library to collect the student nominations, and in June I awarded the first Hart Campbell Kindness Award. Coincidentally (or not), it went to one of Hart's closest friends, Paolo, who strove to do something kind every single day of the year. He spent his two hundred dollars on a drum kit and named POPS the Club as his charity of choice. POPS the Club aims to transform shame and stigma into dignity for teens with loved ones in prison. It's designed to nourish and empower these students through creative expression, emotional support, and the development of community. Hart would be so proud.

I consider the act of creating the Kindness Award a mourning ritual because it brought a community together, gave everyone a task (perform acts of kindness and nominate others for their acts of kindness), and created a space to share my grief and some memories of Ruby and Hart. Delivering the speech was my performative task.

I have included the speech in Appendix C. It's about how being kind is actually edgier and more bad-assed than being cruel. I talk about Hart and Ruby. And there are some words about grief in there as well.

School Celebrations of Life

When Ruby and Hart's other schools reached out with an interest in holding their own celebrations of life, Gail and I eagerly accepted. Ruby and Hart's elementary school, Hollywood Schoolhouse, had a gathering of everyone from their classes, along with the parents. It is a small, intimate school where every faculty member and every parent knew and loved Ruby and Hart. A podium was set up in the yard, facing rows of mourners. The head of school dedicated a pomegranate tree to Ruby and Hart and planted it next to the swimming pool. Faculty gave beautiful speeches. Parents got up and shared words of love. Gail and I spoke. Some of Hart's friends performed "Wish You Were Here" by Pink Floyd. We all wept together.

Ruby went to two high schools, Pilgrim School and Fusion Academy. Both held beautiful gatherings where students and faculty shared their grief, and Gail and I spoke. At Fusion Academy, everyone gathered on pillows and couches and shared memories. I gave a slide show of Ruby's digital art. It was a wonderful two-way street of sharing, because the students had never seen all of her art, and I didn't always know the backstory to all of her pieces. So as I went through the slide show, I had students tell me if they knew anything about a particular painting. It felt like we were all working together, sharing stories, to paint a more complete picture of Ruby. Ruby had a favorite couch in the "homework café," and they officially declared it to be "Ruby's Couch." Above it, they hung a framed collage that her art teacher made in her honor, and that featured a photo of Ruby's self-portrait.

At Pilgrim, students and faculty gathered in the chapel for a more formal and somber gathering. I again shared a slide show of Ruby's art, but this time I knew more about the backstory of each piece. My father was an art historian, and I felt as though I was channeling him as I talked about Ruby's works. Pilgrim framed two of Ruby's digital paintings, which she had titled *Koi Wolves*, and hung them together in the Art Center, Ruby's favorite place on campus.

Being able to hold multiple memorials for our kids was invaluable to Gail and me. Each gathering was an opportunity for us to take an active role in our grieving and was a new way to push back against denial as we celebrated Ruby and Hart with each community.

Fear of Mourning

Sadly, Ruby's middle school, Marlborough, declined to hold a celebration of life for Ruby. We spoke with the head of school in August, and she promised us they would hold an assembly to honor Ruby "when the time was right." She didn't want the students to be hit with such a somber and upsetting topic at the beginning of the school year, when she wanted the assemblies to all be focused on the "core values" of Marlborough. I thought that having an assembly that pointed to the dangers of drunk driving would be an excellent segue into core values. I also believe that honoring the dead is an important core value to hold as a human being. But the head of school disagreed.

Months went by and we heard no word from Marlborough. I reached out again at the start of the spring semester. I listed all the celebrations of life that their other schools had held, and how important and moving they all were. I never heard back from the school. Ruby had several incredibly close friends who still went to Marlborough in the high school program. Those friends were in deep mourning, but the school never publicly acknowledged their loss and pain. The school was too frightened of mourning, and as a result they dishonored my daughter's memory and they neglected their own living students, some of whom continue to get therapy to cope with their grief. The following spring, when Ruby's class graduated from high school, it was during COVID-19 and the ceremony was a prerecorded video. The school sent us a copy in which the head of school briefly mentions Ruby. She tells the graduates that they lost a classmate, Ruby Campbell, and "that is now a part of your story." I don't know what that means or how that is supposed to help her friends in mourning who have to navigate the pain and guilt of graduating and going to college without Ruby. Sadly, Marlborough is a reminder that many of us in mourning are going to be let down because people and organizations are simply too frightened of grief, and they would prefer to deny it.

The Afterlife as a "Quick Fix" and a Denial

Some religions offer beliefs about an afterlife, which can help many people in grief. But an afterlife doesn't solve our pain. It doesn't fix our loss. When people tell us that our loved one is in a better place and that we will get to see them again as soon as we die, it can often feel as though they are trying to get us to deny our grief and to stop mourning. By offering the quick fix of an afterlife, they are essentially saying that we have no business being so upset. But you can believe in an afterlife and still feel the pain of your loss.

The idea that you might get to see your loved one in heaven doesn't mean you can't weep for all you and they have lost here on earth. These well-wishers may imagine they are cheering us up, but people who are grieving don't need cheering up; we need to be allowed to feel and express our pain and loss. If you derive comfort from the thought of a heavenly reunion, that can be helpful, but it doesn't negate the pain you are feeling now in this life. You need to be allowed to grieve and process your loss regardless of your religious beliefs.

Acceptance of Our Reality

If part of our journey through grief is to move away from denial, then what are we moving toward? I used to imagine that "acceptance" implied a sense of feeling okay about whatever it was I was accepting—as in "I can accept your criticism," or "I can accept that deal," or "I find those terms acceptable." It seems to imply that I am okay with them. But using the term "acceptance" in relation to my catastrophic loss does not mean I am okay with it. It means I am no longer actively denying its reality. I will never be okay with Ruby and Hart's deaths. I will never find it acceptable that a woman who had lost her license as a result of a prior DUI decided to get drunk and high and get behind the wheel anyway, and drive ninety miles an hour, and now my beautiful children are gone forever. No, that is not acceptable.

But the fact that Ruby and Hart are dead is a reality I have to accept if I want to live in the real world. And this act of acceptance is heroic. It is a fierce, ongoing battle against denial. Sometimes, in the first year of my grief, I would force myself to remember details of the car crash as a way of proving to myself that Ruby and Hart were really dead. It was so hard to believe. It was so easy to feel untethered from this reality. Even now, I don't believe I have *completely* accepted the truth that they are gone forever from my life. It feels to me as if, in the way back part of my brain and heart, there is still some expectation that this nightmarish chapter in my life will end someday and they will be returned to me. And I am scared to completely lose this reassuring bit of denial.

I actually found it hard to write this chapter. I noticed that I was stalling. Clearly, exploring denial made me uncomfortable. I think I still harbor an unfounded fear that if my denial were completely stripped away, I might not be able to bear the pain. Or maybe if my denial were completely gone it would mean that Ruby and Hart's spirits were also gone from my life. But neither fear is true. There is no "other shoe" that is going to drop. I am bearing the full weight of my loss right now. And Ruby and Hart will never not be a part of my life. I take them with me wherever I go.

What Is Our Reward for Confronting Denial?

In the early days of grief, there was a part of me that felt as though if I suffered enough and grieved for all I was worth and did it "right," I might be rewarded and get Ruby and Hart back again. On a subconscious level, that thought made a lot of sense to me. There must be some kind of reward for enduring so much pain, right? It must be for a reason.

I now know that the reward we get for leaning into our pain and battling our denial is simply the ability to continue living in reality. Our reward is one that we don't actually want but must accept: the awful truth that to love is to lose, and that there is no such thing as safety in this life. The ancient Greek playwright Aeschylus said it best some twenty-five hundred years ago. In his play *Agamemnon*, he wrote, "He who learns must suffer. And even in our sleep, pain that cannot forget falls drop by drop upon the heart, until in our own despair, against our will, comes wisdom to us by the awful grace of the gods." Robert F. Kennedy quoted that same passage at Martin Luther King Jr.'s memorial.

We all desperately want to go back in time and be the people we once were, who believed that bad things only happened to other people and not us. I have a visceral memory of my past life. I can *feel* what it was like to sit by the pool and just simply be at ease, swaddled in the security of my family's permanence. Now I ache for that carefree naïveté. But then again, as my friend Christopher points out, "Who really wants to be carefree? Don't we want to care?" Maybe our unwanted wisdom has shown us a powerful truth that people who have never grieved can't know. And maybe, on some level, our grief has made us more alive to the world as it really is. Of course we want our loved ones back, but maybe we don't actually want to go back to being the people we used to be.

We might wish we could live in denial forever. But we cannot. We are alive and we have a purpose in this world. We are empowered now because we truly know what it means to love. So the question becomes, what are we going to do with the precious time we have left to us?

Actions

- **Engage with the reality of your loss.** Visit the cemetery. Tell a stranger about your loss. Avoid euphemisms and try instead to use direct words such as "dead" or "killed." Try sharing the specific manner of their deaths as a way of banishing any fear or shame you might hold, using concrete words such as "suicide," "drug overdose," "drowning," and so on. It gets easier the more we do it.

- **Purposefully choose actions that maintain continuity with your past.** Return to an old hobby, continue a Sunday morning tradition, reengage in your previous volunteer work, or political activism, or church or temple, or social group, or favorite pastime, or sports team, and so on. Your habits of the past may at first feel meaningless, but allow yourself to try to reengage and reconnect. You are changed, but you are also still you.

- **One at a time, reconnect with the people in your life, taking the time to incorporate the reality of your loss into your new relationship.** Your relationships need to be redefined. How does your grief fit into each one? You may find that it sits more comfortably with some friends than others. Even so, each prior relationship has value, as it holds a link to your past. Each relationship offers something different.

- **Hold memorials with different specific communities.** The problem with having only one memorial, and holding it right after the funeral, is that you, the mourner, are not necessarily in the right frame of mind to receive all the love and support that is there for you. Months, or even years after their death, you will inevitably be in a different, more receptive place in your grief. Perhaps holding additional memorials later on would be even more emotionally valuable to you. You may want to hold a memorial just for work colleagues, or one for school friends, or one for the neighborhood. These could be simple, small rituals or more elaborate, structured events.

Journaling Prompts

- How is denial manifesting itself for you? What is it preventing you from doing? What people, places, or things is denial encouraging you to avoid?

- In what ways is denial causing you unnecessary suffering?

- What helps keep you tethered to reality?

- Write down every detail you can remember of the day they died. This is perhaps the scariest, most awful day of your life. Facing it early on and not allowing it to feel secretive or taboo can be a powerful way of neutralizing some of its terrible power. This is not an easy journaling prompt, and it may not help everyone. But I believe that writing down those terrible details helped give me some sense of agency early on in my grief. But be careful not to retraumatize yourself. You are writing out the trauma in order to let it go, *not* obsess over it. This may be best done with a therapist.

- What are some of the ways you can maintain continuity in your life?
- Who are you, now that you have lost one of the most important people in your life? How are you changed, and in what ways are you still you?
- What does your grief look like today?

CHAPTER SIX

Holidays

Holidays Are Brutal

There is just no getting around it, every holiday brings with it an extra level of pain to those in mourning. After all, holidays are meant to be shared with our loved ones. These are the occasions each year when we focus on spending time with the people we call family, so the absence of someone so central to our lives is inevitably excruciating. And not just the holidays themselves but often the days and weeks leading up to a holiday can be particularly painful. We remember all the years when we joyfully prepared for the festive day. Maybe we decorated with our loved one, or went shopping to buy them gifts, or simply enjoyed the anticipation of the extra time we were going to spend with them.

Now that they are gone, we are instead anticipating an extra dose of anguish. How are we going to get through these days without them? Even simple holiday greetings can cause grief. People wishing us a "Happy New Year," a "Merry Christmas," "Happy Mother's Day," or a "Happy Valentine's Day" can seem like a slap in the face, mocking our pain. Holidays can make us feel out of step with the rest of the world, and even more alienated from our community. There will be times when we wish that some of these holidays would simply disappear from the calendar and never come back again. After his wife Suzanne died, my friend Stuart and his children kind of wanted Mother's Day canceled for everyone. They argued it's not really a real holiday, most moms don't need it, and it causes horrible anguish for everyone who has lost their mom.

And yet the holidays can also be an opportunity to actively mourn our loss with structure and support. Celebrating holidays can bring us solace in the midst of our pain.

Rituals and Traditions

Another way to look at holidays is that they are each a collection of rituals. They are, therefore, opportunities for us to process our grief in an active way. The challenge is to find new meaning in old holiday rituals, or to invent new holiday rituals that can somehow incorporate or acknowledge our new loss. Denial, and our natural fear of pain, may urge us to avoid gathering with people on these difficult days, and yet these may be the times when we could use their support the most. If you are able to celebrate a particular holiday with friends and family, it can be yet another opportunity for people to bear witness to your loss and for you to find the words to express your grief.

Holiday traditions provide continuity with the life we led before our loss. That is, after all, what a tradition does: it creates continuity in the life of a family. It can be very hard to engage in these traditions, especially the first time after a loss. But hopefully we can find, over time, more solace than suffering in these practices. Gail and I found this to be true in our continued celebration of Shabbat.

Shabbat Shalom

Shabbat is the day of rest for Jews. It begins at sundown on Friday and continues till sundown on Saturday. Observant Jews light candles and say a few prayers over wine (or grape juice) and challah (traditional braided bread) and lay hands on their children and bless them as well. The four of us celebrated Shabbat almost every Friday night, taking turns saying the prayers. We gave the ritual our own spin. First, Hart would lower the lights in order to, as he said, "set the mood." Then we would take three deep breaths together as a family. After lighting the candles and blessing the wine, Ruby and Hart would begin the Hamotzi, the prayer over the bread. When they reached "our voices join in happy chorus . . . ," Ruby would always frantically gesture for Gail and me to join in. It was something she did as a little girl, and we all got such a kick out of it that she went on doing it, channeling her little Ruby self, even as she got older. It was as though she was, on the one hand, making fun of that younger, earnest Ruby, but at the same time allowing herself to be that little eager girl again for a moment. It was a beautiful tradition all her own. And because our dog, Orso, would always howl during the ceremony, we would often change a line of the prayer in Hebrew from "Eloheinu melech ha'olam" to "Eloheinu melech *howl* olam." It was silly, but it always made us smile.

The four of us created a family ritual that belonged to us. We made it special. Every family builds its own traditions. One of the main functions all our traditions share, regardless of cultural differences, is the creation of family. For me, as an atheist, Shabbat was never about god; it was always only about love and family. So with Ruby and Hart dead, how could we possibly go on celebrating the holiday? It seemed like it would bring us nothing but pain.

Yet Gail and I both quickly realized that continuing to celebrate Shabbat every Friday night would be an opportunity to connect back to the love the four of us shared. The first dozen or so Fridays were full of aching and tears. When it came time to say, "our voices join in happy chorus," of course we wept. And on some Friday nights, I still tear up at that line, imagining Ruby gesturing to us to join in. Initially, it was hard for me to have that vivid image of Ruby in my mind. But the more we did it, the more I took comfort in picturing her sweet, eager face.

Nowadays, I experience more solace than pain during Shabbat. I value it as a special time carved out of our week where we can connect. I imagine Ruby and Hart with us; I visualize them standing around the table, just as they had done for years. On good days, I can see their faces and almost hear their voices as we say the prayers. On bad days, they feel so very far, far away.

It could have easily gone very differently. Gail and I could have decided that celebrating Shabbat was a thing the four of us did, and now we would never do it again. We might have felt as though we never again wanted to share that ritual with anyone else. But in doing so, we would have consigned it to storage. In trying to protect our memories, we would have inadvertently closed ourselves off from experiencing those memories on a more regular basis. That is the irony of locking away the past. It may feel as though we are protecting our relationship with our dead, but actually we are missing out on having a more visceral connection to the life we once shared with them.

Creating New Holiday Rituals

I believe it is worth examining each holiday to see what we can change or salvage. That said, it's not easy to change a holiday when extended family members are involved. Even under the best of circumstances, planning holidays can be a complicated negotiation between people who may not all get along so easily. But mourners, especially those of us in fresh grief, are in crisis. We are going to need our families to cut us some breaks if they want us to participate. This requires us to clearly articulate what we want, in order for them to be able to help us. While it may seem obvious to us, we can't assume other people know what we need.

Gail and I thought hard about what our holidays should look like now, in order to best help us get through them with the least amount of suffering. Here I share how we navigated three different holidays in three very different ways: Thanksgiving, Christmas, and Passover.

Ritual: Reinventing Thanksgiving

Thanksgiving was the first family holiday Gail and I had to face after our loss. We were dreading gathering with our extended family, knowing there would be two empty places at the table. We did not feel particularly grateful or in the mood to be giving thanks for anything. It would be the first time we would be seeing many of our family since Shiva, and it all felt too emotionally taxing to endure. Once again, our initial impulse was to retreat from life, and avoid the holiday altogether.

In the past, we alternated each year between Gail's family and my family for Thanksgiving. This year, Gail's sister Betsy offered to host both our families. This was clearly an important opportunity for all of us to grieve together. Gail and I knew that we would have to find some way to make the holiday bearable and also meaningful to us in our grief. We would have to come up with a plan to modify the holiday and then convince both our families to go along with it. Gail and I are the youngest of our siblings. We are not usually the ones who call the shots in family gatherings. But this year was going to have to be different. We had some ground rules that we needed to put in place for us to be able to participate.

Large family gatherings inevitably involve some tension. I think most families can take it for granted that during the holidays someone is going to get upset, or say something that will get taken in the wrong way. Between jet lag, chores, and long-standing grievances, tempers are bound to flare. But Gail and I felt fragile. We didn't think we could tolerate any sniping or snide comments. We didn't have the bandwidth for familial tension. So we preemptively asked people to forgo saying anything inflammatory to anyone else for the entirety of the holiday. Maybe our request wasn't necessary. Perhaps if left to their own devices no one would have said anything upsetting anyway. Perhaps we insulted our families by even suggesting it. But it was too important to us. We had so much free-floating rage at the universe, we needed to make sure nothing our family did would set us off. Either way, it helped us to verbalize this need for peace and civility. It gave us one less thing to worry about it. Our families happily obliged.

We also knew that it would be unbearable to us if family members avoided talking about Ruby and Hart out of a desire to avoid pain and grief. In order to ensure that that wouldn't happen, we told everyone that instead of going around the table and saying what we were grateful for, we would share a memory we each had of Ruby and Hart. The structure was helpful, since some of them can be reluctant to speak aloud about their grief. Hearing them share their pain helped Gail and me feel like we weren't so alone in our sorrow. The shared ritual brought us all closer as a family. It felt good to hear all the stories of Ruby and Hart, even though it was also awful. It was so hard to believe that all we had left of them were our memories.

We wanted to make sure there was an active component to our mourning, something physical for everyone to do in honor of Ruby and Hart. We decided we would all plant daffodil bulbs in Betsy's backyard. Everyone dug holes in the earth and placed bulbs in them. Gardening can be a beautiful gesture of nurturing, in honor of those we have lost. It gives the earth new life and growth. Now, every spring, Betsy sends us pictures of the first two daffodils to sprout and bloom. They are a sweet visual memorial to Ruby and Hart.

Afterward, we all took a long walk. We started in a big cluster but gradually separated into smaller groups. I found myself walking with my niece-in-law Freddie. I hadn't spent any time with her one-on-one since the crash. It was nice to talk with her, both about our grief and also about her life. It was a good reminder that performing these rituals doesn't mean that we are staying "trapped in the past" or "locked in grief." These rituals enable us to be both in grief and in life at the same time.

We were very fortunate in that our families gave us the support we asked for. It was uncomfortable telling them how we needed to structure the holiday, but it paid off. It was not an easy day, by any stretch of the imagination. But we managed to avoid a lot of suffering, and we got a fair amount of solace.

Of course, not all families are so supportive or understanding about the needs of grieving people. You can educate some people all you want, and they will still think that it's better not to talk about grief, lest you "get stuck in it." Some people are unable to accommodate others' suffering and think only of their own comfort. If you find that your family is unwilling or unable to support your holiday needs, you may have to excuse yourself from the gathering and find support elsewhere. You may need to find a different "family" of people to mark the holidays with, ones who can better walk on this journey of grief with you. But keep in mind that you may feel very differently next year. You don't necessarily need to break forever with a challenging family member. You might just need to take a break for this particular holiday, this year.

Ritual: Canceling Christmas

A month later it was Christmastime. In the past, every year Gail and I would take the kids to Maine, where my mom has a house by a beautiful lake. My sister Cathy, my brother Christopher, and his wife Lisa would join us, and we would spend a week in a winter wonderland. The lake would often freeze, allowing us to ice skate or go cross-country skiing, if there was snow. We would build an igloo, go sledding, and build a bonfire out on the ice and toast marshmallows. Each year we would venture into the woods on our property and top off a pine tree, bring it into the house, and light candles on it, creating a storybook, old-fashioned Christmas setting. When Ruby and Hart got old enough, they helped cut the tree down and carry it into the house.

Ruby and Hart were the only grandchildren, so the holiday was centered on them. Each year we'd all listen as they read aloud from "'Twas the Night before Christmas." For me, Christmas Day meant watching Ruby and Hart open a flurry of presents and then rush outside to use whatever crazy dangerous gift their uncle got them that year—a blow dart gun, a BB gun, a bow and arrow, throwing stars, and so on. Christmas was always magical.

Now the thought of gathering with my family in Maine and unwrapping presents with no Ruby and Hart felt unendurable. By now, Gail and I had fully embraced the idea of leaning into our pain. And yet forcing ourselves to endure this holiday seemed like a form of self-punishment. It would be an exercise in longing, with no upside at all. It would lead to more suffering than grieving. We didn't think we had the strength to endure it that first year. We decided to cancel Christmas and run from the holiday as best we could.

I know this choice is counter to everything else suggested by this book. We didn't lean into the pain, we didn't use the holiday to create meaningful traditions, and we didn't pull our community closer. We fled to Rome and Naples instead. And it was absolutely the right choice for us. I don't regret it at all. It is a good reminder for me that leaning into the pain isn't always the right choice, because sometimes it simply involves too much attendant suffering. We knew we were only postponing the inevitable, and at some point in the future we would need to gather with my extended family and experience the agony of Christmas without Ruby and Hart. We would need to eventually integrate that holiday with our new grief-stricken reality. But that first year, we just didn't have it in us.

The trip we took to Rome and Naples was helpful to us. It made Christmas and New Year's Eve bearable. Friends had offered us vacation getaways earlier in the year, but those didn't feel right at the time. I was in no mood to be vacationing. But suddenly, in December, it felt right. Wandering around the ruins of a long-gone ancient civilization suited our mood. We derived some solace from all the ancient carnage of Pompeii. Being in Naples on Christmas Day, surrounded by throngs of locals, cloaked in anonymity, made the day bearable. We wept as we watched the New Year's Eve fireworks erupting over Rome, but we could also appreciate the view.

We still grieved while in Italy. We didn't actually escape the pain of our loss. We talked every day about Ruby and Hart and our shattered lives. We revisited parts of Rome that we had taken the kids to in the past. We wept. But we were also kind to ourselves on that trip. We indulged in nice dinners. We walked all over the city. We went to obscure art museums and saw two plays. We ate gelato every day.

Other grieving people I spoke to also dramatically altered their first Christmas after their profound loss. After his wife Carolyn died, James took his daughter Lola shopping for brand-new decorations, and they purchased a life-size Christmas pig. It is pink, lights up on the inside, and has a Santa Claus hat and scarf. For James, it was a way to mark the change: "It became something different, it was what we did now. You couldn't not notice the pig." For the actual day, James took his daughters Ruby and Lola to Berlin. He thought, "I am just going to take us all out of the situation. We went away to *not* be here." My friend Stuart and his two children decided they would do something that his wife Suzanne would have hated, so that it wouldn't feel like she was missing out. They went on a Disney cruise for Christmas—which Suzanne would have detested. My friend Gretchen's family escaped to Europe for their first Christmas. And then to New Zealand for their second one after Dana's death.

I realize that trips to Europe or Disney cruises are extravagant, and not everyone in grief can afford such a luxury. But regardless of one's economic situation, the *emotional* challenge of giving ourselves permission to take a vacation in our grief and cancel a holiday can be daunting. For me, it is easy to slip into a self-punishing mode. My survivor's guilt, coupled with my tendency to be overly dogmatic, can often lead me into a practice of relentless mourning, in which I carry the horror of my loss with me at all times. This is something I am actively working on as I grieve. Maybe it comes from a place of being scared I will forget Ruby and Hart (which intellectually I know is impossible). Or maybe it's my guilt preventing me from fully enjoying the life I have left.

Christmas was another lesson in the complexity of grieving. There is no simple "correct" course of action as we navigate our loss. We mourners are always confronted with the challenge of striking a balance between facing the healthy pain of loss and leaning so far in that we cause ourselves undue suffering.

Ritual: Altering Passover

After canceling Christmas, Gail was tempted to keep going and cancel our first Passover as well. A Passover without Ruby and Hart struck Gail as particularly pointless and painful. The centerpiece of the holiday is the Passover Seder. It's a long meal shared with friends and family full of rituals, prayer, and feasting. During the Seder, everyone reads aloud from the Haggadah, which tells the story of the Jews' escape from the slavery of a cruel Egyptian pharaoh. The thought of "celebrating" an escape from bondage seemed particularly galling to Gail, now that it felt as though we were forever in bondage to our grief.

One ritual of the holiday is reciting the ten plagues that god inflicted on the Egyptians because their pharaoh refused to free the Jews. The last plague is the death of the firstborn child. Gail insisted there was no way she was going to sit through a Seder meal talking about the deaths of firstborn children. After we railed against the newly felt cruelty of this holiday, we began to ask ourselves which of the Seder traditions might still have meaning and value for us.

After all, Gail had celebrated the Passover Seder every year for her entire life. She used to love this holiday. Instead of throwing the whole day out the window, could we design our own version of the Seder meal that would work for us? Was there a way to simultaneously keep some continuity, honor Ruby and Hart, connect with her family, and also, crucially, be kind to ourselves? Could we get any solace from this first Passover without Ruby and Hart?

The difficulty was compounded by the fact that the holiday took place during the COVID-19 lockdown, which meant we would be Zooming over computer screens with the other members of Gail's family. Ultimately, we came up with an extremely abbreviated Seder. Instead of the traditional three-hour meal, it would last about forty minutes. Gail sent out detailed instructions to her entire family, explaining who would read what parts of the Haggadah, what prayers would be said, and by whom. Certain parts were cut out completely—the four questions, the escape from Egypt—and other new elements were added in. In between each section of the Haggadah, Gail asked us all to share a memory from a past Seder. She sent her instructions a day in advance, so people would have time to prepare.

The Seder has a number of old songs that are traditionally sung, but instead Gail asked her niece Raffaella to close out the meal with "Little Green" by Joni Mitchell. Raffaella had sung this song at Ruby and Hart's funeral, and it is hauntingly sad. By the time she sang about how life will give you icicles and birthday clothes and sometimes sorrow, we were all weeping. It was a struggle for Raffaella to sing through her tears, but she managed it. Weeping together as a family was a beautiful way to grieve and bring our loss out into the open to be shared. It felt important to us to incorporate our loss into this holiday. It was now part of our Passover story.

If you are Christian, you may face similar challenges celebrating the first Easter after a loss. You may feel able to attend Easter services but need to skip the Easter egg hunt. You may want to forgo dyeing eggs but take solace in other family traditions. The holiday's theme of resurrection and rebirth may be too difficult for you during that first year of loss, but your feelings may evolve over time.

Post-Holiday Crash

I often experience intense anticipatory anxiety in the days and weeks leading up to a holiday. I worry about how awful I will feel waking up on the actual day, knowing I have to spend the holiday without Ruby and Hart. I can get so worked up imagining worst-case scenarios of unendurable pain that when the actual day arrives, it often feels relatively "easy." I am usually surprised that night at how the day that I had been dreading had passed so quickly. It was, after all, just another day.

And then I get hit with the post-holiday crash. It feels almost as if "I did it, I made it through this incredibly painful holiday, but so what? My pain hasn't lessened. My loved ones are still dead. The stress, anxiety, and sorrow that I just endured was all for nothing." These thoughts can be so disheartening and demoralizing that it can feel like I am taking a step backward in my journey through grief. Post-holiday crashes can often send me into a spiral of despair.

However, I would argue that there *is* a benefit to enduring the holidays. It wasn't all for nothing. Processing our loss through the framework of holiday rituals is an important part of active grieving. These holidays help us stay alive and engaged in life. They are an important piece of continuity and connectivity.

Knowing that there will be a post-holiday crash is helpful to me. It allows me to anticipate the extra wave of grief and hopelessness. When I find myself in one of these waves, I think about Ruby's "Ocean" essay, and I take heart.

> *This would be a peaceful life, a good life, and I will only have to brave one more wave.*
>
> *I see it approaching, slowly building, and so I swim forward to meet it, the taste of salt on my tongue.*

Día de los Muertos

There is, of course, a holiday that is specifically designed for us, the Mexican tradition of Día de los Muertos, or Day of the Dead. Traditionally celebrated on either November 1 or 2, it is a day to remember and celebrate people we have lost. Participants build an altar for an offering, or ofrenda, which often includes photos of their loved ones, along with their favorite foods or personal items. These altars are decorated with sugar skulls, or calaveras, and marigold flowers, or cempazúchitl. The tone of the gatherings is often irreverent and celebratory.

My friend Mike has been hosting a large gathering for Día de los Muertos for more than twenty years. He started celebrating it to honor his mother, Sally, who died of suicide when Mike was about to turn twelve. "What began with a few people has built into parties of fifty or sixty. It starts with a convocation. I tell the crowd that you die three times: the first, when your heart stops, the second, when they put you in the ground, and the third, when the last person who can tell a story about you is gone from the earth. And then I tell a story of my own for whoever I lost that year. Or I might tell someone else's story who is not there. And then I ask, 'Does anyone want to say a name? Does anyone want to say something they remember about them?' People say a name, and then of course, the stories come. And over the years people have invited others who have lost someone that year. Often people are talking about their loss for the first time. I have veterans who have come to this ceremony for years and years who know to be quiet and to listen and to honor them as they explore their own feelings. There are very funny stories and there are a lot of tears. And almost inevitably someone new shows up at my door every year that I may not even know, but they've been invited for that very purpose. Those pictures and those items that they bring stay on the altar. Every year I send a photo out of the altar so that they can find their own people on it and know that, 'Hey, even if I wasn't able to go this year, my aunt is still on the altar, and she's still next to Christine's friends, just like last year, and she's next to Kelly's dad, and she's near Colin and Gail's kids, and they always have the candy over in that corner.' We survive through ritual. We build ritual in an attempt to understand grief, but grief is not understandable. Death and loss—in the end, we can't process them fully, so we have to come up with artificial ways to try our best, you know?"

On Mike's altar, next to Ruby's photo is a set of plastic vampire teeth, because Ruby loved vampires and for her last Halloween, she put in red contact lenses and fake vampire teeth and looked perfect. And next to Hart's photo is a bag of Flamin' Hot Cheetos since he loved them. Whenever he was enjoying a bag, he'd insist I try one, because he was convinced that if I just tried enough of them, I would eventually realize they were delicious.

Navigating the Next Holiday

Now, when the next holiday approaches, I feel as though I have tools to navigate it, including a checklist of questions to ask myself. I carefully assess where I am at emotionally. I contemplate what sort of ritual I would like to perform. Is it a private or public ritual? How elaborate do I want it to be? What parts of the holiday do I want to change or skip? How can I be kind to myself even as I grieve? There is clearly no "correct" way to get through any holiday. And our relationship to each holiday changes every year. I believe the important thing is to pay close attention to where we are and honor our emotional needs in that moment. And avoid, as best we can, any feelings of guilt about our choices. If we need to cancel a particular holiday this year, so be it. For the third Christmas after the crash Gail and I included my family in a discussion about the best ways to incorporate Ruby and Hart into the holiday. It was nice to brainstorm ideas. It felt like we were grieving together as a family. My sister Cathy had the beautiful idea to hang Ruby and Hart's stockings and to build a small altar with their photos, a sort of Christmas ofrenda.

Hopefully, each new holiday will bring us all some solace amid the pain.

Actions

- **Design your own version of the next holiday.** Redefine a family tradition in a way that incorporates your loss and honors your loved one. Create new holiday rituals that hold a special meaning for you.
- **Find continuity in some traditions or rituals from your past.** Maintain some of the traditions or rituals you used to do with your loved one, even though it may seem too painful at first. Use these traditions as a way to stay connected to your loved one and the life you shared. Treat these traditions as an opportunity to carve out a special time in which to focus on the person you've lost.
- **Allow yourself to cancel a holiday this year.** You can engage in the process of reintegrating it into your new life some other year. Don't worry about it.
- **Allow yourself a vacation.** Not a vacation from your grief, because it will come with you on vacation, but a break from some of your suffering. Take a vacation from your guilt and self-punishment. Allow yourself to experience pleasure alongside your pain.

Journaling Prompts

- What has this holiday meant to you in the past? What can it mean to you now, in your new reality?
- How would you transform this holiday so as to honor your loved one and also provide an opportunity to share your pain with your family? Can you create a new holiday ritual that has meaning for you? What would your loved one want you to do for this holiday?
- In what ways do you imagine your family will rise to the challenge of making space for your grief during the holiday? In what ways do

you anticipate them failing you in this time of need? Can you design a holiday that mitigates your disappointment and discomfort?

- What would make this holiday less cruel for you? Can you change some of its elements in order to make it more bearable?

- What are some of your favorite memories from past celebrations of this holiday?

- We know intellectually that our loved one would want us to feel pleasure, and yet it is hard to allow ourselves that indulgence while we are in mourning. What are some of the ways in which you have been able to experience pleasure? What does it feel like to hold joy and grief at the same time?

CHAPTER SEVEN

Guilt

Survivor's Guilt

Survivor's guilt can take many forms and infect almost every aspect of our new lives. It can make it emotionally difficult to maintain basic levels of care, such as exercise and sleeping. Even the simple act of feeding ourselves can feel like a betrayal of the one who died. I can feel guilty for enjoying a beautiful sunset, or for taking a walk, or for enjoying a movie. I can feel guilty over doing something that I used to do with Ruby and Hart, and I can also feel guilty over doing something new that Ruby and Hart never got the chance to experience. I can feel guilty simply for surviving the crash when they did not.

I remember in the early days, both Gail and I felt incredibly guilty about our crying. We wept almost every day and yet we felt as though we weren't crying enough. We each thought the other was crying more. Survivor's guilt can turn grieving into a "damned if you do, damned if you don't" situation. We desperately struggle to not be overwhelmed by the pain of our loss, and yet the minute we experience any respite, we are immediately crushed by feelings of guilt. It can make grieving feel relentless.

Not only do we feel guilty that we have survived, but we can also feel that we are somehow responsible for their deaths. We think we could have, and should have, saved their lives. Our brains will very quickly find an action we might have taken that would have kept them alive, no matter how absurd or unrealistic. I remember my sister Cathy telling me, with anguish in her voice, that she wished she had called me on the night of the crash and told me not to go to Joshua Tree. But Cathy lives across the country from me and didn't even know we were going to Joshua Tree. Why on earth would she have suddenly called me up and told me not to do something she didn't know anything about? How could she possibly feel guilty? Yet she does. Clearly, our brains will work overtime finding inventive ways for us to feel as though it were our fault they died.

Sometimes guilt can be a useful emotion. It can remind us of our obligations to other people. Guilt over past actions can encourage us to behave better in the future. But survivor's guilt seems largely useless. Any remorse or regret we have concerning our actions in the past can't help us now. Death cannot be reversed by a change in our behavior. It's too late—our loved one is gone. Survivor's guilt creates suffering with seemingly no remedy or purpose.

A Misguided Sense of Obligation

Ruby's OCD therapist, Dr. Grayson, once asked me if I could imagine ever not wanting to feel guilty. And at the time, I couldn't. I clung to my terrible guilt as if it were an important connection to Ruby and Hart. In my mind, feeling guilty was a way of still actively being their dad. If I ever gave up my guilt, it would mean that I was no longer behaving like their father. It would mean that my kids were dead and gone.

But of course, they are dead. And yet I am still their father. But I am no longer actively parenting them, because they don't need any more parenting. Sadly, Ruby and Hart don't need anything from me anymore. My guilt doesn't help them; it only mars my own life. My guilt narrows my range of experiences by preventing me from being fully open to what life might still have to offer me. My guilt doesn't honor Ruby and Hart. They don't need it and they don't want it. So how do I give myself permission to let go of it?

I often think about Megan Devine's idea of suffering versus the healthy pain of loss. In her book, *It's OK That You're Not OK*, she writes, "Pain is a healthy, normal response when someone you love is torn from your life. It hurts, but that doesn't make pain *wrong*. Suffering comes when we feel dismissed or unsupported in our pain, and when we thrash around inside our pain, questioning our choices, our 'normalcy,' our actions and reactions." In that context, I find it useful to think of these pangs of guilt as unnecessary suffering. They are not a part of the productive pain of grieving. It's not helpful to dwell on feelings of guilt and remorse. These emotions can, in fact, be a distraction from the grieving process.

My friend Lindsey, who lost her sister when they were teenagers, has been struggling with feelings of survivor's guilt for twenty-five years. As a teen, she took her grieving cues from her mother, who felt tremendous guilt over Casey's death. Lindsey felt that "if it's her fault, then maybe it's also a little my fault and we should both stay in secret blame and shame forever." Lindsey's guilt had given her a lot of obsessive-compulsive beliefs about how she should behave and what her obligations were in the world. For many years, she believed, "If I am in pain, maybe that will keep other people safe." She feared what might happen if she ever stopped being in pain because that might be "a betrayal of the people I have lost." It's only recently that she has been able to shake some of these guilty feelings. Her therapist asked her what would be the worst, most taboo, and guilty thing she could possibly do. Lindsey replied that it would be to dance on the anniversary of Casey's death while eating Casey's favorite candy, Skittles. At her therapist's urging, Lindsey did just that, and discovered to her surprise that it actually felt really nice. It felt like she was celebrating Casey, not betraying her. It helped her to see that Casey's life was not solely defined by its painful end, but also contained joy and happiness. Doing the "most blasphemous" thing was a real turning point for Lindsey in terms of processing her feelings of guilt and loss. Dancing while eating Skittles was, in effect, a powerful mourning ritual.

Guilt Is a Form of Denial

My therapist offered me the helpful idea that guilt is actually a form of denial. While I am busy being guilt-ridden, thinking about what I could have done differently to save Ruby and Hart, I am imagining an alternate reality in which they are still alive. I am living in a "what if" universe in which I still have time to save them. Because I am so desperate to imagine them still being alive, I will happily punish myself with guilt if that is what it takes. Even though it is gut-wrenching to blame myself for their deaths, it is a way for me to stay in denial. And denial has a powerful allure. But as we know, denial is ultimately not our friend. So I take some comfort in knowing that as I struggle to not dwell in feelings of guilt, I am actually doing the heroic work of confronting denial.

I sometimes find that whole hours of my day disappear in guilty ruminations. My mind gets stuck on a loop as I think, over and over again, about how I should have never made that turn. Or I should have just stayed in the turn lane another few seconds and then that car would have harmlessly flown past me and my whole life would be different. Or I think how I should have made that turn faster, and raced into the gas station, and that car would have harmlessly crossed behind me. Having these guilty thoughts cycle over and over through my mind is exhausting and pointless. It doesn't bring Ruby and Hart back to me. Eventually, I manage to pull myself out of this self-punishing trap. I force my mind to shift the blame back where it belongs—onto the drunk driver and her many, many terrible choices that night. Choices I had absolutely no control over. Letting go of the guilt allows me to return to life. It lets me live in the present and not dwell in some alternate universe that is not real.

Even my feelings of survivor's guilt are a form of denial. They are an attempt at denying the reality that life goes on for everyone who is still alive, regardless of how they feel about it. Those guilty feelings are keeping me tethered to a past that no longer exists. I need to accept that my guilt can't find a way to bring them back. I have to say goodbye to Ruby and Hart over and over again.

We Are Not in Control

Another powerful thought my therapist offered is that it may be easier for me to feel guilty for Ruby and Hart's deaths than it is for me to accept the reality that I am not in control of what happens in my life. Terrible things happen all the time. Plagues, fires, drunk drivers, diseases, accidents, wars, crime—these are not things that we can stop. It is terrifying to contemplate how vulnerable life can truly be. Sometimes feelings of guilt give us the false sense that we are in control of our fates, when the reality is that there is uncertainty in life. As the editors of *Treating Traumatic Bereavement: A Practitioner's Guide* write, "Self-blame serves the purpose of shoring up the belief that there is some controllability in the universe and that what happens is not completely random. . . . Despite the anguish that typically accompanies feelings of guilt, it is easier for survivors to find themselves guilty of some sin of omission than to acknowledge how helpless they truly are." It can be hard to acknowledge how little control we actually have over our own lives.

Helen Keller wrote, "Security is mostly a superstition. It does not exist in nature, nor do the children of men as a whole experience it. Avoiding danger is no safer in the long run than outright exposure. Life is either a daring adventure, or nothing." I was first introduced to this quote by Ruby. Dr. Grayson had given it to her weekly OCD adult group meeting to discuss. Even though Ruby was only sixteen years old when she joined the group, she quickly became an outspoken leader and often shared inspiring insights. This quote meant a lot to her, and she tacked it onto the corkboard in her bedroom. It helped her with her compulsions. Now Helen Keller's quote helps me with my grief. For my birthday, Gail had an artist hand-paint the lettering onto a wood panel. It hangs in our living room. It gives me some solace and inspiration. In the face of uncertainty, I choose daring adventure.

Ruby and Hart's Love

Ruby and Hart loved me and were rooting for me in life, just as I was rooting for them. Sometimes it helps me to think of their sweet faces as they shout encouragements to me to pull myself out of these self-punishing thoughts and get back to living my life and honoring their memories. I can imagine Hart teasing me to "Get up off the couch, old man!" and Ruby coaxing me, "C'mon, Papa, c'mon, you can do it."

There Is Comfort in Knowing I Am Not Alone

In grief groups, people often share their feelings of guilt and responsibility over the deaths of their children. As I listen to their stories, it's easy for me to see how irrational it is for them to blame themselves. I often find myself thinking, "They shouldn't feel guilty at all." Which, of course, I should also in theory be able to say about myself. If I think they clearly shouldn't feel guilt, then why can't I accord myself the same courtesy?

I also see how hard it is for them to believe the rest of us when we tell them they are not to blame. Witnessing their struggle to cut themselves a break helps me to put my own difficulties in perspective.

It's Not So Easy to Dispel Guilt

All of these thoughts are nice, intellectual rationalizations, but they don't actually succeed in causing my feelings of guilt to magically disappear. I wish it were that easy. Guilt accompanies me every day. I find that it comes in short waves, and that the best way for me to navigate them is to have one or more of the thoughts I have discussed, namely:

- Guilt is a distraction from grieving.
- Guilt adds to our unnecessary suffering.

- Guilt is a form of denial.
- Guilt is a way of hiding from the truth that we are not in control.
- Our guilt doesn't honor our loved one.
- We don't owe anyone our guilt.
- Our loved one wouldn't want us to waste time in guilt.
- Survivor's guilt is shared by many others who have lost someone.

All of these thoughts help me, but one of the most effective ways of mitigating my feelings of guilt is to engage in some form of active grieving.

When Survivor's Guilt Can Sometimes Be Useful

There are times when feeling guilty can actually be useful. The tug of guilt can keep us tethered to the reality of our loss. It can work to prevent us from ignoring, or compartmentalizing, our grief. Guilt can act as a healthy reminder that we need to honor our grief and the love we shared. I find that my guilt often builds up when it feels as though I have been neglecting my grief. Let's face it, it's not "fun" to grieve. It can be a relief to take a break from it and allow myself to feel a little enjoyment and pleasure. It's nice to not dwell so much on my loss. But at a certain point, my grief demands attention. I can't hide from it for too long. I need to carve out some time and energy and simply grieve for Ruby and Hart and all that we have lost. Guilt is one way that grief steers me back to face the pain. It is a way for my heart to tell me that I need to do the hard work of grieving.

I definitely feel less guilty after I've cried, or visited their grave, or held some ritual in their honor. It doesn't have to be an elaborate public ritual. It could be something small and private. It can even simply be talking about Ruby and Hart with a friend or family member. I don't need to cry either. I could have a happy conversation about Ruby and Hart, in which I share a funny story. What matters is that I listen to the prompt my heart is giving me. Feelings of guilt don't have to send me down a self-punishing spiral of suffering. Instead, guilt can guide me toward action.

Ritual: Visiting Their Graves

I am often reluctant to visit Ruby and Hart's graves. Their burial was an extraordinarily agonizing event. I remember bits and pieces of the day very clearly, but I was also in a lot of physical pain from the car crash and a little out of my mind with shock and disbelief. I can be certain that a visit back to the cemetery will bring on tears and aching and a fair amount of despair. It's not exactly a calm place of rest for me.

And yet Ruby and Hart are there. At least their physical bodies are there. As my friend Shirley says about her son, "I know his skinny bones are there. I think, 'Yeah, I know you're not here, your soul is somewhere else. But if I opened the coffin, I know your skinny bones are gonna be there.' So in that way I feel peaceful that I have a place to cry for him." Shirley goes to the cemetery almost every Sunday with a blanket, lies down, and talks to Jon. She tells him about her life and how his baby daughter Jimena is doing. She pours out onto the grave a little Coke and a few chips of Flamin' Hot Cheetos (he and Hart had the same taste!) and she listens to his favorite song, which he dedicated to her, "Una Cancíon para Mamá" by Boyz II Men. "In the summer I bring his favorite ice cream and I have my ice cream. His ice cream is melting and I'm eating mine, but I know he's enjoying it. That's what I like to believe, you know?"

The Jews have a tradition of leaving a small stone on top of the headstone each time they visit the grave of a loved one. It's a nice tradition for several reasons. It gives the mourner something physical to do, yet another ritualized task to perform in grief. We have to choose a specific stone and bring it with us. The act of laying the stone on top of the grave is a physical gesture of love. Stones allude to the timelessness of that love; they aren't going anywhere any time soon. The accumulation of stones atop Ruby and Hart's headstones also gives me some solace. Their numbers are a testament to all the other people who have visited their graves and left stones behind. Sometimes when Gail and I come to the cemetery, we notice new rocks that weren't there before. Seeing the physical expression of so much love is helpful to me. One rock atop Ruby's headstone has the word "rebel" painted on it. Another rock is in the shape of a heart. All the rocks are beautiful to me.

Ruby loved succulents. She tended to a large succulent in our kitchen, which absurdly she named Maurice. On our many desert hikes, she would admire the succulents and cactuses we passed by. So Gail and I thought it would be beautiful to have a small desert garden built into their graves. We had a single cement planter installed in front of the two tombstones, linking them. We filled it with a variety of succulents.

So now, when we visit their graves, Gail and I tend to their succulent garden. We bring a blanket and lie down on top of their burial plots and cry as we weed and water the plants. And we talk to Ruby and Hart. We tell them a little bit about what we're doing and how we miss them.

Our visits to the cemetery are a private ritual. They involve a physical action, a verbalization of our loss, and an opportunity for us to mourn. Going to the cemetery is a way of carving out time for Ruby and Hart, and for our grief. We are able to honor the place that they hold in our hearts and in our lives. After a trip to the cemetery, my feelings of guilt usually subside. For a little while, I feel as though I am moving through life with grief at my side and not on top of me.

A Grave That Glitters

My friend Jesse has a beautiful graveside ritual for her son Gidi. He loved glitter and, really, anything that sparkled. So when Jesse and her husband Amit visit his grave every Wednesday, they always sprinkle it with glitter. And on his yahrzeit, the anniversary of his death, they hand out baggies of glitter to everyone who comes, and by the end of the day, "his whole grave sparkles. There's so much glitter it's blinding. It's actually funny because when we were getting his gravestone made, we asked if there was a way that we could get glitter embedded in the headstone somehow and they looked into it and they were like, 'We can't get it done, no one does that. To somehow put glitter on the stone itself and then cover it—there's just no way for us to do it.' So we said okay. But we have sprinkled so much glitter over the years that it has permanently stuck onto the headstone and now people ask us, 'How did you get a headstone with glitter on it?' They said it couldn't be done, so we did it ourselves!"

The Guilt of Regret and Remorse

I have so much unfinished business with Ruby and Hart. We had our whole lives ahead of us. There was so much that I was looking forward to, so many milestones that I was eager to share with them: their first true loves, marriage, careers, grandchildren. But most of all, I was excited to see what kind of adults they would blossom into. Now, with that future stolen away from us, I find myself instead replaying, and regretting, many of my worst parenting moments. As I remember those low points in my life, I ache for the opportunity to apologize to Ruby and Hart. I wish I could go back in time and make better choices and be kinder and more understanding.

I wish I hadn't pushed Ruby so hard at school. I wish I had not been so scared of mental illness when she began presenting signs of OCD and needed my help. I wish I could have been able to see earlier that she needed to be pulled from her toxic middle school. I wish I had celebrated her incredible talents more. We have her artwork all over our house now, but I wish we had hung more of it while she was still alive. I told her I loved her every day, but I wish now that I had told her even more often than that. For several years her OCD made it difficult for her to receive hugs, but now I wish I had fought harder to hug her. I wish I had found a way to make it okay for her.

I wish I hadn't pushed Hart so hard at school. I wish I had found more patience when teaching him math. I wish I hadn't pushed him so hard to go on school overnight field trips when he was feeling fragile and scared because of his sister's mental health struggles. I wish I had talked to him more on those rides home from school. I wish I had spent more time with him doing whatever he wanted—which probably meant playing more video games.

The remorse I feel at all these failures is magnified because I can't ever make amends. It is too late for me to apologize to Ruby and Hart, or to make it up to them. I didn't know we had so little time left to us, but then again, no one ever does. So now what do I do with all these guilty feelings and thoughts? I wish I had some profound piece of advice to offer, but I don't. I know that sharing my feelings of regret and remorse with others helps. So does journaling about these complicated feelings. Writing this chapter has been painful, but helpful. It doesn't make these feelings go away, but it does allow me to live side by side with them. Accepting my remorse is part of my journey through grief.

The older sister of a friend of Ruby's, whose name is also Ruby, lost her mother, Carolyn, when she was nineteen years old. Carolyn battled breast cancer for five years, so according to Ruby, "I had years to do all the things I wanted to do with her, and ask all the questions I wanted to ask her, and I still didn't do it." Yet as a teenager she was largely shielded by her parents from the gravity of her mother's condition. In fact, her mother often urged her to stay focused instead on college admissions and on having developmentally appropriate experiences. Life is always more complicated and challenging than regret would have us believe. As Ruby shared with me, "Grief and death compress the time we spent with our loved ones down to a point, and make us demand perfection of our past selves, and feel grief and guilt for the ways we failed to live up to that perfection. It's important to remember that we are whole people with reasons for acting the way we did at the time. It's unfair of me to expect so much of myself when I was essentially a child in a very difficult and stressful situation."

I think Ruby is right. All we can do is have appreciation for the challenges we were operating under, along with compassion for the limitations we had at the time. Of course we would do things differently now, but while they were alive we did the best we could.

Guilt and Rage Intertwined

There is one particularly strange manifestation of my guilt that occurs frequently enough that I believe it bears mentioning, as I suspect it's not unique to me. Every so often, I will catch myself thinking about a friend, or even a stranger, who in my imagination is somehow failing to understand the depths of my pain and grief. I begin to have an imaginary conversation in my head with this person, in which I attempt to get them to grasp the ungraspable, namely just how badly I ache for Ruby and Hart to still be alive.

I become frustrated with this theoretical person because they don't understand how trivial their problems are compared to mine. I tell them that I would be willing to sacrifice my own life if it meant Ruby and Hart could return. I then descend into absurd depths of violence, shouting at this imaginary person that I would gladly set myself on fire and slowly roast to death if it could bring Ruby and Hart back from the dead. Not only that, but I would brutally murder all my friends and family to get my two children back. As this imaginary conversation continues to spin out in my mind, I become progressively more and more furious and unhinged. It's at the point when I begin to actually shout out loud, that I catch myself and realize I need to find a healthier outlet for these outsized emotions.

Obviously, these outbursts come from all the free-flowing rage that is bouncing around inside me. But they are also clearly a manifestation of my guilt. Even though I would have done anything in my power to keep Ruby and Hart alive, ultimately, I failed to save them. They died while in my care. They died while in my car. I think these imaginary conversations are really expressions of my own internal struggles with guilt. Understanding where some of my misplaced anger comes from can be helpful in dissipating it. It's not a good feeling to be caught up in so much fury at the rest of the world. I don't want to turn bitter and full of hate. I don't want to be that guy who walks down the street talking to himself, caught up in an imaginary shouting match.

It takes so much stretching of my heart to accommodate the reality that I am alive, and Ruby and Hart are not.

Writing the Story of My Life

I sometimes think about my life as if it were a story. I don't want my story to be: "Colin and Gail's two beautiful, loving children were killed by a drunk driver and so then their lives were over. Colin and Gail retreated from the world and lived out their remaining years shrouded in grief and doing nothing but weeping." I don't want to live the rest of my life "shrouded in grief." It's an apt but terrible phrase. It evokes the image of someone prematurely wrapped in a burial shroud, living in permanent semidarkness; they can't see the light shining because they are already halfway dead.

I may feel broken and aching for something that is gone forever, but I refuse to write off the rest of my life like that. My story is not over. I intend to continue to live a full life. I want to keep making connections to students, I want to make more theater and films, I want to have more adventures with Gail. I want to love more. I want to make a difference in the world. I want to make Ruby and Hart proud.

When Catastrophe Is No Longer a Crisis

As time passed and we moved out of the acute stage of grief, Gail and I faced a new emotional challenge. We were no longer in a state of crisis. By late August we no longer needed either of her sisters to live with us. We were able to cook and do laundry for ourselves. We ended the incredibly generous meal train that Ikar and Campbell Hall had organized. We both returned to work. We were able to have conversations with friends that were about subjects other than Ruby and Hart and our grief. In other words, we were able to function again as "normal" adults. We were no longer in emergency mode. Our pain and aching hadn't disappeared at all, but to the outside world we appeared as if we were doing okay. Which made us ask ourselves, how could we be suffering such a catastrophic loss and still manage to seem okay?

As I continue to move forward through grief it can be emotionally confusing to feel less and less in crisis. The more adjusted I become, the more emotional dissonance I experience. And with that dissonance comes guilt. How can I be laughing with Gail? How can I be teaching? How can I be writing a book about grief? Shouldn't I be out of my mind and wailing uncontrollably? Ironically, the better I am able to navigate my grief, the more guilt I feel.

I remember I was at a Compassionate Friends grief group meeting early on and Jesse said that she missed the days when she cried every day. At the time, I was crying every day and I couldn't imagine that ever changing. And yet I remember thinking that I couldn't imagine that I would ever *want* to go back to this state of constant pain, because it felt so awful.

But now I understand how she was feeling. In a way, the focus of early grief can be comforting. There is clarity in its all-consuming nature. There is no room for anything but grief. In a way, Ruby and Hart were still with me in those early days, because I had not accepted the reality that they were truly gone forever. I can see now why it might feel nice to be able to return to that early state of fresh agony.

In early grief I believed that I had the right to insist on the terms of my social interactions. I felt it was appropriate for me to tell people what we could and couldn't talk about. I was in crisis and my needs clearly outweighed anyone else's. If they couldn't cater to me, I would walk away from the situation, or the entire relationship if necessary. Acute grief is extremely selfish. It needs to be.

But nowadays, it's more complicated. Often my grief needs to take a back seat to the ebb and flow of life and other people's needs. Sometimes it can feel like I am neglecting my grief, and thus neglecting Ruby and Hart. What is worse, sometimes I *want* to neglect my grief. Being in the flow of life can feel nice. It can feel good to take a break and just enjoy myself. And that, of course, brings on feelings of guilt.

And yet I have done all my grief work for precisely this very reason. By repeatedly leaning into the pain and processing my loss, I have enabled myself to return to life and experience pleasure and laughter again. So why can't I let myself off the hook? After so many months and years of grieving, haven't I earned a break?

As time goes on, my feelings of guilt change and evolve, but they don't disappear. I need to accept this reality and learn to live with guilt, just as I need to live with grief. Guilt is a complicated feeling, and it requires our attention and self-analysis. Just as untended grief can turn us bitter, angry, and self-destructive, so, too, can our feelings of guilt.

It's Not Your Fault

If you were responsible for the safety of the person who died, if they were a child under your care, or a soldier or first responder under your command, or a sibling or partner you felt responsible for, then I am so, so very sorry. I know the terrible burden you carry. But the fact is, we can't actually guarantee the safety of anyone. No one is ever truly safe. Terrible things happen all the time and there is not a lot we can do about it. You are not responsible for your loved one's death. There were other, more important factors at play over which you had no control.

It's hard to hear, so I'll say it again.

You are not responsible for your loved one's death. There were other, more important factors at play *over which you had no control.*

Actions

- **Articulate your feelings of guilt.** Write about them in your journal. Share them with people you trust. It can help take away some of guilt's power over you, and it can enable you to put your feelings into perspective.
- **Create a counternarrative to your thoughts of guilt.** Incorporate the truth that we are not always in control, and that terrible things happen all the time, and that love involves loss.
- **Seek out other mourners who are also grappling with guilt.** Many people in grief struggle with guilt. Join a local grief group and share your feelings. It helps to not feel so alone.
- **Perform another mourning ritual.** Carve out the time and space to perform some physical act that commemorates

your loss and celebrates the love you shared. It can be a private or public ritual. Honor the dead and the place they hold in your heart.

Journaling Prompts

- Write about your feelings of guilt and remorse. Explore your most taboo and secret self-punishing thoughts. Get it all out on the page. Expose it to the light of day. Keeping feelings of guilt and shame hidden away will only make them more dangerous and overwhelming.
- Explore all the ways in which you are not responsible for their death. These rationalizations won't make your feelings of guilt magically disappear, but they can help mitigate their negative effects. They can provide some perspective. A reality check can reveal how little control we truly have over another's life and death.
- Write a letter to your loved one. Share your feelings of guilt and remorse, but also your love. Tell them what you are doing to cope with the pain of your loss. Tell them how you are honoring them in the small moments of daily life, and also in the larger life decisions you are making. Tell them how you hope to make them proud of you.
- Write a letter from your loved one to you. (You can channel them because, after all, they are a part of you. They helped shape who you are.) Let them write about anything they want, but also let them weigh in on your guilt. Do they forgive you? Do they want you to suffer? What advice would they give to you?
- Does some of your guilt come from mixed emotions you have toward your loved one? Are you struggling with feelings of anger toward them? Do you have specific regrets or frustrations?

We all have complicated feelings toward the people we love. Yet complex feelings toward people who have died can make us feel guilty or ashamed. Journaling is a way to safely express and explore those mixed emotions in a place of no judgment.

CHAPTER EIGHT

Rage

When Anger Is a Primary Emotion

There is an oft-repeated therapeutic refrain: "Anger is not a primary emotion." The idea here is that when you feel anger it is really that you are struggling with another, deeper emotion that you don't want to examine, and you are obscuring it in anger. But sometimes that is simply not the case. Sometimes we mourners are just plain angry. We have been robbed. Life has taken something precious from us. Our loss is unjust and can leave us feeling helpless. According to Gwen Schwartz-Borden, in an article about grief for *Social Casework*, "Often this helplessness is linked with an incredible sense of rage, and it is not unusual for the survivor to want to vent his or her anger at someone. This expression of their rage may help counter the feelings of helplessness they are experiencing."

For those of us who have been brought up to not show our anger, these feelings can be challenging. The clinical and forensic psychologist Stephen A. Diamond writes in *Psychology Today*, "Anger is a primary emotion that tends to be repressed in most patients. . . . For many, to feel angry is to feel out of control, irrational, unenlightened, uncivilized, and this frequently leads to fear, shame and anxiety. And more repression."

Friends and family get uncomfortable when Gail and I express our anger. Just as people feel an impulse to "fix" our grief, they often also want to "correct" our anger and steer us back toward safer, more socially palatable emotions like sadness. Rage can be hard to accept. At times Gail and I are angry at the rest of the world. And that includes our friends and family, and everyone we know. That doesn't make us easy to be around.

Free-Floating Rage

In theory, my anger should be focused exclusively on the drunk driver who killed my children. She destroyed my past, my present, and my future. She wanted to get high and drunk and drive really, really fast out of town, leaving her own children at home, on a Wednesday night. Never mind that her license was suspended for a prior DUI and she had no insurance, she felt entitled to get wasted and then get behind the wheel. Even though the bar she went to was only three blocks from her house. She could have easily walked there, gotten drunk, and then walked home. But for some reason, she decided it was okay to risk my children's lives simply because she felt like it. When the police asked her where she was going that night, she told them she didn't even remember. And now my whole life has been stolen away and my sweet, loving wife feels broken. And I feel broken. And my children are six feet underground. And I am so, so incredibly angry.

But my anger doesn't just stay focused on her. It's always there, bubbling away just beneath the surface, waiting to spill over onto anyone who crosses me. I want to smash just about anyone who gets to go through life without enduring my heartbreak and pain. I catch myself having conversations in my head with strangers who, in my imagination, dare to piss me off or threaten me. I imagine lunging at them, gouging their eyes out, punching their windpipes, jump-kicking them in the stomach, and then stomping on their faces. Over and over and over—

And then I catch myself, realizing I have yet again veered off into Rage. When I snap out of these trances, my heart is racing, my teeth are clenched, and my hands are balled up into tight fists. This formless rage does not feel good.

Anger Needs to Be Expressed

Just like grief, anger can't be bottled up or compartmentalized without causing suffering. Repressed anger can drive us toward self-abuse, in the form of either drugs and alcohol or ulcers and cracked teeth. We need to express our rage. We need to find healthy outlets for all that fury. As Dr. Mary S. Cerney and Dr. James R. Buskirk write in "Anger: The Hidden Part of Grief," an article for the *Bulletin of the Menninger Clinic*, "Anger, under any circumstances, is difficult to experience and understand. When associated with grief, anger seems startling and somewhat inappropriate. Yet the failure to recognize, and the inability to work with, angry feelings may compromise and inhibit the necessary grieving process. If not confronted directly, anger emerges in a variety of disguises such as disabling illness, maladaptive behavior, and chronic unhappiness."

Sometimes I think that an army of mourners would be the deadliest force imaginable. We are full of rage and not particularly afraid to die because we have nothing left to lose. But aside from becoming a mercenary army, there are healthier, safer outlets for our rage. And I believe it is important to seek them out. All too often, angry mourners lash out at the very people who are closest to them and trying to help. And right now, we need all the support we can get. Gail and I have found a number of ways to vent our rage without harming others.

The Gift of a Target

Two days after the car crash, Gail and I had to go to a cemetery to choose burial plots, caskets, and a location for the funeral service. It was an inconceivably awful day. Our rabbi, Sharon, drove us to the cemetery and helped us negotiate these emotionally wrenching tasks. She physically and metaphorically held our hands through the worst moments of our early grief.

The mortician who helped us was particularly bad at his job. Shockingly so. He made numerous outrageously inappropriate comments to us. Which is strange, because he should know better, given that his job is to talk to the freshly bereaved. He started off by telling us he could get us a "deal" on the caskets since we needed two. Then he complained about how inconvenient it was for him to have to get two hearses. He explained that the parking logistics were a nightmare. When we realized the cemetery chapel would be much too small for the funeral, he said with a disapproving sneer, "Let's not make this a big Hollywood thing, let's keep it small." Did he think he could shame us into turning away Hart and Ruby's friends, just to keep the funeral more convenient for him? When Gail asked if we could see our children's bodies one last time, to say goodbye, he gave a disapproving frown and commented that "after a car crash, it's not a beauty pageant." He capped the morning off by cheerily telling us that since he had about an hour of paperwork to do, we should go off to lunch with our rabbi and "enjoy" ourselves. Our children were killed less than forty-eight hours ago and here he is smiling and urging us to *enjoy* ourselves?!

As soon as he left the room to do his paperwork, Sharon suggested we view this man as a gift, because we could direct all our immense formless rage onto him. And she was right. It helped us to rail against his incompetence. It felt good to later vent about this terrible encounter with all our friends and family. The mortician became a target onto which we could all unleash some of our vast cosmic fury.

The Hate du Jour

Gail is normally a kind and compassionate person able to see the best in everyone. But now, in grief, when someone crosses her, she feels an uncontrollable rage build up inside her. In these moments, she will often turn to journaling as a way of getting all the venom out of her system. She applies her rapier wit and wry humor to eviscerate her target on the page. She describes sections of her journal as a "burn book" of grief. I eagerly embraced the practice as well and find much solace in being unabashedly, gleefully vitriolic in my journal entries. We often regale each other with our tirades. Gail's sister Betsy dubbed these our Hate du Jour—the hate of the day. The phrase stuck with us. Something about labeling it with a sassy French "du jour" made our venting more pleasurable. It was as though we were serving up a savory dish of rage.

The Hate du Jour goes to whoever has pissed us off that day. The mortician was our very first one, and deservedly so. But sometimes the object of our rage is actually quite innocent. It may be that their only offense was that they looked at us with too much pity, or they tried to commiserate with us by talking about their grandmother who died. Sometimes it almost feels better if our attack is completely unwarranted, and our choice of target is totally irrational and unfair. And that's okay. We have a lot of rage, and it has to go somewhere. If we can find some form of perverse enjoyment in the harmless venting of our fury, so much the better.

Ford v Ferrari—March 18, 2020

Here is an excerpt from my journal entry for March 18, 2020. I chose this Hate du Jour because it also happens to be about the depiction of grief in popular culture, so it seems particularly relevant (it contains spoilers about the film *Ford v Ferrari*—so skip it if you don't want to know how the film ends). I apologize for the expletives.

> *Just finished watching "Ford v Ferrari." Okay, so good movie, but what the hell is happening at the end? Here we go with another unbelievably shitty depiction of grief! So Matt Damon goes to visit Christian Bale's widow, and you think, oh, this is gonna be a great scene, where he opens up about his feelings and tells the widow a wonderful story about her dead husband, and maybe connects with her poor kid who just lost his dad who he idolized. And Matt Damon gets to the house and sees the kid and gives him . . . a wrench! What is this grieving kid supposed to do with a fucking wrench?? That's idiotic. It's just a regular wrench. Maybe for Matt Damon it's special—it's the wrench that Christian Bale threw at him, like, twenty years ago. But it's not*

going to mean shit to the ten-year-old kid! And then the widow appears on the porch and Damon fucking waves at her and then jumps in his car, snuffles back a tear and drives off erratically. And we're supposed to think wow—this guy loved Bale so much he can't even face the widow. How strong and manly of him. No! It's not manly. This chicken-shit just ran away! He is supposed to be this macho guy who risks death behind the wheel, and then he can't even just fucking talk to someone in mourning? And the woman's husband died in a car crash for chrissake. So seeing Damon speed off erratically is going to retraumatize her! Thanks for that, Damon. The poor woman is from England, so there is no family to visit her, she's all alone in this foreign country, no one to grieve with, and here comes her husband's best and only friend, and this asshole just waves and drives off! After giving her son a goddamn wrench. And he's supposed to be the hero of the story?! Man, fuck him and his bullshit cowardice.

Identifying with Hulk

Gail has done a lot of thinking on anger and its superhero avatar, the Hulk. "I have a friend who writes comic books, and he told me that people whose favorite superhero is Hulk tend to have a lot of anger issues because they identify with undefined, boundaryless rage. Hulk is out of control in his anger, and I feel that way now. I have so much rage I feel like I could stomp on a city. I could just bring down the world and not care if I crush people or cars or buildings. I feel like I can relate to Hulk, even though I don't like him. I actually aspire to be Batman. Batman's parents were murdered and he tries to honor them by doing good in the world, and that's what I want to be. I want to be Batman, but I feel like Hulk. I was talking to a friend who also deals with a lot of rage, and we were talking about Hulk. He mentioned that in the final credit sequence of the original Hulk TV show, Bruce Banner walks down an empty road all by himself as music plays. And my friend said it was the saddest, loneliest song in the world, and how ultimately, that is the message—that anger isolates you and keeps you from connecting. And I couldn't remember the tune, so we looked it up online and it turns out that the name of the song is 'The Lonely Man.' I found it interesting that even the name of the song about a character who's full of rage is actually about loneliness. At first when the kids were killed, I was scared. But what it has evolved into is less fear and more just pure loneliness. I think that's why I shout to the kids, 'Where are you?' and 'I miss you.' I think a lot of anger is loneliness. There is no one for you."

Ritual as an Outlet for Rage

Injustice feels particularly acute to me now. I find I can't watch films in which someone is bullied or discriminated against. I can't stand the sight of abuse. About a year after Ruby and Hart were killed, George Floyd was slowly and deliberately murdered in broad daylight. I couldn't watch the video, even though I knew it was important. I was filled with murderous rage at the injustice, and at the white supremacists who went on to murder peaceful protesters. I spiraled into dark fantasies of revenge killing. I felt ugly inside. Gail and I knew we needed a healthier outlet for our rage. It went beyond Hate du Jour. There was nothing funny or entertaining about this anger.

Ritual: A Fund-Raiser for Black Lives Matter

At the one-year anniversary of the car crash we were once again hungering for some sort of action we could take. We wanted to do something that had meaning, in honor of Ruby and Hart. We wanted to reach out to our community and give them an action they could take in their grief. Gail connected with one of the co-creators of the Los Angeles chapter of Black Lives Matter and was able to start a fund-raiser that directly linked to the official BLM GoFundMe campaign. My sister-in-law Lisa created a beautiful image of two red flowers, ranunculuses, on a black background with the tagline "Nobody's Kids Should Die." Gail wrote this to go with it:

> *My husband Colin and I are white. Just putting it out there. It'll be relevant in a minute. One year ago today, our two teenagers, Ruby and Hart Campbell, were killed when a drunk driver crashed into our car, ending their lives and destroying ours. Since the sickening moment of impact, we have been relentlessly heartbroken, furious, rarely able to imagine a future with any joy in it, and sick with survivor guilt in the moments we can.*
>
> *I thought Colin and I would be spending this painful week thinking only of the unending pain we suffer as grieving parents. Instead, I find my mind and heart consumed with thoughts of other mothers who grieve young children and teenagers as well: Tamir Rice's mother, Samaria; Trayvon Martin's mother, Sybrina Fulton; Michael Brown's mother, Lesley McSpadden, and countless other black parents who mourn children of all ages.*

We all have the single most terrible thing that can happen to a parent in common, but because of our race, we have little else.

Ruby and Hart's deaths were immediately condemned as senseless and tragic. Police and onlookers converged upon their bodies with the sole intention of saving their lives. We believe that the police are doing their best to bring their killer to justice, and we have been treated with respect and courtesy. Our children are being remembered solely as the wonderful, loving, kind people they were. No one would ever consider blaming them for their own deaths. Colin and I had the financial safety net and medical access needed to take time off work and seek the therapy that was crucial in helping us survive this catastrophe as best we can. Our privilege is apparent even in our devastation. We are asking everyone in our small and large communities who have loved and supported us this past year to love and support the grieving parents of murdered black children by making a donation to Black Lives Matter in memory of Ruby & Hart Campbell. Please share! Thank you.

Within three days we had raised over forty-five thousand dollars. The fund-raiser gave Gail a chance to share her pain and to put words to her grief. And she got back a whole lot of love from our community in the form of Facebook reposting and text messages to us. I include this fund-raiser in the list of mourning rituals, because it helped to organize our days and gave purpose to us as we pined for our kids. It was another opportunity to take action in our mourning, and to share our pain and loss.

Resenting Family and Friends

One of the most complicated feelings of anger I have is that toward the people closest to me. I resent that they get to go forward in their lives relatively unscathed. I don't mean to minimize their pain. They are devastated by Ruby and Hart's deaths. Some of them have started therapy to manage their intense grief. They ache for Ruby and Hart, and they think about Gail and me every day. And yet they get to go on with their lives. They get to have children and grandchildren. They get to have moments of unbridled joy and happiness. Their lives are not destroyed in the way Gail's and mine are. There is simply no comparison.

This difference creates an awful rift between me and the people I love and need the most. It is so complicated to resent the very people who are trying so hard to help me, and yet I can't make my feelings go away. On the one hand, it is so helpful to still be in the mix with all our friends whose children were friends with Ruby and Hart. These people make up some of our closest community. It helps our sense of continuity to still be a part of holiday gatherings and social activities. And yet these same events are a brutal reminder of our loss. Seeing Ruby and Hart's friends getting older and becoming interesting young adults is wonderful and awful. Sometimes just mostly awful.

Joining our extended family for holidays and summer vacations is a beautiful way to be back in the flow of life. These gatherings create opportunities to reminisce about Ruby and Hart, and for Gail and me to get much-needed love and support. But at the same time, it is a painful reminder of how different our lives are from those of the rest of our family. What am I supposed to do with all my anger and resentment?

Sometimes friends and family seem oblivious to our painful situation.

They blithely offer up delightful stories of their children or grandchildren as a way to cheer us up and entertain us. On the other hand, sometimes friends are overly aware of our pain, and they carefully monitor themselves to never mention their children or grandchildren to us, as if we can't handle it. It feels like a no-win situation. I get upset no matter what they do.

The reality is that life goes on even though my children are dead. The people I love get to continue their lives and so do I. It is painful, but that is my reality. I have a choice to either engage with life or allow my resentment and rage to curtail the rest of my time on earth. On the balance, I would rather lean into discomfort for the opportunity to be with the people I love. I do want to enjoy my grandnephews, even though they remind me of when Ruby and Hart were little kids. I do want to stay in the lives of Ruby and Hart's friends and celebrate their milestones. I do want to keep my family and friends.

James's daughter Ruby shared that in her early grief several of her friends weren't able to show up for her when she needed them. Ruby came to feel that she didn't have the right to expect her friends to help her in her grief, so she stopped asking. And then she became even more resentful when they didn't anticipate her needs. "I became more isolated. My response was not super healthy. You can't resent not getting something you didn't ask for. But now I am discovering that you have to keep asking for what you need and try to work on acceptance when you get turned down. It's easier to become okay with any individual person not giving you something because you can trust that you'll get it from the larger group of people in your community."

No matter how supportive our friends and family are, they will inevitably, over time, check in on us less and less. I try to look at it not as an abandonment, but simply a reflection of the reality that life goes on. No one else needs to talk about Ruby and Hart as much as Gail and I do, so it makes sense that people's attention shifts elsewhere. If I can manage to not hold that against them, it makes my life better. I simply enjoy myself more if I am hanging with friends rather than isolating myself. And I can often sneak in enough talk about Ruby and Hart to feel okay.

Wanting to Really Let Them Have It

Because my boundless rage is always there, close to the surface, I often imagine turning on my friends and family and "really letting them have it." I have heard numerous mourners use this very phrase. It even appears in Elisabeth Kübler-Ross and David Kessler's *On Grief and Grieving*. I am not exactly sure what we all imagine "really letting them have it" means. I guess there is a sense that we are always holding back from unleashing the full extent of our daily horror onto our closest loved ones, and that if they only had an inkling of our true suffering it would crush them. This desire to "really let them have it" feels full of rage and cruelty, but I think it is really about simply needing our pain to be witnessed. Now I use that impulse as a barometer of sorts. If I catch myself wanting to punish the people closest to me, it is a wake-up call that I need to take a walk with a good friend and talk about Ruby and Hart a little. I find it radically reduces my rage.

Handling the Hurtful Things People Will Say

Because there is so little guidance out there for how to talk to the grieving, mourners are subjected to a shocking amount of hurtful "advice." Most people are very uncomfortable with death and become quite desperate to "fix" our pain. This leads them to try to cheer us up, or snap us out of grief, or encourage us to "get over it." It can also lead people to try to put a positive spin on the death of our loved one. We've had people tell us how much more they appreciate their own life after learning of Ruby and Hart's deaths. But my kids didn't die just so you could have an epiphany! Others have told us that Ruby and Hart are in a better place. Maybe some people find comfort in that thought, but I find the idea offensive. For me, there is no better place for my kids than being alive and in my arms.

Even more upsetting to me is the idea that Ruby and Hart's deaths are all part of god's plan. If that's his plan, it's a terrible plan and I want nothing to do with it. In fact, now I get angry hearing that *anything* in life was "destined to happen" or "meant to be." As my friend Stuart points out, watching athletes thank god for helping them win is infuriating. "When somebody scores a touchdown and thanks god, it's like, wait, god wanted you to score the touchdown, but *not* the other team? God was like, right, I didn't want the other team to block you and I also didn't want to stop Suzanne from dying. If god is really focused on your touchdown, that means god took his eye off all these other things, like COVID-19. Millions of people died from COVID-19, but you got a touchdown?! Or people who say, 'Ooh! A parking spot! Thank you, god.' And I think, 'Fuck you! No. God is not giving you that parking spot!'"

Clearly, we grievers can have anger issues about the language people use to talk about loss or fate. So how do we handle this rage? Often I find that I need to take a breath and try to appreciate that these people don't intend malice, they are just trying to help me in any way they can. It is hard for them to see people in so much pain. It's natural that they would want to try to make my awful situation better somehow. Sometimes I need to modify my grief spiel so as to cut these hurtful, "helpful" words off at the pass. If someone's words keep getting under my skin, I find it very useful to simply tell them up front. Or send it in an email.

Offering Criticism to Friends

We have a close friend who is always there for us and so eager to be a loving and supportive companion in our time of grief. But she had an odd habit. Instead of asking us how we felt in our grief, she would preemptively tell us how she imagined we felt each time she saw us. She has a gift for vivid words, which only made it more upsetting for us to hear her interpretation of how she assumed we were feeling. We were always caught off-guard in the moment and could never seem to find the right time to tell her this habit was hurtful. Besides, our complaint seemed so strange and specific that it almost felt rude to tell her, especially when her intention was to be supportive. And yet it made us so angry. So for a while, we found ourselves avoiding her. We realized we were in danger of writing her off as a friend without even ever telling her why. How could we hope for her to change if we never even gave her the chance? So Gail and I made a date to take a walk together with her, and then sent her this email:

> *Subject: A little heads up and we love you*
>
> *Hey, we're psyched to see you today, but there's something we've been wanting to bring up that we think might be easier in an email. We know that you only want to love and support us, and we feel loved and supported, but we've also noticed that you have a tendency to tell us how*

we feel, or to describe our situation in vivid and poetic terms that are hard for us to hear. For example, instead of telling us that being at our friend's Shiva "must be devastating," please just ask us how we feel. Or, for example, saying "it's like someone pushed 'stop' on Ruby and Hart's lives," while true in many ways, just underscores and adds to our sorrow. This email isn't to say that we don't want to talk about this with you. In fact, we think it would be better if we do. It's just that we don't want to blindside you.

See you soon. We love you,
Gail & Colin

She wrote right back:

Thanks Gail and Colin, I really appreciate you telling me that! I'll do my best to not narrate your experiences. I've never walked with a friend through something like this and I'm sure to fall flat on my face several times, but I really appreciate knowing when and why that is, so I can be a better support for you. It means a lot to me that you told me, and I take it to heart.

Xxxx

On our walk later that morning, she thanked us for sending the email and said it was a true sign of our friendship that Gail and I were willing to reach out, rather than just walk away from an uncomfortable situation. She understood right away that it is hard to send that kind of an email, and that we wouldn't have gone to so much effort if her friendship didn't mean a lot to us.

I think she zeroed in on such an important truth when she wrote,

"I've never walked with a friend through something like this and I'm sure to fall flat on my face several times, but I really appreciate knowing when and why that is, so I can be a better support for you." It's so easy for me to forget that no one I know has ever had to be friends with someone who lost both their children. And the fact is, if the situation were reversed, I would never have known what to say to such a friend either. We remain close with her, and she has never again tried to narrate our experience or made us feel uncomfortable.

Writing Out the Rage

A week after the car crash, I began writing a one-person show with some very dark humor. I let all my bitterness and rage out on the page in disturbing and offensive rants. I let myself be as raw as I wanted. By writing out my darkest and ugliest thoughts, I took away some of their frightening power over me. I'm a theater artist, so it makes sense that I gravitated toward performance as a way of exorcising my rage. It was a natural fit for me. Over the following months, I kept adding to the monologue. I didn't know if it was something I might ever perform, or even show other people. But I kept writing. It went from being a two-minute monologue to becoming a full-length show. I shared it with friends who encouraged me to keep developing it. I submitted it to a solo performance theater festival, and it got accepted in New York and London. I began spending hours each day memorizing it and tinkering with it. I was about to try it out for the first time in front of an audience when COVID-19 arrived and shut every theater down. The festivals were both canceled.

At the time, I didn't know if I would ever perform my monologue in front of an audience, but working on it was an important part of processing my grief and anger. The act of memorizing the words meant that I spent hours with them. I got to articulate my rage and then exorcise it for as long as I wanted. I cried every time I rehearsed the piece. But it was a way of staying close to my kids. I put some sweet Ruby and Hart stories into the monologue, which gave me some solace.

As soon as the country went into lockdown, I put my monologue away and began writing a first draft of this book. That early draft was too infused with rage to be useful to other people, but it allowed me to write out some of my anger. It helped me process my grief in a way that was different from my journaling.

As soon as I finished the first draft of the book, I began writing a screenplay. As a screenwriting professor, I encourage my students to exorcise their demons in their scripts. I suggest that they explore topics that push their buttons and keep them up at night. I followed my own advice and wrote a script about a couple whose two teenage children are killed by a drunk driver. It's a dark revenge thriller that allows me to explore the outer limits of my rage. I got to sublimate my anger into the actions of my protagonists. I also got to rail against people who have pissed me off in my grief.

For example, right after the kids were killed, someone sent me a lengthy email that suggested I see a psychic so I could receive a message from Ruby and Hart. The email included photographic "proof" of this psychic's abilities and went on at length about how they had helped a friend talk to their dead father. I knew the email was intended to be helpful, but it enraged me. So in the film, I included the following scene. In it, the grieving couple, Charles and Gwen, are playing poker with their friends Leslie, Sarah, Brian, and Rick.

INT. LIVING ROOM—NIGHT

The six friends are mid-poker game. Charles and Gwen are clearly in emotional pain, and the others feel desperate to help. Leslie seizes on an idea.

LESLIE

I've been meaning to tell this to you guys. I think it might help.

Charles and Gwen look up at her, hopeful.

LESLIE

A really good friend of mine from college, she lost her dad a year ago, cancer, tragic, but she's been seeing this psychic who is, believe it or not, able to channel his spirit.

The others don't notice Gwen and Charles tensing.

SARAH

Oh my god. Really?

LESLIE

My friend's not some new age kook, but she swears this psychic knows stuff about her dad and their relationship that no one else could possibly know.

RICK

Is this Suzanne?

LESLIE

Yeah. And get this—and this is crazy, but real—while the psychic is channeling him, Suzanne's taken a photo of her dad's favorite chair, and there is a glow—

RICK

No way—

LESLIE

Yes! I swear. In the photo! I've seen it.

SARAH

Whoa, amazing.

LESLIE

And maybe this psychic could help you guys.

They all look expectantly to Gwen and Charles.

CHARLES

Are you fucking kidding me?

The looks of excitement wither on their faces. Gwen puts a steadying hand on Charles' arm.

GWEN

(cautioning)

Charles—

CHARLES

You want us to talk to a psychic? You think we're down for some parlor tricks? Some fucking dime-store conman talking to us about our dead children? Like it's some kind of entertainment?

They all stare at Charles in horror and shame.

BRIAN

Charlie—

CHARLES

Let's all get our palms read, and oh, by the way, Becca has a message for you from the grave.

LESLIE

Shit, sorry, I—

CHARLES

Do you have any idea how we yearn, fucking YEARN, for our children? Like it's ripping our hearts apart.

The doorbell rings. Loud. Everyone jumps. Charles shakes from adrenaline and rage.

CHARLES

Fuck.

The doorbell rings again. Charles leaps up and strides to the door. Gwen is on her feet after him. The other four stand, awkward—it's not like the game is going to continue. Charles opens the door to reveal two POLICE OFFICERS.

I don't know if this film will ever get made, but writing this scene helped. I got to articulate what was so upsetting about this person's offer of a psychic two days after my children were killed. Ruby loved supernatural horror films that involved ghosts and hauntings. If she wanted to contact me from beyond the grave, she'd find a way on her own. She wouldn't need some "psychic" to reach me.

All of my writings—the one-person show, the book, the screenplay, the journaling—are all attempts at processing my complicated feelings, including my anger. Dr. Mary S. Cerney and Dr. James R. Buskirk write, "The resolution of grief depends, in major part, on the willingness of an individual to recognize, own, and resolve feelings of anger."

Sublimating Our Rage

Clearly, writing and performing are my preferred outlets for channeling my rage. Another person might express themself through dance, music, painting, martial arts, video games, sports, swimming, jogging, yoga, or tai chi. But we all need some way of sublimating our rage. In psychology, sublimation is understood as a defense mechanism in which socially unacceptable impulses or thoughts are channeled into more socially acceptable actions. This can sometimes result in a lasting conversion of the initial impulse. Sigmund Freud popularized this understanding of sublimation. According to Freud, "Sublimation of instinct . . . is what makes it possible for higher psychical activities, scientific, artistic or ideological." In other words, by sublimating our rage (our unacceptable impulse to "unleash" on the people around us), we are able to instead transform that energy into something that may be useful to the rest of society.

I have never been particularly comfortable with anger. I have usually avoided confrontation and used comedy as a way to defuse tension. I don't like being so angry all the time. My current free-floating rage makes me feel ugly, isolated, and out of control. By sublimating some of my anger into healthier outlets, I can feel a lot of that rage drain away. I can let go of some of it. Exorcising my demons gives me some solace.

My friend Jesse vents a lot of her anger in Facebook posts. "I think the reason I like to make those big emotions public is because I think people don't understand that A) we're feeling those big emotions, and B) that we are entitled to. The cult of positivity that's out there wants us to hashtag 'be blessed' or hashtag 'be grateful'—they are so busy trying to get us to feel okay about our lives. I do think it's a bit of a calling for many of us to educate people that we can be blessed and pissed at the same time. I actually try to make my big feelings public because our society, our culture, is so uneducated about grief. Especially grief over the loss of children. It's a grief that is typically hidden in our society—people don't like to talk about it and don't like to hear about it. And I think people need to hear about it. For all sorts of reasons. One, so they can be more empathetic, compassionate humans and two, because as we've seen, we're not going to be the only ones that experience this kind of catastrophic loss. And would that there were more people in this world whose hearts were open to sitting with us." Jesse also often wears a rhinestone necklace that spells out "FUCK." That helps her, too.

My friend Jen recently had an interesting revelation about her anger. "It's weird but I feel like I am less angry now than I was before Luke died. It's strange. I was on this track before and when things would sideline me, I would feel very angry about it—because I was getting behind my schedule! That was when I still felt in control. But this meteor—this nuclear explosion—just wiped that out, and now I understand that I'm not in control. I used to have this 'Karen' inside me, this entitlement, and now I understand I am not guaranteed anything. It feels like a revelation. You would think I would be more angry. It's not like I am not angry at what happened, I sure am. But there is something inside me that just is clear acceptance about that which I can't control. It's about trying to go through your life experiences with some sort of grace about it all instead of just punching the walls. Grace. Maybe that's the only thing I am in control of: how I choose to deal with it. We read that [in Viktor Frankl] and then we learned it the hard way."

I think both Jesse and Jen are absolutely right. We've got big emotions that need to be shared, and at the same time, we also have a perspective on life that helps us to see what truly matters and what really doesn't. There is a grace and wisdom that comes from grief, whether we want it or not.

A Raging New Year's Eve

When Ruby and Hart were alive it had been our annual tradition to throw a big New Year's Eve party. It was a real family-friendly affair. We'd hire a bartender and a lifeguard and heat our pool to a ridiculously high temperature. It made for a chaotic night of adults partying and children running around dripping water everywhere. I'd stock up on confetti cannons and by the end of the night our house and yard were trashed. It always felt like a glorious blowout to the year. Ruby and Hart loved those parties and so did Gail and I.

After our kids were killed, we no longer felt like throwing parties. We spent our New Year's Eves alone. Each year, fewer and fewer friends reached out to check in on us around the holidays. As we approached the third New Year's Eve after the crash, Gail and I began anticipating that we would, once again, not hear from most of our friends. As we got closer to the holiday, Gail and I became angrier and angrier. How could all those dozens of friends—some of whom had spent their New Year's Eves with us for twelve years in a row—how could they *not* be thinking about us?! How could they *not* reach out? It sent both of us down a dark path of anger. When we shared our fury with our grief group, our friend Lisa gently suggested that we reach out to those friends rather than stew in our own righteous rage. It was, of course, exactly the sort of advice this book keeps offering, yet both Gail and I hadn't thought of it. We were so busy feeling hurt and betrayed that we forgot we could take action on our own. We didn't need to wait for our friends, we could simply reach out first and ask for what we needed.

The reality is that the attention of friends and family will inevitably taper off as time goes by. That can be hard to accept, and sometimes it can feel easier to just stay angry at the world. There is a seductiveness to righteous rage. It feeds on itself. It feels good in the moment, but ultimately it sabotages any chance of getting the support we need. We can either become embittered and rageful or accept our situation and ask for what we need. We took Lisa's advice and sent out the following email at noon on New Year's Eve:

Beautiful Friends,

Before we ring out 2021, we'd like to ask a favor of you.

While every day has its challenges, one of the hardest of the year is the last.

We desperately miss our annual New Year's Eve party.

Some of you came for nearly every one (12? 13 years running?) and some of you were new friends who only came to what we never dreamed would be our last with Ruby and Hart.

It was an annual shebang we loved—all of you, all our children, the chorus of noisemakers, and the mountains of confetti.

We even loved waking up to the wreckage and cleaning up together.

We never thought we'd see our children fighting over a broom, but it happened every New Year's Day.

We miss them, we miss you, and we miss feeling uncomplicated happiness.

We cling to our memories, but this time of year makes it harder to remember the joy, because our sorrow crowds out almost everything else.

Because you're the people who've celebrated with us for so many years, please take a minute today and email us a memory you have of them, or a thought you have about them.

It can be one sentence—whatever it is, we'll cherish it.

Please forward to your kids, too. We'd love to hear from them.

Sorry to be the ultimate buzzkill.

We wouldn't be asking if we didn't really need it.

Thank you. We love you.

Wishing you all a safe, healthy and happy 2022.
—Gail & Colin

We got several dozen beautiful responses. Some people shared moments they'd had with Ruby and Hart that we never knew about; others simply shared their pain. Their emails helped us get through the tough holiday. They made us laugh and cry, and at the end of the day we didn't feel quite so alone.

Kindness as an Antidote to Rage

Gail says that performing small acts of random kindness helps her contain her rage. In particular, she likes to be extra courteous behind the wheel. Nowadays, she tries to always let merging drivers enter her lane. It is a useful bulwark against her own potential for road rage. And the small friendly waves she receives in return are a balm. I, too, find that I drive more courteously these days. I am careful to make way for motorcycles as they pass me on the freeway. They often flash me a peace sign and it does help calm my anger. My friend Lisa's daughter Serena started a Kindness Project in honor of her brother

Hunter, as has my friend Jesse in honor of her son Gidi. And of course, we started the Hart Campbell Kindness Award.

I don't think it's a coincidence that so many of us mourners turn to random acts of kindness to commemorate our losses. I believe that performing acts of kindness can function as an antidote to our rage. It is akin to the axiom "Fake it till you make it." If we keep ignoring our angry impulses and instead respond to the world with kindness, our inner rage loses some of its steam. The more kind we act, the more kind we become.

Our loss is unfair, it's true. But sadly, the universe is not fair. As Lisa put it, "I grew up thinking that if you did the right thing, the right things would happen to you in your life. But I learned at some point that life isn't fair. It's not fair for a lot of people. It's not fair for whole countries of people. So we have to take responsibility for our life and try to make it the best we can given our circumstances."

Two Wolves

Ruby made two digital paintings of creatures she called *Koi Wolves*. She outlined the wolves and then used koi fish color patterns to fill them in. They are beautiful and strange, with long koi fish whiskers. They inspired her middle school, Pilgrim Academy, to frame them with an accompanying Cherokee legend, titled "Two Wolves." The idea of the legend is that we each have two wolves fighting inside us. One wolf is Rage, Resentment, and Envy. The other is Love, Compassion, and Kindness. A child asks which wolf will win the fight, and a Cherokee elder replies, "The one you feed."

The legend has been co-opted by cheesy inspirational poster companies and become a goofy meme. Googling it just now, I came across a version that would have delighted Ruby. It reads, "There are two wolves inside you. One wolf is gay. The other wolf is gay. You are gay." Ruby, a proud lesbian, would have gotten a kick out of that. I don't know how she would have felt about the original legend, but I imagine she would approve of it being paired with her two Koi Wolves. Either way, the message resonates with me in my grief and rage. I try not to feed that other wolf. Instead, I try to let it run out in the yard where it can tire itself out without hurting me or anyone else.

Actions

- **Notice when your unexpressed rage is building up inside you.** What are your warning signs? Do you find yourself yelling at other drivers? Lashing out at loved ones? Fantasizing about "really letting them have it"? Identify when you are about to explode, and then channel that rage into a constructive creative expression.
- **Find a creative expression for your rage.** What is the best way for you to transform all your rage into something artistic or useful or interesting to you? Is it drawing, painting, dance, song, theater, writing, building, gardening, sports? Don't judge yourself—it's not about how "good" or talented you are at any of these activities. It's a tool to exorcise your rage.
- **Exercise.** It's a great immediate release of anger. Especially high-impact exercise. It can also help your mood and give you the strength to cope with your grief. I enjoy a good three-mile run. Even a short walk can be helpful.
- **Find a Hate du Jour.** Allow yourself to metaphorically rip someone to shreds. Feel free to eviscerate them on paper. Or find a trusted friend you can freely rant to without judgment. Maybe

your target deserves to be dragged, or maybe their "crime" is simply that they lead a seemingly happy and carefree life.

- **Create a ritual that has meaning for you.** Translate your grief and anger into an action that somehow honors your loss.
- **Talk to people who have suffered a similar loss.** They understand your rage in a way that no one else can.
- **Perform random acts of kindness.** If you are feeling unkind toward the world, sometimes the best cure is to act as if you care. Act kind to become kind, because being kind feels so much better than being angry.
- **Get a night guard for your teeth.** Many mourners grind their teeth at night. If you wake up with a sore jaw or suspect you are grinding your teeth, go to your dentist and get fitted for a night guard. You don't want to have to deal with cracked molars right now. Or ever, really.

Journaling Prompts

- What happens to you when pent-up rage builds to a boiling point? What are the signs that you need some form of creative release for all that anger?
- Who is your Hate du Jour today? Sometimes my Hate du Jour is a famous comedian who made homophobic comments that would have infuriated Ruby. Sometimes it's a kind, well-meaning member of my synagogue who lists his good deeds a little too ostentatiously. Sometimes it's the principal at Marlborough who didn't honor Ruby properly. Allow yourself to vent all your fury on the page; be as vicious as necessary. Let yourself be a little transgressive, and a little childish.

- What are some of the hurtful things people say to you? Is there anything constructive you could preemptively say to them to get them to change their enraging behavior? How can you best protect yourself but still stay in life?

- In what ways do you resent the people closest to you? In what ways do they understand your pain, and in what ways do they simply fall short? How does that make you feel?

- In what ways does it hurt you to gather with friends? And with family? How is it helpful?

- In what ways are you less angry than before your loss? How has grief given you perspective on life? In what ways do you now find yourself living with more grace and wisdom?

- What does your grief feel like today?

CHAPTER NINE

Despair

Suffering versus Despair

Despair is not simply a bad case of suffering. To my mind, suffering is something we can avoid or mitigate. I can usually think my way out of suffering (the flip side is that I can think my way *into* more suffering if I'm not careful). But when I am hit by despair it feels entirely out of my control. I can't rationalize my way out of it. Grief will come in waves. It will pull me under but always bring me back to the living. Despair doesn't seem to work that way. At times, it feels as though despair can grab me and hold me for as long as it wants. Despair makes me want to give up on life because it just feels too damn hard.

Actively grieving brings me closer to Ruby and Hart—closer to the joy and love they brought to my life. Despair pulls me further away from them. I am left feeling so despondent that I can't really focus on them; I am too wrapped up in my own hopelessness.

Gail often thinks about a poem by her friend Albert Goldbarth. "After the kids were killed, Albert sent me a note that said, 'There are no words.' And I wrote back to him—we write letters to each other—and I said that's not enough, you can do better. I said, send me a poem. And he sent me a collection of his poems and said look at the last stanza of 'Sleep & Wake.' And I think about it a lot. I think about what it takes for me to wake up every morning. The simple act of opening my eyes every day feels as hard as lifting marble eyelashes."

> We wake, and . . . often a day is so large,
> is so imposingly vast, it's better to linger
> for a while in the clouds of after-sleep than it is
> to stride out boldly. I can't explain it clearer
> than a statue in the Vatican,
> *Sleeping Ariadne*, that some experts suggest
> is the only classical marble statue
> with eyelashes. That's it:
> marble eyelashes. Every morning. That's
> our unacknowledged courage:
> lifting marble eyelashes.
>
> —ALBERT GOLDBARTH

The Unpardonable Sin of Despair

I don't think it's a coincidence that Christians have labeled despair as the one unpardonable sin. To Christians, despair means losing all faith in god, in his mercy and forgiveness. To be in despair is to be without faith in anything. I am an atheist, so I don't see despair as a sin against god, but rather a sin against the children I am mourning. How can I squander my time and energy in despair? How can I not take heart and feel gratitude for having gotten to know and love Ruby and Hart? After they have been robbed of their lives, how can I not value my own? To be in despair feels like a betrayal of my children.

Sometimes it helps me to take a step back and imagine my own death. What would I want from the people who survived me? I like to imagine I really matter to the people I love, and that if I suddenly died they would be devastated. Selfishly, I would want them to weep a lot. But I would want more than that. I would want them to keep thinking about me and honoring me by making life choices that would make me proud. I would want them to lead rich, full lives in which they were often reminded of me. I would want them to remember me not just with sadness but also with joy and a twinkle in their eye. I would want them to do crazy, outrageous things and think, "This is for you, Colin!" I would want them to dedicate a portion of their life to the philanthropic and political causes I believed in. I would want them to tell hilarious and inspiring "Colin stories" to people for the rest of their long lives.

I definitely would *not* want them to collapse despairingly in their bed for weeks at a time. I would *not* want them to fall away from life and not talk to anyone about me ever again. And I would certainly not want them to take their own life! That would leave no one to mourn *me*, no one to tell the world about *me*. Clearly, suicide is the enemy of mourning. Suicide is the ultimate avoidance of grief.

"I Would Have Just Died"

I have had people look me in the eyes and tell me, in a deep heartfelt tone of voice, that if their children were ever killed they "would simply die." But of course, instant death is a fantasy. No one just magically dies from grief. We all go on living, no matter how terrible the loss. Other acquaintances have declared melodramatically, "I would just kill myself." A friend of my sister-in-law's even casually inquired, "Have they considered suicide?"

What happened to Gail and me was clearly so awful that these people imagined they would rather die than find a way to live with our pain. The very thought of losing their kids was so terrifying that their minds simply leapt to oblivion as a way out. They would rather have the erasure of death than even *contemplate* the amount of psychic pain we actually endure every day. Instead of engaging with our pain, these people make what amounts to self-aggrandizing and flippant comments about taking their own lives. The implication is that they must love their children more than I love mine, and that killing themselves is some sort of heroic tribute to their imaginary dead kids. They have the luxury of not actually having to deal with losing their children, so they feel they can make offhand comments that don't take real life into account. If I killed myself, how would that actually help anyone? All the people who loved and were grieving Ruby and Hart would now have to grieve me, too. I would simply be adding to the misery in this world. No thanks.

Of course I have had thoughts of ending my own life. Everyone suffering a profound loss will experience times when they wish they weren't alive. But those moments all pass. They always pass. If you allow yourself to truly feel your emotions, even the scariest ones, eventually those emotions will shift. One of the best ways to help that shift happen is to forge our own connections to life. An essential part of our work as we journey through grief is to find our own reasons to live. We're not dead. We weren't killed. So it's our job to be alive to the fullest possible extent. To quote the character of Maude in my favorite film, *Harold & Maude*, "A lot of people enjoy being dead. But they are not dead, really. They're just backing away from life. Reach out. Take a chance. Get hurt even. But play as well as you can. Go team, go! Give me an L. Give me an I. Give me a V. Give me an E. L-I-V-E. LIVE! Otherwise, you got nothing to talk about in the locker room."

Suicide Is Not an Option

Ruby struggled with suicidality because she had a mental illness. She had a severe case of OCD, which led to depression and self-loathing. Ruby struggled for several years with this illness. But she fought hard for a better life for herself. She tried over a dozen medications, a half-dozen therapists, a residential program, two partial-hospitalization programs, and any number of therapeutic practices. In the end, she got back her life. Her depression lifted and she was managing her OCD. The week before she was killed, she teared up over breakfast at a diner as she shared that she had finally gotten all her feelings back. Ruby was a fierce warrior for life. She used her artistic talents to create a beautiful and moving comic that captured the hopelessness of despair. It is titled *Hyperion* and on the back cover Ruby wrote the following words: "*Author's note* This comic was written during a very difficult part of my life. Thankfully, things have gotten *much* better for me. On that note, if this comic hits too close to home for you or someone you know, it would be a good idea to talk to a loved one or a professional. If no one is available to you, the 24-hour suicide hotline is 1-800-273-8255. Thank you for taking the time to read my comic! ♥ ♥ ♥ —Ruby." She finished this comic the day she was killed.

I could never betray Ruby or Hart or Gail by killing myself. I would not do that to them. Not after Ruby fought so hard for her life, only to have it stolen away by a careless, thoughtless drunk driver. I hope that hearing Ruby's struggle for life inspires anyone who is wrestling with suicidal ideation. In the name of all those who have fought so hard to live, let's agree that suicide is not an option.

You can't control when despair will hit. Despair is always waiting in the shadows, poised to pull us into the darkness. So how can we get out from its clutches? How do we climb back out of the abyss? I believe one answer is active rituals.

Two Birthday Rituals

Ruby and Hart were born three years and one day apart, March 29 and March 30. And every year their birthdays would fall during spring break, which was our favorite time to travel. So we celebrated them all over the world: Rome, Tokyo, London, Costa Rica, Yelapa, Lake Powell. Then we'd return home and throw pool parties with their friends. And now, in 2020, we had to celebrate their birthdays without them. It seemed unimaginable. How would we get through those days?

Ritual: Birthday Card-Playing Tournament

Ruby, Hart, Gail, and I loved a card game called Michigan Rummy, which was taught to me by my grandmother, Granny Maddy. It is a simple gin rummy game with five rounds, and each round has a slightly different goal. There is some strategy involved, but it is the kind of card game that is conducive to talking and joking around while you play. It is not that mentally taxing. Every time we went to a restaurant, we always brought cards and would play a few rounds while we waited for our food to arrive. We played in airports and hotel lobbies. We played when friends and family came to visit. We played countless rounds on our dining room table. It was our game.

So in honor of their birthdays, we planned to hold a massive card game tournament. We invited a hundred friends, both kids and adults. We rented a hall with fifteen tables. The idea was that each table would share how they knew Ruby and Hart, and everyone would tell a Ruby or Hart story. And after each round, everyone would rotate tables. After five rounds, each person would have met and talked to around thirty different people, and everyone would hear new stories and memories about our kids.

And then the coronavirus pandemic struck. The tournament was scheduled for the end of March, right at the start of the lockdown. Our intimate, rotating tables would have been the perfect super-spreader of COVID-19. So we had to cancel. We still hope to hold it sometime in the future, plague permitting.

Ritual: Birthday Letters to Ruby and Hart

When our birthday card-playing tournament had to be postponed, we grew concerned. How were we going to get through both of their birthdays with no ritual, no shared communal activity, no way to have others bear witness to our loss? We were all isolated in the early days of COVID-19. No one was socializing in late March. The entire country, and most of the world, was in lockdown. It seemed as though everything we had learned about mourning rituals couldn't help us.

Then Ruby's friend Yaya texted Gail and asked if she could write Ruby a letter on her birthday. Gail realized that Yaya had a brilliant idea. We reached out to family and friends and asked them all to write birthday letters to Ruby and Hart. We knew we wanted people to share stories in these letters. We didn't want a bunch of birthday cards that just said "Thinking about you and missing you." We wanted details. And by now, we knew how to ask for what we wanted. So Gail sent an email out to everyone, with clear instructions:

Beautiful Friends,

> *We are so disappointed to have had to cancel the Michigan Rummy Tournament. We were excited to have a fun, joyous way to commemorate the brutal pain of enduring Ruby and Hart's first birthdays without them. (March 29th and 30th! One day apart!)*
>
> *Inspired by a friend of Ruby's who told us that she was planning to write Ruby a letter for her birthday, we're asking you all to help us commemorate the day in a social distancing-worthy way.*
>
> *To honor their love of scrambling in the Joshua Tree desert, will you please write a letter to Ruby or Hart (or both) that we'll put in a time capsule and nestle in the rocks at the top of a high, scramble-worthy peak near our house out here. We'll send you all the coordinates, and if you ever find yourself out this way and in need of a Ruby and Hart fix, you can stop by for a visit, climb up to the cache of letters, and read them in the beautiful place that we as a family loved so much.*
>
> *We know a lot of you have had a hard time putting your feelings about this terrible loss to words, so we're making*

this as easy as possible. Here are some very simple guidelines and a tight deadline so you can't overthink it!

The letter should be written on 8 ½ x 11 paper (lined or unlined) and can be as simple as (but not necessarily limited to):

Dear Ruby/Hart,

I remember when we/you ______________________.

I miss when we/you ________________________.

I'll always think of you when _______________________.

This last one can be as profound or ridiculous as you like. Some examples might be:

Ruby, I'll always think of you when I hear a fake Russian accent.

Hart, I'll always think of you when I drink chocolate milk.

Ruby, I'll always think of you when I see someone with bright blue hair.

Hart, I'll always think of you when I do something kind for someone.

It's easy and it will mean so much to us.

Please take a few minutes today to think of Ruby and Hart and please mail your letters by this coming Tuesday, March 24th!

Thank you for being part of this! We love you! Hope everyone is staying safe and healthy and enjoying your time being home together.

Much love, Gail & Colin

We wound up getting one hundred forty letters. Some were pages long. All of them were from the heart. Many friends thanked us for giving them the opportunity to write to Ruby and Hart. It was very clear that the action of writing these letters helped our friends and family. It was yet another opportunity to put words to grief, to convert pain into action. We took the letters high up into the rocks of Joshua Tree National Park and read them aloud to Ruby and Hart. And we wept and wept. It truly felt as if we were speaking aloud to our children, and that they heard us. We could only read about six to eight letters each day, because it was too emotionally overwhelming. But it was such a help to us. So many of the letters held stories of the kids that we didn't know or had forgotten. Each letter was a precious gift. They made us feel so much less alone, as we could hear our friends' palpable grief in their words. We spent the entire month of April slowly reading aloud all the letters, including our own, as we sat up high in a special nook among the beautiful rocks. And now that spot feels holy to us. It is yet another special place where we feel close to our kids.

It took us a full six weeks to read aloud all the birthday letters. On Mother's Day, we read the final two letters, and then placed all of them in a weatherproof box and tucked it into the rocks for safekeeping.

A Little Glitter against the Loneliness of Despair

Grief can be so lonely. And despair can exacerbate that loneliness by causing us to withdraw and isolate. Grief compounding grief. My friend Jesse has a sweet daily fashion ritual that keeps her engaged in the world and connected to her son at the same time. "I have a strand of glitter in my hair. It's hair tinsel tied in, like an extension. My son Zeve gets it, too. We started it weeks after Gidi died. Gidi loved anything sparkly, so I try to carry him with me everywhere I go and in everything I do. Another thing that Gidi did was he talked to strangers everywhere. He would be waiting in line in a grocery store and tap the person in front of us on their shoulder and say, 'I love your pretty dress,' or he would see a mom come to pick their kid up from preschool and he would say, 'Ooh, are those new shoes?' He would constantly talk to strangers and compliment them on what color their nails were painted, and from those little compliments would come huge conversations. We got to know so many random people because Gidi would say, 'I love your pretty dress,' and they would look at this little four-year-old boy and they would say, 'Well, thank you. How old are you and what's your name and where are you from?' And he would say, 'Where are *you* from?' because he wasn't shy of anyone, and before we knew it, we knew the person in front of us and where they lived and how many kids they had—and he would spark conversations all over the world. This kid just made friends with anyone. So now I have the glitter in my hair and every single day I am stopped by someone who will say, 'Wow, what's that in your hair?' And I have a little moment's interaction with them. I call them my Gidi moments because those are the moments we don't have anymore because we don't have Gidi talking to strangers. And sometimes I tell them about Gidi and sometimes I don't, but they are my Gidi moments. Those were the moments he always added to our lives, and I like to think I still get them."

Asking Friends for Help

In March 2020, just as America went into its first lockdown, it felt as though the whole world was struggling with despair. Everyone was isolated in their homes and coming to terms with the fragility of life. On the one hand, Gail and I felt like saying "Welcome to our world."

But on the other hand, we felt more alone than ever. A group of our friends organized a Friday night Zoom as a way to stay connected and share some much-needed laughs and cocktails. Gail and I knew these friends because our children had all gone to elementary school together. We assumed that in addition to talking about life in lockdown, someone would ask us about our grief, or share a story about Ruby and Hart. But no one did. Afterward, I was furious and sad. How could they have talked for over an hour and not mention our dead children once? Our only connection to them was through Ruby and Hart. They had each hosted our children for sleepovers, shared holidays with them, and seen them grow up. I was tempted to never talk to them again. It seemed too painful to endure another session of superficial chitchat about politics and the struggles of Zooming to work. But I knew that I would regret cutting them out of my life. They knew and loved my children. They were part of my community. So I took a breath and sent out the following email:

Subject: Friendship

Dear friends—

It was very nice seeing all your lovely faces on Zoom. But I do have to share that it was difficult, too. No one mentioned Ruby or Hart, or asked how it was for us, in this time of everyone hunkering together with their families—everyone having enforced family time—which to us is what we yearn for desperately every moment of every day. Gail and I are discovering how to integrate our pain with our daily lives and work and friends. And luckily, I feel like I can break our needs down pretty specifically. It would mean the world to us, if each of you would check in with us, in the first five minutes of a conversation, to see how we are handling our loss. And literally mention Ruby and Hart's names at least once. It doesn't need to dominate the conversation or even last more than a few sentences. It's just the total absence of talk about Ruby and Hart that is so hard for us.

And the other need we have is, if we mention Ruby and Hart, it would mean the world to us if you would follow up with a question or comment that continues the thought or thread of conversation. Otherwise, we wind up mentioning Ruby and Hart and then the conversation continues on to another subject and we feel like crazy people who keep talking about their dead kids.

Maybe you are worried that it feels like mentioning Ruby and Hart will remind us of our loss and be painful for us—but trust me, we never don't want to talk about Ruby and Hart.

And we're not looking to bring everyone down, or make people feel bad. We still like to laugh and be ridiculous. But we just have these needs.

I know it's a little odd and demanding for someone to tell their friends what they need, and to be so specific, but that's our deal now. I hope you guys can all roll with it. It's a little scary to write this potentially alienating email, but your friendships are too important to us.

Much love,
—Colin

It was indeed a scary email to send to old friends, but I felt I couldn't come away feeling so upset and not address it openly. Here are some of my friends' beautiful responses:

Colin and Gail,

An email like this is not alienating; it's the opposite. It would be a terrible thing if unspoken needs or unintentional wounding drove us apart. Thank you for telling us what you need. We miss Hart and Ruby every day; a gut-punch waits for us each time we think about it. But we make a point to say their names, especially to the kids. We goad them into recounting hilarious Hart stories from school and sleepovers, and we summon the awesome inspiration of Ruby when we talk to them about their art.

I'd like to think that, in a more organic setting, we would have done better by you the other day. But we'll try harder next time. Love you both.

Gail and Colin—

You are absolutely right. I can only speak for myself, but I have to say that you two and Ruby and Hart are ever present in my thoughts, and it is a coping mechanism to not talk about painful things in my family (don't get me started), which is something I bristle at with my relatives, so I am mortified to see that behavior in myself.

Dude, we love you guys and your kids. Roll with it? ABSOLUTELY.

Please feel free to give me shit for being an asshole when I don't realize it. Trust me, you won't be the first person to call me one. :)

Gail and Colin,

I want to apologize for our insensitivity and wanted to echo what J said about how we deal with painful situations in our family as well. I can say for myself that I didn't ask for fear of upsetting you, although after reading your email, I understand completely why not acknowledging Hart and Ruby was so much worse. We think about you two and Hart and Ruby often throughout the day, every single day.

I am so very sorry. And yes, feel free to call me out for being an asshole as well. I often say I was raised by wolves but then if I was, I would probably have better social skills.

I love you both and Ruby and Hart. I miss you all every day. Thank you for sending this email.

Colin,

Thank you for being so direct and letting us know so clearly what you need. It should have been obvious to us, and I am sorry that we didn't do what we knew was important, but hard. I'd like to consider myself a better friend than that, thank you for giving us the opportunity to do better.

Hart & Ruby have been so on my mind especially lately. They always are, but as each of us find our regular stress coping habits in these crazy times, it is so clear that Hart would have lifted everyone's spirits in bizarro non-sequitur ways. And I know that Ruby would be processing all of this world turned upside down craziness with insight, wit and her sense of humor that could cut right through bullshit. I am missing them so much right now.

I should have said that. I was a chickenshit. I'm sorry.

I'm so glad you took the risk in communicating to us. I wish we'd been braver with you.

Sooooooo much love to you both!

I share this email exchange in the hopes that some of the specifics are helpful. There is so little written about what mourners actually *do* to navigate this challenging landscape of grief. My specific words may not apply to other people's relationships, but I hope they nonetheless inspire better words from someone else.

This email exchange didn't solve everything, but it kept our friendships intact, and it meant that over the next few months of Zoom cocktails I got to talk a lot more about Ruby and Hart.

The Despair of Backsliding

I find that no matter how many times I tell myself that grief comes in waves, it always surprises me when I am hit hard by a fresh dose of it. It makes me feel like I am backsliding, and that all the "progress" I have made in grieving is for naught. I have managed to navigate my loss for a couple of years now; how is it possible that I can still suddenly become so despondent? What was the point of enduring all that pain and weeping if I can be brought so low all over again? This continued vulnerability to grief can fill me with despair. In these moments of backsliding, the future can appear too bleak to endure. Sometimes in these moments Gail turns to me and says, despondently, "We could live another forty years." I know this despair will pass in a day or two, but it is an awful place to be in for even a minute.

I was tempted to make "Despair" the last chapter of the book. It seemed to be too naïvely hopeful to end the book on a chapter with an uplifting title such as "Meaning and Purpose." I didn't want to imply that we can get to a point where we are able to leave despair behind as we happily find our reasons to live. I didn't want to whitewash the pain and paint an unrealistically rosy picture of grief. On the other hand, despair is not the final word. It may keep coming at inopportune moments in our lives, but it doesn't have to control the narrative. There is so much life to live between each wave. And I am confident that, over time, those waves will be fewer and farther between.

Ironically, I began writing this chapter while in the midst of a bout of despair brought on by the second anniversary of Ruby and Hart's deaths. I had just finished the previous chapter and we had gone up to Joshua Tree to observe the awful day as best we could. I made it through the day by swimming and texting back to well-wishers and watching some of the kids' favorite films. And then, the next day I was hit with despair. Just as I was supposed to start this chapter. How fitting. Instead, I slept ten hours and awoke feeling exhausted. And empty. And overwhelmed. And full of a terrible longing. I couldn't focus on anything. I felt unproductive and adrift. I stalled by playing Spelling Bee in the *New York Times* for hours. Finally, at five thirty in the evening I wrote this paragraph and called it quits. Everything simply takes longer in grief.

Even though I know from experience that every bout will eventually pass, when I am in despair it feels timeless. It feels like it will go on forever, because the root cause of it (Ruby and Hart's deaths) will never change or get better. And yet that bout of despair did pass. Two days later, I was able to get back to work. Because I had a purpose. I was writing a book that I hoped would help other people. That sense of purpose helped me out of my despair and back to life.

And that is why the final chapter of this book is titled "Meaning and Purpose." And not "Despair."

Actions

- **Notice when the natural pain of loss slips into something darker and more debilitating.** Lasting despair can be a warning that you need help, either from your community, from medication, or from a professional therapist.

- **Reconnect to something meaningful.** Before your loss, your life had meaning and purpose beyond your loved one. Reconnect to something that you used to care about and that gave your life meaning in the past. It may not seem to matter to you anymore, but it still does. Give it a chance. Give it time.

- **Allow yourself a guilty pleasure.** Grant yourself permission to engage in something frivolous and fun. Rewatch a favorite film; read a trashy novel. Do an enjoyable activity that maybe you used to do with your loved one, or maybe it has nothing to do with your loved one. Either way, it can help pull you out of the despair you are feeling right now. Stay focused on the immediate present; don't catastrophize about the future.

- **Ask again for what you need.** You may have already told friends and family how to best help you. But time has passed, and they may have drifted back into less helpful patterns of behavior. Even though your needs may have changed, your grief has not gone away. Find a way to ask for what you need now.

- **Connect with your community.** Isolation can lead to despair. And despair makes it even harder to reach out to people right when we need them most. Schedule time with a friend or family member even though it feels like you'd rather be alone.

- **Seek out other people in grief.** Connect with someone from your grief group. Sometimes they feel like the only ones who can understand the depths of our despair.

- **Put yourself out into the world.** Encourage yourself to interact with friendly strangers. Do whatever your equivalent is to wearing tinsel in your hair.

- **Exercise and practice self-care.** Go for a jog, or a swim in the ocean. Move your body. Stay healthy. Stay away from drugs and alcohol. Take good care of yourself.

Journaling Prompts

- How do you navigate despair? What seems to pull you out of it and back into the flow of life?

- What triggers your despair? Is there anything you can do to stay on the course of productive grieving and not fall into the abyss?

- Are friends and family members slipping back into the habit of not mentioning your loss? Have they stopped saying your loved one's name? Do they change the subject whenever you bring your loved one up in conversation? What would you say to encourage them to be with you in your grief and not avoid it?

- What are some of the people or things that used to give meaning to your life, aside from your loved one? Make a list. Which might still give you a sense of purpose?

- What does your grief look like today?

CHAPTER TEN

Meaning and Purpose

Meaninglessness

Gail and I lost the two most important people in our lives. All of our hopes and dreams were about them and the life we were going to share together. Any thoughts I had about the future all revolved around them. Without Ruby and Hart in the world, that future now seemed pointless. Most days it felt like I was merely going through the motions of life but that I was not actually alive. Joan Didion captured this feeling so well in her memoir about the loss of her husband of thirty-nine years, *The Year of Magical Thinking*. She describes it as "the unending absence that follows, the void, the very opposite of meaning, the relentless succession of moments during which we will confront the experience of meaninglessness itself."

A central part of our journey through grief is our struggle to reconnect to a sense of meaning. To do so, we need to have faith that meaning is still even possible for us. Rabbi David Wolpe, in his book *Making Loss Matter*, cites as inspiration the dying words of the early nineteenth-century scholar Rabbi Nachman of Bratslav, "Don't despair! There is no such thing as despair at all." According to Wolpe, "Rabbi Nachman's teaching is the very foundation of faith, that for all the trials of the world, life can be made worthwhile if only we do not abandon the belief that life can be made worthwhile. We are prophets of our own destinies, that which we believe will be meaningful will be meaningful. When we despair, we empty the world of meaning for our lives."

Having that faith and trusting it enough to search for a purpose to our shattered lives is not easy. I don't think meaning and purpose just come to us. We can't find them by looking inward. We must go out into the world to find our purpose.

Viktor Frankl, the psychiatrist and Holocaust survivor, writes, "The true meaning of life is to be discovered in the world rather than within man or his own psyche . . . being human always points, and is directed, to something, or someone other than oneself—be it a meaning to fulfill or another human being to encounter." Frankl developed a theory of psychiatry, which he called logotherapy, based on the idea that the fundamental drive of human beings is not for sex or power, but for meaning. Interestingly enough, he developed this theory and was writing a book about it when he was arrested by the Nazis and sent to Theresienstadt, then Auschwitz and then Dachau. In the concentration camps, he saw his theory put to the test in the sense that the prisoners who were able to hold on to a sense of meaning and purpose were the ones who had a chance at survival. Those who tried to comfort themselves by repeatedly retreating into fantasies about the past, rather than focusing on a possible future, were the ones who died the quickest. Frankl writes in *Man's Search for Meaning*, "It is a peculiarity of man that he can only live by looking to the future."

Honoring Those We've Lost

Many mourners start their search for meaning by thinking of ways to honor their loved one. For example, my friend Marc's son Noah, a gifted young musician, was killed by a drunk driver. Marc has joined the national board of Mothers Against Drunk Driving to advocate against driving under the influence of drugs or alcohol. My friends James and Jen's son Luke was a brilliant cyberpunk jewelry and clothing designer. James and Jen now operate the Corrosive Complex Project, which sells jewelry and clothing inspired by Luke's designs and artwork. The young people who shop at the online store call Jen and James their "Fairy Goth Parents." All the money they raise is split between three nonprofits: a women's shelter called the Downtown Women's Center; End Overdose, a Los Angeles program that provides Narcan and other support for people struggling with addiction; and My Friend's Place, a shelter for unhoused youth.

Mourners often set up scholarships to memorialize the dead. As with the Hart Campbell Kindness Award, it's not about the amount of money involved, it's more about accurately reflecting the person who died. My friend Abraham set up a scholarship to support LGBTQ students at his alma mater, Boston University, in honor of Ruby and Hart. And Jen and James established a scholarship in Luke's name at the ArtCenter College of Design in Pasadena that "celebrates and supports the self-proclaimed: rebel, out of the box thinker, the misfit, the freak, the underdog, the uniquely multidisciplinary designer that has no boundaries or edges, and feels limited by thriving in just one discipline."

My friend Jesse created a Kindness Project in honor of her son Gidi. Every year in the weeks between the anniversary of his death and his birthday, "we ask people to do an act of random kindness during those weeks—and people have done unbelievable things. People have stood on street corners with coolers of cold water and handed them out on hot days, people donate books to libraries, they make goodie bags and deliver them to friends or teachers. We've had people who have paid a whole street's worth of meters—people get really creative. We have little cards they give out that say 'This act of kindness has been done in the memory of Gidi Zilberstein,' and it has a website on it and the people who get the card can check out the website if they choose to. And then we ask the people who have done the act of kindness to post about it on social media and it lights up our internet during those weeks when we are feeling exceptionally shitty and we get to see some really great things happening in the world because of Gidi. And oftentimes, and this is my favorite part of the project, we get alerted that somebody has posted on Facebook saying, 'I was the recipient of this act of kindness and I looked it up on the internet and I am going to pay it forward and I am going to start doing acts of kindness in Gidi's memory.' Those are the things that always mean the most to us, when we see that it's made an impact on someone who never knew him. So now there is someone else in the world who knows him. Nothing is going to take away the pain that we feel every day, but there is a remarkable sense of adding joy or relief or happiness or a sense that he is still alive somehow in the world to those moments of pain. So it doesn't take the pain away. I don't think it even softens the pain, but it allows there to be something sitting next to the pain that is, not in opposition to it, but that complements the pain. I think that is important. Because if we don't have the ability to complement the pain with another emotion, that pain can very easily overtake us." Jesse was inspired by Dr. Joanne Cacciatore, who wrote

Bearing the Unbearable and created the MISS Foundation, a nonprofit dedicated to supporting bereaved parents. Dr. Cacciatore's original Kindness Project was in honor of her daughter Cheyenne, who died in childbirth. It was so successful that word of it spread through the bereaved community, inspiring thousands of new Kindness Projects and generating millions of acts of kindness all over the world.

In honor of his mother, Sally, my friend Mike made a darkly comedic documentary film, *Don't Change the Subject*, about her suicide. Making the film allowed him to exorcise his demons and process his grief in a way that he didn't get to do as a child in mourning. The film gave him a chance to talk to his family more frankly than he had ever done before. And the film, by speaking so openly about the often taboo subject of suicide, has helped many people. Mike told me, "A lot of people have talked to me about how they were able to talk to their families for the first time after seeing the movie, how they called up their mom, or they called up their brother, and they talked about these things, they honored the people they lost. Dozens and dozens of people. I still get calls, people contact me even now, and the movie is just on Vimeo, it's not out there being publicized, but people still find the movie, because someone tells them or because some algorithm leads them there."

Being of Service

My friend Ruby said it so clearly: "Our sense of purpose always lies with other people. Human beings are meant to live in community. There has been a lot that capitalism has done to explicitly take that sense of community away from us. I think that's why a lot of people feel so lost a lot of the time. We don't know each other. We don't have other people to lean on. As a result, feeling isolated in grief has become very normal. But within the course of human evolution, grieving alone is not normal. We need stronger communities. We do actually need a lot of support during grief." Ruby devotes her time to working with environmental activists and is studying to become a nurse.

Many of us who have suffered a profound loss feel a desire to be of service to others. We want to help our community. We want our lives to matter. We want to help others in pain. My friend Steve talks often about how precious life is, and how important it is for him to be of service. "The greatest joy I get in life is to help others. Whether it was as a lifeguard, pulling people out of the ocean or performing CPR, or as a lawyer just helping people, especially people that can't afford representation. Donating blood, donating platelets, donating money. It's helping people. Complimenting them, sending them jokes. Helping a woman in the store last week who couldn't reach the broccoli on the top shelf. And then there was a woman on the beach the other day who couldn't get up a sand dune and I just grabbed her and pulled her up—little things like that help. It's those random acts of kindness that help me a lot."

My friend Eric has told his daughter's story many times, to Alcoholics Anonymous (AA) groups and other support groups and advocacy groups. "At USC, the heads of the School of Medicine were having a dinner with the surgeon general, and I was invited to speak. One of his agendas was the opiate epidemic. So he used Ellie's story to give an example of how normal everyday people are affected by it. And earlier in the day I went to a group of film executives, about two hundred showrunners, studio execs, and producers, and used Ellie as the example of why we need to destigmatize the disease of addiction. We need to see the epidemic as what it is—an epidemic and a disease. Being of service. It's changed my life. Losing Ellie has changed my life to one that is finally aware of being of service. I just didn't think about it before. I was distracted in my stupid Hollywood life and my little semicapitalist ambitions, and I just wasn't giving. So it's really changed my focus."

My friend Lisa finds meaning and purpose in her work. Working at the Center for Living and Learning, she teaches financial literacy to unhoused people and people who are coming out of drug treatment centers and moving into sober-living homes. "It's the perfect moment, when they're vulnerable enough to want to do something different. I start out by having them think about their values—what's important to them. And then we set some goals that are related to that. It really works. Then we go on and talk about other aspects of financial literacy—credit, budgeting, debt management. With Hunter, he would get a job while he was in the sober-living homes, but then start using again and get kicked out of the facility, so it became a spiral. I watched my son do it over and over and over. At the time, I couldn't do anything more than watch in horror. But now I can turn it into something and help other people. So that's a lot of how I work my grief out. What did I learn from this terrible experience? And how can I make it productive and help other people that are just like my son? I have grown to believe that having a values-based job, a job linked to my values, was going to give my life meaning."

Writing *Finding the Words*

As I went from grief group to grief group, I kept hearing similar stories of people in mourning feeling abandoned by their friends and families. They described not being able to talk about their loved one to anyone in their lives. Many of the grievers complained about not knowing how to even start to talk about their grief, so instead they never spoke about it at all. I saw a need in my new community, and I thought I could be of service. So I started writing about my grief in the hopes that my journey might be a source of help to others. This book gave me a sense of purpose. It kept me engaged in life and working toward a goal. It gave me a task and helped me process my loss. It was also nice to be able to insert a few Ruby and Hart stories. Thank you for taking the time to read a little about my beautiful children.

Finding Purpose Outside of Grief

Honoring our loved ones, translating our grief into art, helping others through their own grief—these are all wonderful actions that can give us a powerful sense of purpose. I think it can also be helpful to find a purpose that lies outside of grief. Our loss is a central part of our identity now, but it is not the limit of who we are. Even Viktor Frankl, who dedicated himself to helping others find meaning and purpose in their lives, also found other additional purposes in his own life. He lost his wife in the Holocaust, but he remarried and had a daughter and grandchildren. He learned to fly planes and he climbed mountains.

My friend Christopher began painting for the first time in his life. It has nothing to do with the son he lost; Charlie wasn't a painter. But it has opened Christopher up. As he shared, "On some level I feel like I'm connecting with Charlie by making art—I'm trying to capture some far-off spirit, some animating force that's just beyond what we see. But more than anything, it feels good to have something else to do besides feel terrible."

Gail told me, "Hart had to do this written interview for his Bar

Mitzvah pamphlet. And it asked, 'What's your life goal?' and he said, 'To make someone laugh every day.' And I feel like I want to do that. I wanted to do that before. But now I really want to do it in his honor. And when I write, even though I am a very sad and angry person, I write funny things. It's how I cope. I think writing sad things would drag me down. But writing funny things, life-affirming things, makes me feel good. So right now, I am making movies for children, and I am writing books for children. I had a test screening for a new film, and I heard a room full of two hundred children laughing, and it made me feel great. It made me feel like I was honoring Hart. I am writing a book right now that I hope parents will read to their children at bedtime. I hope it creates a space for parents and kids to be together at bedtime, laughing and snuggling. That was one of my favorite things with my mom, and it was one of my favorite things with Hart. I feel like giving that to other families has meaning and purpose."

My friend Lindsey finds meaning in the "really, really small things . . . being with the people you love and telling them you love them. A lot. Because people forget to say, 'You matter to me, you're important to me.'"

Love as Meaning

One morning at Auschwitz, Viktor Frankl had an epiphany. As he exited the camp on an early-morning work detail, he found a renewed sense of strength and purpose thinking about his wife and the love they had shared. "A thought transfixed me: for the first time in my life I saw the truth as it is set into songs by so many poets, proclaimed as the final wisdom by so many thinkers. The Truth—that love is the ultimate and the highest goal to which man can aspire. Then I grasped the meaning of the greatest secret that human poetry and human thought and belief have to impart: *The salvation of man is through love and in love.*"

We who have suffered a profound loss know the truth of Frankl's words. The fact that the death of our loved one is causing us such staggering pain is proof of the primacy of love. No other loss would affect us so deeply. What Frankl offers us is a path forward through grief. Our search for meaning begins with love.

Being Open to More Heartbreak and Loss

One of the scariest aspects of offering up our hearts to more love is that we are opening ourselves to the possibility of yet more loss. We now know that no one in this world is truly safe. Anyone can die. So how can we be such suckers that we would ever make ourselves vulnerable to feeling this loss *again*? It would be so much safer to protect ourselves by resolving to never love again. And yet that is no way to live.

My friend Lindsey shared the following fable:

> *There was once a woman who walked around all day, every day, in a raincoat and rain boots, holding an umbrella because she was convinced it was going to rain. Everyone in the town thought she was crazy. For weeks the sun shone and the whole town enjoyed the lovely weather while the woman was miserable and sweating in her rain gear. Then, one day it rained, and the woman shouted in triumph. "Aha! I told you it was fucking going to rain. And now look! I was right!" And her neighbor replied, "Yeah, congratulations, but you missed out on all the sunny days."*

As Lindsey points out, "There is a big cost to coming at life with the strategy that you are always prepared for the worst, as if by mentally assuming the worst you are somehow protecting yourself from the pain of loss. But it doesn't work. You can't minimize the pain of loss by being pessimistic. It's still going to hurt just as bad. But you will miss out on all the joys of life as a result."

It seems to me that the lesson my life with Ruby and Hart has given me is not that loving another person is a mistake, but rather the exact opposite: loving is the only choice that makes sense.

Parenting as a Purpose

About a week after the crash, I turned to Gail and said, "You know, we can foster-adopt. We can be parents again." I saw her face flood with relief. She was thinking the same thing but was scared that I might not want to go back down the path of parenting. The thought of being able to have children in our house again someday gave us a lifeline. It offered us a glimpse of a future with purpose.

In that moment, we were clearly not in any shape to be parenting new children. Our days and nights were consumed with grieving. At that point, we couldn't even feed ourselves—our community of supporters was bringing us nightly dinners. And my two sisters-in-law were taking turns staying with us to make sure we were okay. We were in two grief groups and both of us were seeing two therapists to help us get through our days.

Our initial desire for more children was intense and complicated. Perhaps, on a subconscious level, we were trying to somehow get Ruby and Hart back, or maybe we were hoping that new children would distract us from the agony of our loss. Either way, our desperation felt unhealthy. In dark moments, we would troll foster-adoption websites like AdoptUs.org and look at photos of children in need of parents. It was clear we were looking to these traumatized youth to rescue *us*.

And yet Gail and I had trouble visualizing a future without children. We realized that losing both our teenage children put us in a rare category of grief. Most parents who have lost a child have other living children. Or they lost a young child and are able to have more biological children. Or they lost an older, adult child who had already moved out of the house, and they were no longer actively parenting them.

Losing both our teenagers meant that our roles as active parents were cut short unnaturally. Our days were abruptly and unnaturally empty. We ached to parent. But we were too old to have more babies. Besides, we pined for teenagers, not infants.

One morning, I went for a jog in the park and passed an older couple on a walk. For all I know, they might have been blissfully happy, leading full lives brimming with meaning and purpose. But in that moment, they seemed to me as if they were in their own little irrelevant bubble, separate from and unseen by the swirl of life all around them. I was suddenly struck by the thought that this couple was like the Ghost of Grief Future. I had a dark vision of Gail and me as a desolate and disconnected old couple, pulling further and further away from everyone, sunk in our eternal sadness. I didn't want the next forty years to be a slow, sad drift away from life.

Raising Ruby and Hart had kept us feeling relevant. Thanks to them, we were up on the latest music and catchphrases and culture. I wanted to stay in the mix. I wanted to still be a parent and stay connected to the future. I knew that our immediate desperation for more kids might be unhealthy, but I was resolved to stick it out and find a way to get to a more grounded place. The idea of foster-adopting was actually first proposed to us by Ruby. When she was fifteen, she suggested that we foster-adopt because she thought our family was so awesome that we should spread the love. So we feel as though we have her blessing. And Hart's, too, since he usually approved of his big sister's choices.

I know that foster-adopting is a radical choice to make in the face of profound loss and is not something most grieving people are even considering. But many of the emotional hurdles that Gail and I faced on our journey toward foster-adopting are ones that all of us in mourning must confront. As we move back into life and begin to pursue a new sense of purpose, all of us will have to wrestle with some of the same issues that Gail and I struggled with as we contemplated becoming parents again. If you have lost a spouse, you may find yourself wanting to date again. If you have lost a sibling, you may find yourself looking for someone else to confide in and connect to in a similar way. If you lost a parent, you may find yourself reaching out to others for guidance, or you may find yourself stepping into a parental role for someone younger. If you lost your best friend, you may one day open up to a new intimacy with someone else. If we are truly entering back into life again, it means we are opening ourselves up to love again, and that is a very challenging process. I share some of the details of our foster-adoption journey in the hope that they might be relevant to your journey back into life.

Foster-Adoption

In California alone there are about sixty thousand youth in the foster care system. These children have been removed from their homes for any number of reasons and are living with foster parents. The majority of these kids will wind up being reunified with their families or taken in by a relative. But several thousand of these children will remain in foster care for the rest of their childhood, until they age out of the system and are sent into the world largely unprepared and unsupported. These children are in desperate need of adoption into loving homes.

A year after Ruby and Hart were killed, Gail and I discovered an organization in Los Angeles called Kidsave that allowed us to meet teenagers in the foster system whose permanency plan was no longer parental reunification but adoption. Kidsave organizes afternoon retreats where these teenagers get to play games with adults who are interested in possibly becoming adoptive parents. These retreats are opportunities for kids and adults to connect. At the end of the day response forms are handed out. The kids are asked to circle the names of any adults they enjoyed hanging out with, and the adults do the same for the kids. If kids and adults circle each other, then clearly there is a good match.

We connected with a thirteen-year-old girl. She was smart, funny, engaging, and eager to play. After each event, we circled her name and she circled ours—it was a match! We discovered how resilient, strong, and spirited she was. Like us, she got dealt a very hard hand from life, but she was determined to thrive. We found that we shared a wicked sense of humor and similar values. Not only was she extraordinarily perceptive and quick-witted, but she was incredibly emotionally intelligent. She was also fierce and had a finely tuned bullshit detector. She was not afraid to speak her mind. She was an impressive kid. Gail and I found ourselves falling in love with her.

She started spending weekends at our house, where we binge-watched the first three seasons of *Stranger Things*, played games, and slowly bonded with each other. Then, the day after Christmas 2020, she moved into our home and officially became our foster daughter.

As we brought this child into our home and our hearts, we encountered some specific questions that all of us face as we try to simultaneously live and mourn.

What to Do with All Their Stuff?

Every mourner is faced with some version of this quandary: what to do with all their things? After they were killed, Ruby and Hart's rooms stayed exactly as they were the night of the crash. We could lie in their beds and still smell them. I would occasionally pull an old T-shirt from their dirty laundry hamper and breathe deep and weep. It made their absence all the more surreal; it was as though they had just stepped outside and would be back at any moment.

But after a few months of not touching anything in their rooms, it felt like the spaces were in danger of becoming dusty mausoleums. It started to seem as if we were compartmentalizing our life with them and sealing it in their rooms for safekeeping. We decided that we didn't want to keep Ruby and Hart locked away in the past. We wanted to feel them with us as we moved forward in our lives. As Elisabeth Kübler-Ross and David Kessler write in *On Grief and Grieving*, "The ritual of dealing with a loved one's clothes and belongings facilitates the grieving process, partly by helping us to accept the reality of the loss."

Yet we kept dragging our heels, not feeling ready to touch Ruby and Hart's belongings. As we began the process of getting certified as potential foster parents, we realized that we would need to have empty bedrooms ready for any potential new kids. This meant that we had to take all of Ruby and Hart's things out of their rooms. We had to make space for whoever might be coming. This was the impetus we needed. We slowly began the difficult process of going through their rooms and designating what to put in storage, what to throw away, and what to keep. As Gail and I sorted their things, we set aside any clothes that might fit us, or objects that we might continue to use ourselves. We find that any time we can incorporate something of theirs into our day-to-day activities, it allows us to feel Ruby and Hart's presence in our lives. It gives me solace to wear Ruby's shirts and to sit at Hart's desk. My friend Irwin wears his son's bracelets and rings. "Somebody asked me the other night at dinner, why do I have two wedding rings? And I said, it's just part of Russell." Keepsakes can help us feel connected to those we've lost.

So even though it was terribly painful for Gail and me to empty all their drawers and sort through all their belongings, we trusted that seeing their bureaus being used by a future child would keep us closer to Ruby and Hart. We wanted them to have a younger brother or sister. We wanted to expand our family.

Once we met our foster daughter in person, we realized that it would be too upsetting to have her sleep in Ruby's old bed. We then realized that she might also be disturbed by the sight of the empty bed that belonged to her new dead brother. In the end, we took apart both Ruby and Hart's beds and put them away. It was brutal. I remembered so clearly putting those two beds together, bolt by bolt, in another, easier life. I remembered how full of promise for the future I felt back then. I remembered all my hopes and dreams for little Ruby and Hart. And now here I was, dismantling that life in order to prepare for a different one.

Bringing a foster daughter into our house meant leaning into the pain on a whole new level. Making breakfast for her, sitting at the dinner table together, giving her a hug goodnight—everything I did with her inevitably reminded me of Ruby and Hart's absence. Every act of parenting I performed brought my former life back into painful focus. How could I not be constantly thinking about, and aching for, Ruby and Hart? With a teenage girl in the house, sleeping in Ruby's old room, the pain was unavoidable.

But at the same time, it was so sweet and nourishing to have a teenager in the house again. It felt good to stretch my heart.

Are We Too Broken to Love Again (Live Again)?

Reengaging with life means that we are opening ourselves up to new heartbreak and even more emotional turmoil. How can we know if we'll ever be strong enough to withstand it? In some ways, my loss has made me tougher, and fiercer. But in other ways, I am much more fragile. Everyday life struggles can suddenly feel overwhelming. I don't have a lot of extra bandwidth to cope with additional emotional challenges. And on a day-to-day basis, I am just less productive. It feels like I pay a "grief tax": every day, a certain amount of time and energy gets drained away simply by being in grief.

So will Gail and I be able to balance both being in mourning and being foster parents? All children in foster care have suffered terrible trauma and loss, which understandably leaves them with emotional issues. They present challenges to any prospective caregiver. Will we have the strength and ability to be good parents even as we continue to grieve? Will we be able to make room for both? Will we be able to open our hearts to another child? Are we ready? Well . . . we definitely became foster parents before we were ready—because no one can be truly ready for something like this. At a certain point, you just have to go for it. Resolving to open my heart is aspirational. If I behave as though my heart is open, then eventually it will open. I want to love again, so I am *choosing* to love again. It's frightening, but I am not going to let fear get in the way of love. Or life.

How to Handle "the Question"

This past summer, my foster daughter and I hung out at a park with a mother and daughter from her new school. I was eager for my foster daughter to get to know some kids before the fall term. The mom asked me, "Do you have any other kids?" Normally, I would talk about Ruby and Hart, but in that moment, I didn't want to further burden my foster daughter's story with the story of my grief. I decided I would tell the mom about my other kids later, after my foster daughter was more settled in her new school community. But it is not easy for me to stay quiet about Ruby and Hart. Not talking about them can feel like an erasure.

For grieving parents, the simple question "Do you have kids?" can become so complicated and fraught. We don't necessarily want to get into the specifics of our loss every time a random stranger asks us a casual question. It's our right to respond in whatever way we want. Sometimes, I feel like giving a full disclosure: "I have three children, one living, and two, named Ruby and Hart, who were killed by a drunk driver." Sometimes, I just want to say "three" and leave it at that. Other times, I want to say "One." All three answers are true.

Grieving spouses are hit with the same problem when people ask if they are married. Grieving siblings have to wrestle with "Do you have any brothers or sisters?" Grieving children have to deal with "What do your parents do for a living?" In each instance, we get to decide what level of detail to respond with. There's no wrong answer.

Future Thinking

When we started down the path of foster-adoption, we didn't know with certainty that we would wind up bringing a child into our home. In fact, when we started the process, we were clearly not ready for it. We knew that we might at any moment change our minds and decide to not ever adopt. That uncertainty was okay. Becoming certified as foster parents and spending countless walks in the desert of Joshua Tree talking over our fears and hopes allowed us to future-think. Simply having a plan for the future—even one that we might discard later—helped to organize our lives. It gave us something to look forward to and a reason to live.

It also kept us in the flow of life. We realized that a large portion of the kids in foster care in the Los Angeles area were Hispanic. There was a strong possibility that we might foster-adopt Spanish-speaking children. Gail and I started taking Spanish lessons to be better prepared. We had no idea if we would ever actually foster children, let alone what language they would speak, but it didn't matter. Studying Spanish gave our lives a focus. It added to the structure of our weeks. Learning a new language kept our brains engaged and gave us another reason to get out of the house.

And it introduced us to the idea of having new experiences without Ruby and Hart. Taking Spanish lessons was the first real new thing we had done since the crash. Ruby and Hart knew nothing about this. Gail and I were having a new life experience that was wholly separate from our lives with Ruby and Hart. It was painful to be doing something without them, but the rest of our lives were going to be lived without them. It was something we were going to have to learn to accept. Taking Spanish lessons was an important early step in reorganizing our identities.

We were also learning about the foster system in Los Angeles. It opened our eyes to a whole other side of life that we were barely aware of. It helped to have something else to talk about besides our grief. It meant that there was more to us than just being grieving parents. On a very basic level it made our conversations more interesting.

I realize that foster-adopting is not a typical response to loss. It is certainly not something everyone in grief should do. But being able to envision a future, any future at all, can help us survive our loss. It's not easy. Even taking small steps toward a possible future can be painful. Taking Spanish lessons was emotionally challenging for us. We struggled over whether to tell our instructor about Ruby and Hart. In the end, we shared our story and bonded with our teacher. She shared her own losses with us, and we became friends. She is yet another source of support for us.

No Longer Lost at Sea?

At Ruby and Hart's funeral, our rabbi, Sharon, quoted a story from the Talmud, a collection of rabbinic discussions of Jewish law and theology. In the story, Rabbi Akiva is in a terrible shipwreck but survives. His friend asks, "What happened? Who brought you up from the water?" Rabbi Akiva says to him, "A plank from the ship floated by me, and I clung to it. Holding it tight, I bowed my head with each wave that came toward me, and let it pass over me knowing I'd once again be brought to the surface." Sharon then turned to us and said, "Gail and Colin, if you can, take a look around the room today. I know everything is shattered around you, but there are hundreds and hundreds of planks floating by you. Your family, your friends, your community. We are here for you to grab us and hold on. We promise you that we will do our best to help you catch your breath as each wave passes over you." I learned to appreciate those planks. I learned to cling to others in my time of need.

Early on in grief, I was struck by another boat analogy. I imagined that I had navigated my whole life aboard an ever-growing ship. I pictured my teenage self aboard a small lifeboat setting out from my parents' steamship. For a few years, I drifted in the wide-open ocean. Then I fell in love and married Gail, and my boat got bigger and started moving with direction and purpose. When Ruby and Hart were born, my ship got even bigger. As they grew older, my hopes and dreams for them expanded my boat even more. It gained speed and was charting a clear course through the waters. I had a future I could see for miles. It took me all the way into old age with loving children and grandchildren. I was moving swiftly toward a beautiful life aboard my now-enormous vessel.

After the car crash, that future was gone. I could no longer keep going toward it. I had no choice but to change direction. But a big boat doesn't turn so easily. It takes a lot of hard work to fight against all that forward momentum. And I didn't want to do that work. I didn't want to change direction. I desperately wanted to keep going forward in my old life. That is how it felt to me to be engaged in my grief work; I had to work very hard at something I desperately didn't want to do. And besides, I didn't even know the new direction I was supposed to point my boat toward.

But then suddenly it felt as though our foster daughter was on our boat with us. And we were headed somewhere new with her. It was not quite clear where we were going, but it felt like together the three of us were charting a new course. I had a reason to change direction. I had a reason to do the hard work of grieving. I could glimpse a future. It was still so hard to be turning away from that beautiful life with Ruby and Hart, but I had to. That future was gone forever. I couldn't get it back.

More Loss as the Journey Continues

Sadly, after living with us for eighteen months, our foster daughter decided she no longer wanted to be adopted into our family. She requested to move on to another foster home with the intention of eventually aging out of the system. She told her social workers that she didn't want to be part of a family at all. Her decision was hard for us and her social workers to understand. Ultimately, the love we offered her felt too uncomfortable. She couldn't tolerate feeling vulnerable and dependent. It was important for her identity to feel self-sufficient and remain emotionally apart from us. Our love asked too much of her. The intervention of therapists and social workers was all to no avail. The fierce compassion we worked so hard to cultivate was not something she could accept. Sometimes all our hard work will not always be fruitful or wanted.

Gail and I thought we were building a new family. It was heartbreaking to realize we were headed instead for yet another loss. But loss is a part of life. Just because we lost our children doesn't then make us karmically immune to future loss. All of us who have lost loved ones will encounter future losses as well. These losses compound our grief. At each new loss, we re-experience our prior losses. But that is no reason to avoid love and vulnerability. Love is inherently risky. We who have lost loved ones all know this to be true. Yet love is still worth the risk. Besides, now we are experienced in mourning. We know what we need to do. It's not so scary or confusing. The pain is familiar and navigable. It feels like we and our foster daughter have found a way to part on good terms with a very real intention of staying connected for the rest of our lives. The future is unknown, but right now it feels reasonable to assume our lives will remain entwined in some way or other. And that feels good.

Gail and I are going to take a break from fostering to lick our wounds. It hurts to be rejected and to feel like we failed. We need some time to recover. We might try again in the future. I would like to think we will. But we are not going to pressure ourselves. We'll wait and see. Fostering these past eighteen months certainly helped give our lives purpose and meaning. I don't regret opening my heart and home, despite the pain. The three of us had many wonderful adventures. We traveled to Hawaii, Maine, Cape Cod, Las Vegas, and San Francisco. We went to a baseball game, a soccer game, and a football game. We went to amusement parks and saw stand-up comedians. I gave her driving lessons in an empty parking lot. We helped with homework and watched many movies together. We hosted many sleepovers with her friends. We swam together in pools and lakes and the ocean. We took her out to the desert. We shared a lot of laughter. We also struggled together as Gail and I did the heavy lifting of parenting a teen with a lot of trauma. It was rewarding and also very challenging. We were in life, and life is messy. Now we must just keep going. No feeling is final.

Life Is Meaningful, Not Death

It is tempting to try to understand why someone "had to" die. Our brains always search for a way to make sense of the world, and to put the events of our lives into a coherent narrative. We all construct stories to explain our existence. For example, it can feel as though we were "fated" to fall in love with our spouse, or "destined" to accept that job. After all, everything that has happened to us has, in one way or another, led us to who we are today.

That same optimistic desire to make sense of the world runs into trouble when we try to explain why someone died, especially if they died young. Mourners can become desperate in their search for a silver lining. They might tell themselves that god needed their loved one to die for some mysterious reason. Or maybe their death influenced some wonderful act of charity, or inspired a moving piece of art, or provided an important philosophical insight.

I don't buy it. I think searching for meaning in death is more likely to feel fruitless and as a result only bring on more despair. I don't think you can ever find a satisfying "reason" that someone you loved had to die. In *Treating Traumatic Bereavement*, the editors cite a number of studies showing that most grievers fail to find meaning in their loved one's deaths even four to seven years after. "Moreover, among those who seek meaning, the inability to find it is a significant predictor of poor post-loss adjustment in the majority of these studies." In other words, many of those who do search for a cosmic reason behind their loved one's death just wind up feeling worse.

I say, don't even bother trying to answer the question "Why?" Skip it. I think it is much more fruitful to look to their lives for meaning. Ruby and Hart's *lives* mattered. They deeply affected hundreds of people. Their creativity, their spirits, their humor, their compassion and wisdom made an impact. If they had gotten to live full lives, they would have impacted even more people, but their lives were brutally cut short. So the world will just have to embrace what we got from them. Ruby and Hart's deaths were meaningless and senseless. But their lives continue to resonate and reverberate. Their lives had meaning. Their lives are worth celebrating.

I want to share a dream my friend Jen had recently. She dreamed she was chasing after her son Luke. She saw him run through a yard and then enter a house. She followed after him and came to a blockade of sorts—old cans, planks, debris. As she stepped over the blockade and entered the yard, an old woman waved to her from a window. As she approached the old woman's house, Jen saw a door opening onto a staircase that led down into the basement, and she knew Luke was down there. Suddenly a young woman with blue hair stopped her—it was my Ruby! And next to her was a younger boy—my Hart. Ruby told Jen not to go down into the basement. Ruby said, "That is not where Luke is. You can go down if you want to, but that's not him." Hart nodded in agreement. Jen didn't listen to them and instead went down the stairs into the basement, where she saw Luke dead, stretched out on an autopsy table. It was awful. Jen turned and went back outside. Ruby told her, "If you want to see Luke, you should go upstairs." Jen awoke with the feeling that Ruby had given her valuable advice. The fact is, the basement is always there for us if we feel the need to revisit the trauma of their demise, but there is no reason to dwell there. Jen is not going to find Luke in the terrible memories of his death. Take Ruby and Hart's advice and don't go down there. Spend your time upstairs, in the light of their lives.

My friend Mike offers similar advice. "Try to turn the story away from how they died and turn it back toward how they lived. That's the last line of my movie: 'It's not about how you die, it's about how you live.' What happens when people lose people to suicide is that they stop talking about them, and if they talk about anything, it's about the suicide. It's about the act of their death. And instead, what I'm saying is, let's not just fixate on the noose, or how purple their lips were, or on the whatever. That doesn't matter! Move past the act of death and remember the act of living. Please, please remember the sum total of all these people."

Seeing the World Feelingly

It feels to me as if those of us in grief are given a choice. We can either allow our pain to make us angry and bitter people who shut out the rest of the world, or we can allow the pain we feel to help us grow more compassionate toward others in need. Because we have opened our hearts to the pain of our loss, we can be more understanding of the pain of others. To quote Shakespeare's *King Lear*, we now "see the world feelingly." We have the opportunity to channel those feelings into action and do some good in the world, and honor our loved ones in the process. In *Bearing the Unbearable*, Dr. Joanne Cacciatore suggests that when we fully inhabit our grief, we are granted a form of "fierce compassion," an ability to extend kindheartedness to others who are in pain.

Growth in Grief

It is hard for me to talk about anything positive in connection with Ruby and Hart's deaths. I bristle whenever anyone suggests that there is some opportunity for personal growth or deeper understanding as a result of grieving. I don't want to be better for having lost my children. I find the idea repulsive.

And yet it is undeniable that growth can occur after any new experience, especially the most challenging ones. There are good things that have happened to me in the years since they were killed. I have grown as a person. I am stronger, wiser, fiercer, and more empathetic. I have a deeper understanding of what it means to love someone else. It helps to acknowledge and embrace the positive changes that now enrich me. With so much despondency in my life, I can use all the positivity I can get.

Moving Past Acute Grief and Back into Life

I initially resisted my new identity as a father of two dead children. I did not want it. I went to grief groups and desperately did not want to be there. I didn't want to be a part of "the dead kids club," as one mourning mother called it in a moment of dark humor. I looked at all the other people in mourning and thought I didn't belong. But then gradually I came to appreciate their company. I found solace in being a member of this group of struggling people. I slowly accepted my new identity, as a way of honoring Ruby and Hart. I was the father of two teenagers killed by a drunk driver. It felt like an act of defiance against drunk drivers everywhere.

But after more time passed, my identity started to shift again. My loss wasn't necessarily the most important part of who I was to other people. In the first year and a half after the crash, I told my students on the first day of each new semester that my children had been killed. I was in mourning, and I felt they needed to know. Or, more precisely, I needed to tell them. But after about eighteen months, I was no longer sure it was something I needed to share on the first day of class. I was no longer in acute pain, and maybe these students had their own troubles.

And that was heartbreaking as well. Suddenly I wanted to cling to my identity as the father of dead children. It seemed so important to me, and yet now I had other things going on in my life as well. The impossibility of Ruby and Hart's sudden violent deaths was no longer always the front-page news of my life. I found in my therapy sessions that I was talking more about my foster daughter than about Ruby and Hart and my grief. It feels like yet another brutal goodbye to Ruby and Hart. And yet another betrayal of them. It's not. It's simply what it means to be in life and not in denial. But it sure does hurt.

Part of the work of grieving is the difficult task of stretching our hearts, opening them up simultaneously to the pain of our loss and also to the joy of life. It is so hard to hold both at the same time. It requires a tremendous spirit. And creativity. It is ultimately a generative act to forge a path through life that allows us to bring our loss along with us. Loss tears at our hearts and initially makes them shrink in pain and fear. How can we ever love again, now that we know how terrible loss can be? And yet how can we not risk love again, now that its absence has taught us just how important and powerful love truly is? Our scarred hearts are actually capable of stretching wider than ever before.

A few weeks after the crash someone asked me, in an offhand and casually offensive way, "So do you have any wisdom about life now?" The obnoxious question went unanswered, but I have thought about it. And I think I do have some wisdom about life, because it is suddenly clear to me that at the end of the day, it's the people you call family that matter. Losing Ruby and Hart has shown me how precious—how essential—our bonds of love are. I didn't fully understand just how much of who I am is because of them. I think I know now that we don't really exist as separate individuals. We only exist as a part of the people we love, and who love us. So of course our loved ones are still here, with us. In us. I still share my life with Ruby and Hart.

Ultimately, I believe we do the hard work of grieving, we lean into the pain and banish the denial, in order to be able to hold the spirit of our loved ones close to us and bring them with us as we move forward through life. We hold them close, but not in a desperate clutch. Instead, we hold them *loosely*. They were never wholly ours to begin with. They always belonged to the universe. After all, part of being a parent is learning to let go. Had Ruby and Hart grown to adults, Gail and I would have had to learn to let them live their own lives. In a similar way, in death, I have to learn not to cling. So I strive to hold their spirits close, but loosely.

With open arms. With lightness. With joy.

Actions

- **Find ways of bringing your loved one's possessions back into the flow of life.** Incorporate their photos, clothes, and favorite possessions into your daily life. If they break or get worn out and have to be thrown away, that's okay. As Gail reminds me, "That shirt is not Ruby. That bed is not Hart." We can let go of their physical objects when it is time.

- **Find excuses to keep talking about your loved one.** Even though months or years have passed, and friends and family seem uncomfortable, find a way to bring up your loved one in conversation. Ask others for a memory. Tell a story. It always helps to talk about them. Always.

- **Create small, private rituals just for yourself.** They give you space in your day to accommodate your grief. They allow you to bring your loved one with you as you journey forward in life.

- **Actively search for a purpose and meaning to your life.** Try out different things. You don't have to find the meaning of life; you just have to pursue it. Let that pursuit carry you back into the flow of life. Have faith in life. Your actions have meaning if you believe they have meaning.

- **Be of service to others.** Use your fierce compassion to guide you to a life of meaning. How can you help others? How can you make an impact? Start small; we don't need to save the world in order to matter.

- **Do something new that has nothing to do with your grief or your loved one.** You are still growing as a person. Your grief is only a part of who you are. Allow yourself to discover a new interest, a new experience, a new path.

- **Find someone to love.** You have a lot of excess love coursing around inside you. Find a living person to share it with. Stretch your heart. The pain of loss has made your heart tighten, but somehow as a result it can now stretch even wider than it ever has before. So stretch it. Say yes to more love.

- **Make choices in your life that honor your loved one.** Make them proud. Take an emotional risk in their honor. Even small choices matter. Last year I got on a wild roller-coaster ride that terrified me. I did it for Ruby. It was a connection. And it made my foster daughter happy, too.

Journaling Prompts

- Before your loss, what were some things that gave your life a sense of purpose and meaning? Do any of those things still hold value for you? Can you return to any of those activities, but in a way that honors your loved one?

- What values or interests of your loved one inspire you the most? Is there something you could do that would support that value or interest? What might you do that would make your loved one proud?
- What gets you out of bed in the morning?
- What does Dr. Cacciatore's phrase "fierce compassion" mean to you? Do you ever feel fiercely compassionate in a way you never felt before your loss? Does it inspire you to action?
- What does "stretching your heart" mean to you?
- Has grief given you any newfound wisdom about life? What advice would you give to a young person just starting out in life? And are you able to take your own advice?
- What advice would you give to someone in early grief? If you were writing your own book about grief, what would be in it?
- What does your grief feel like today?

Living with Grief

I am so sorry for your loss. I truly am. I don't know exactly how you feel—no one else does—but I do know the agony of profound loss. I am down there, with you. Try to allow yourself to feel that pain and consider it love. With help from others, the pain can become bearable. Your heart may be broken, but it still works. In fact, it's stronger and more resilient than ever before. It may be hard to believe right now, but you will find that you can live alongside the pain. You have room for more love. And more life.

Time doesn't heal the pain. But time allows our hearts to expand so that there is space for more than just that pain. There is terrible aching, but over time we can also feel other things alongside that ache. The pain of grief is no longer the sum of who we are.

By continuing to live, you are not leaving your loved one behind. You are carrying them forward with you, in your heart forever. Every day that you are living as full a life as you can, you are honoring the one you lost.

Find the words to express your pain and loss.
Tell your grief to others, so that you are not alone.
Teach grief so that the world can be a kinder, more loving place.
Take care of the people in your life.
Be kind to yourself.

And when great souls die,
after a period peace blooms,
slowly and always
irregularly. Spaces fill
with a kind of
soothing electric vibration.
Our senses, restored, never
to be the same, whisper to us.
They existed. They existed.
We can be. Be and be
better. For they existed.

—Maya Angelou

APPENDIX A

Colin's Eulogy for Ruby and Hart Campbell, June 16, 2019

I want to talk to you about love. About the incredible love and generosity Ruby and Hart carried inside them and shared with everyone that was lucky enough to enter their world. And especially about the powerful love they felt for each other.

They had a special, mysterious, intuitive bond. I remember two years ago they played a guessing game with their aunt Betsy and cousin Raffi. They split up into two teams, Betsy and Raffi versus Ruby and Hart. The idea was each team would be told a category and they had to shout out the first word that came to their mind, and they would get a point if they shouted the same word simultaneously. Hart and Ruby had never played the game before, but Betsy and Raffi had played many times and were very good at it and eager to win. But Ruby and Hart destroyed them. They shouted out the same word almost every time. It was so extraordinary, I remember asking them—how did they do that?! And Ruby replied, "Oh, it was easy, instead of shouting the first word I thought of, I just shouted out the first word Hart would have thought of."

Sometimes, when I was helping Hart with his math homework, and I had to help him a lot, I would lose patience with him and he would shout, "What good is math anyway, I'll never use it, it's a waste of time," and that would push my buttons and I'd shout back, and then Ruby would calmly step up and tap me on the shoulder and say, "I got this, Dad," and she would shoo me out of the room and take over teaching Hart math, and she would do such a better job of it.

But then our Ruby entered a dark period in her life. She suffered terribly from depression and anxiety and OCD and suicidality. And when she was hospitalized and had to be away from home for two months, we were all devastated. Hart most of all. Ruby felt hopeless and lost interest in almost everything. To keep herself distracted from her pain she would obsessively read manga and watch anime shows, and she and Hart bonded over them. They would read *Death Note* together and watch *Attack on Titan* and *Voltron* and discuss *Hetalia* fan fiction and eagerly share anime memes. And they both excitedly went to Anime Expo together. It helped pull Ruby out of her depression and sparked her interest in art and animation. Which led to a whole new beautiful chapter in Ruby's life. We were so happy they were able to connect even in the darkest of times. But later, I asked Hart a question about an anime show and he confessed that he didn't actually like anime—he never really had. He just pretended so he could be close to Ruby and spend time with her. He was so smart.

Later, when Ruby emerged from her struggles—and she did emerge, she emerged magnificently—Hart developed a passion for hip-hop music and he desperately wanted to share his enthusiasm for the latest Lil Skies or Ski Mask the Slump God or Juice Wrld track that just dropped. But I would max out at three songs and tell him, "Dude, it's eight o'clock in the morning, this is too tough for me," but Ruby always wanted to hear them. They would each share an earbud on her headphones so they could listen together as they watched a rap video on Hart's phone, their little heads pressed together. But she didn't actually like hip-hop. She liked Queen and Billie Eilish and Madonna. She had zero rap songs on her playlist. But she never told him that. She pretended so she could be close to him.

The only music they both truly loved was the soundtrack to *Hamilton*, which they memorized and played nonstop for a full year, singing together at full volume during every single car ride.

And when Ruby discovered drawing and painting, he was her biggest fan. He loved every single thing she drew. He would greet every new drawing or watercolor or painting with "Oh my God, that's amazing, Ruby," and he'd mean it.

When Ruby came out and embraced her butch plaid-wearing lesbian bad-ass self, Hart became a fierce advocate and ally for the LGBTQ. He would call out his friends for using the F-word and he would call out the casual homophobia and heteronormative bias in movies and TV with incredible sophistication and understanding. And he was fiercely loyal to his haircutter as she transitioned from Seth to Gwen. Hart would casually comment to me, "Oh, did you notice Seth wore a skirt and sandals? Hey, did you see Seth had on a full dress today with earrings, oh just so you know, Dad, her name is Gwen now"—and Hart always, always got her pronoun right. Hair was very important to Hart and he went often to get it cut and shaped just right, short on the sides and back, but long on the top so it would poof to maximum effect. But if Gwen wasn't available that week, he'd wait for her. Unless it was an extreme hair emergency, because this is his hair we're talking about, after all.

I also want to talk about their love for their friends. And how they each found the perfect circle of people to share their lives with.

In Hart's journey to middle school, he had to leave behind his incredible close-knit gang of goofballs from the Hollywood Schoolhouse and go by himself to Campbell Hall. He was vulnerable and struggling and scared to be by himself, but then he found this wonderful strange group of kids who called themselves Mouse Screaming. And at first, he wasn't sure if he was a full-fledged member or just on the periphery—he's always been very sophisticated in his analysis of group dynamics. But then one day he realized he lived at the very heart of the group and that he was beloved by all of them, and by an even bigger circle of friends beyond Mouse Screaming at Campbell Hall. And that close circle of HSH friends never went away—he still regularly got together with them, too. Hart had too many friends.

Because of Ruby's struggles with depression she had to move from school to school to school, before she finally landed at Fusion Academy and truly flourished. And while it was hard to maintain friendships—she did. She arrived at each new place and found a small tight circle of her people: the artsy weirdos. From HSH to Marlboro to Pilgrim to Fusion and Pasadena City College and her adult OCD group, she slowly kept adding new circles of friends till she built herself a real community of love. She discovered herself and embraced who she was with brand-new confidence and power. And when her art professor at Pasadena City College assigned a life-size self-portrait for the final, Ruby painted herself as a woman in a

Renaissance outfit in men's breeches, holding a two-handed sword looking like the sly gay warrior she was.

In the end, both of my children found their true selves thanks to their beautiful friends. Gail and I are so grateful to all of you for loving our children.

I don't want to be up here talking to all of you, but I also don't want to leave. I want to tell you Ruby and Hart stories for hours. And I want to hear all of your Ruby and Hart stories even if they make me cry, because I'll cry, but that's okay because they are tears of love. But I'll tell you one last story in honor of Father's Day—because we've ruined it for you. A few months ago, I told Gail a silly story from when I was seven and my parents took me to a town in France called La Napoule. It's a beautiful old town on the rocky coast, but I hated it because when we got there I was so excited to swim in the pool. I assumed if they named the town after it, it must be the most amazing pool ever. And when my confused parents had to explain there was no pool I was too devastated to enjoy anything there. Gail later told the kids that story and apparently, they thought it was hilarious but they felt for "little me" and said, "Oh, poor Dad." But it inspired them. And for weeks they would whisper excitedly in the other room, as, together, they designed my special Father's Day gift—four hats with La Napoule Swim Club on them. We were so united in our love of imagination and ridiculousness that they made hats commemorating our fun summers spent swimming in a nonexistent pool. I love you, my sweet babies. I love you, and so many other people love you and will cherish the memories of your kind, sweet, funny, sly, clever, weird selves for as long as we live.

APPENDIX B

Gail's Eulogy for Ruby and Hart Campbell, June 16, 2019

My children died on Thursday. Both of them, in an instant. Ruby first, in the same hospital where Colin and I were also being examined. Hart, meanwhile, had been airlifted to a pediatric intensive care unit forty-five minutes away. Mercifully, the doctors went against their better judgment: they looked past our broken ribs and cracked sternums and they discharged us anyway, so we could rush to him, only to be told that his injuries, too, were unsurvivable. Like his sister, he'd never regained consciousness after the other car hit us. They were keeping him alive on a ventilator so we could kiss his forehead and hand, and then he was gone, too. And improbably, in that moment, a line from Shakespeare popped into my head.

As the character Macduff says in the play *Macbeth* when he discovers that his children have been murdered, he cries out not in sorrow but in disbelief. "What? All my pretty chickens, at one fell swoop?"

I've always been moved by that passage. Even long before I had children. In a play full of much more famous speeches, the pure astonishment he feels at the moment of seeing his children dead always jumped out at me. How could it be? All his pretty chickens? In one fell swoop? It was sad and elegant, and it made a fictional scene feel so real.

Now that fictional scene is my reality. Now it's my pretty chickens who've been taken from me in one fell swoop, by a wicked murderer who didn't use a knife but way too much liquor, and a speeding car in the dead of night.

For the past three horrible days, I've spent a lot of time imagining this moment we're in right now: trying to prepare myself for the day when we actually do this: we put my babies in the ground. And I've been reading the hundreds of beautiful emails that have been pouring into my inbox. I've been telling myself that seeing all of you here, your loving faces radiating support, would be a comfort. But I was afraid that it wouldn't be. And sure enough, my worry has come true. I look out at you all and feel envy. I envy you who have living children, who get to come home to kisses, watch way-too-long school plays, and mop up puke at impossibly early hours. And I envy you who have chosen not to have children. When you come back from a trip to Paris unfettered by children's bedtimes, and having eaten in charming cafés, instead of being dragooned into eating spaghetti every night at the only Italian restaurant in Paris because your nine-year-old saw a whole duck hanging in a window and became terrified of French food. This actually happened to us. After three nights of mediocre pasta, the impossibly chic waitress leaned in to me and whispered very gently, "Ah, you know zis ees not French food?" Now, without my pretty chickens I have no noses to wipe, and the beauty of traveling somewhere new and magnificent without children will always come with a searing reminder that Hart and Ruby aren't with us, clamoring for souvenirs and used books they'll never read.

But that's it, I guess. That's my life now. I know there will, at some point, be good moments to go alongside the bad, that I'll be able to listen to the stories of my friends whose children are the same age as mine would be without wanting to throw up, but I also know that I'll never imitate the excited waddle of the dachshund Hart and I once saw, because no one else on this earth would know what that meant or why it was so funny, or hear Ruby's soft call of "Mama" from behind her closed door, which was exquisite because it was so soft and sweet, a reminder of her toddlerhood, even though I knew she was calling to me because she wanted something but, because she was a teenager, was too lazy to get out of bed. I want those things again. And I want to go to my old world, where I didn't envy you all: I could just go back to loving and admiring and enjoying you, all your beautiful faces who have come here to hold me and Colin up while the ground keeps giving out. It's going to be tough being my friend for a while, while this avalanche of emotions is churning inside me. But please stick with me. I want to come back to that world. It'll never be the same again without my chickens, but you guys are my connection to that "before" time, and I'm realizing now that I was wrong. I don't just envy you. I also love you. And in this moment of inescapable darkness, I'm so glad you're here.

APPENDIX C

Speech to Campbell Hall High School Chapel, September 16, 2019

Hi, Campbell Hall. My name is Colin Campbell and I have the honor of being Hart Campbell's dad. Some of you, I am sure, have heard about the terrible tragedy that struck my family. This past June twelfth, our car was hit by a drunk driver. She was driving so fast that both Hart and his seventeen-year-old sister Ruby were killed on impact. I have a few thoughts I would like to share with all of you, as well as a wish. I think both will be of service to this community, Hart's beloved school.

First off, I want to address drunk driving, because it has not only shattered my family but, unbelievably, has struck a second Campbell Hall family this summer. Your community first lost Hart and now Noah Benardout, so I expect none of you to ever drive drunk or high for the rest of your lives. If this isn't a wake-up call, I don't know what is. But preventing drunk driving takes three challenging social skills. If you plan on driving, you have to say no to drugs and alcohol that night, period. Zero tolerance.

But even harder, you also have to say no when all your friends are piling into a car to go somewhere fun, and the driver has had a few drinks, or a few edibles, "but it's no big deal, come on, get in the car." You have to say no. I just met a woman, she lost her daughter and her granddaughter, and her daughter's two best friends, because they got into a car driven by a drunk driver. All four of them were killed, but the drunk driver survived. Which brings me to the most challenging social skill: taking the keys away from a friend who's drunk or high. Yeah, it's tough, but welcome to adulthood. You gotta do it. Not somebody else, you. You step up, and say hey, Hart told me to take your keys. Noah told me you can't drive tonight. Take an Uber. Leave the car and just take an Uber, it's a no-brainer. I promise your parents will approve. And everyone stays alive.

Secondly, I want to address grief. A lot of you are grieving, in the ninth grade and in the twelfth. And I, sadly, have become an expert on grief. I move forward in my life, knowing that not a day will ever go by, for as long as I live, that I won't be thinking about and grieving the loss of my beautiful children. My horrific loss has taught me many things about mourning—insights that I'd like to share with you.

First and foremost I've learned that grief is actually my friend. Because when I am grieving, I am closest to my kids. I am grieving because I love them so much. So even though it's painful to grieve, it's also a way to stay connected to them. Crying is nice.

I've also learned the importance of sharing—telling stories about Hart and Ruby, looking at their photos, sometimes talking to them. Or writing them letters. The important thing about grief is to not bottle it up, or try and push it away, or run from it, or numb it with alcohol or drugs because it feels too scary and overwhelming. I would advise all of you to not be afraid of grief. It might take you to the depths of despair and despondency; it might make you feel like you can't bear its weight. But by giving in to it, by allowing yourself to feel your grief, you will also allow it to pass through you. It will feel more like a companion alongside you, rather than a weight pushing down on top of you. You will emerge feeling stronger and with a bigger heart. Still grieving, but able to bear the unbearable. Also, don't forget, you can laugh. You can enjoy the memories too.

I would encourage those of you who knew and loved my precious boy to keep telling stories about him—his absurd antics, his silly characters, his acts of kindness, and his inappropriately crass comments. Because, even though it can be hard and painful, it feels good to remember him. His circle of friends have made sweet bracelets that honor Hart and Ruby, and also raise money for the Trevor Project—an amazing organization that fights teen suicide amongst LGBTQ youth, a very vulnerable group in America. They're cool bracelets, in Hart's favorite colors—red and black. These friends of his are so wonderfully sincere and genuine and kind.

And that makes me anxious.

Because there is a pervasive culture in American schools that looks down on sincerity, that labels kindness as weakness, that mocks people who share genuine emotions. There is a culture of bullying in American high schools today that has only grown more vicious with the advent of social media. In today's world, showing kindness puts a target on your back.

Even here, in the liberal bastion of LA private schools, a culture of casual homophobia, antisemitism, and racism has seeped in. I know this because, between Ruby and Hart, I've heard stories from six different school campuses. All their schools were on the surface kind, nurturing homes. But underneath each one there lurked an undercurrent of cruelty. A sort of black market in nastiness. At Campbell Hall, Hart witnessed students giving the Nazi salute and saying "Heil Hitler" for a laugh. He heard a classmate say that Hitler should have finished the job. A kid once confided to Hart that he was Jewish too, but didn't dare tell anyone, for fear of being picked on.

Now, my kids were smart. They knew these hateful comments weren't made by actual neo-Nazis. These obnoxious kids didn't know the first thing about the National Socialist German Workers' Party. No. These ignorant kids just thought they were being edgy and cool.

But the fact of the matter is, it's not cruelty, but kindness that is edgy. Any fool can say a racial slur or a homophobic comment. But it takes real guts, real courage to be kind. And Hart was kind. He was funny, and he was kind. Kindness mattered to him.

And he got really pissed off when these quote-unquote "cool kids" used the F-word. Which is not the F-word you're thinking. No, Hart loved to drop the F-bomb, left and right. No, I am referring to the homophobic slur F-A-G. His sister was gay and Hart was the fiercest champion of Ruby. He adored her—was constantly amazed at her artistic prowess, her brilliant insights, and her adventurous spirit. And she thought he was a comic genius. They were a sweet team. So different from one another, but so close and loving.

But Ruby struggled to come out to us. Which was very confusing to my wife and I. I mean, we were so obviously a pro-gay household. But Ruby confessed that it was hard, because she had internalized so many of the cruel slurs of classmates—nasty kids who called her a lesbian as if it were a pejorative term. Even before Ruby knew her own sexuality, kids would sneer at her and call her the F-word. So of course she internalized so much hatefulness. There is a price that is paid for that casual schoolyard homophobia. Some kid thinks it's edgy to be antisemitic, or racist, or sexist, or classist, and there are repercussions. A price is paid.

Hart knew why Ruby struggled and that's why homophobia pissed him off. I don't want to give you the impression that my boy was some sort of prude. Far from it. He loved jokes that Reverend Bull said I couldn't even describe today in chapel, they are so inappropriate. Hart even created a hilariously offensive gay character named Richard. But what made his Richard character so funny was not that he was gay, but that he was so over-the-top macho, so gleefully full of toxic masculinity. Richard wore army fatigues and spoke in a really deep voice about enjoying man-on-man porn, and how hugs and handshakes were for pussies, and how, of course, his husband was straight. The point is, Hart could be delightfully offensive, but at the same time, never put anyone else down for their sexuality. And that's why it's so beautiful that Hart's friends are raising money for the Trevor Project.

But I can see, next week, some of these sweet kids, sharing tearful memories of Hart and selling the commemorative bracelets, and some ignorant kid wandering by, and thinking to themselves—here's an opportunity to be edgy—make fun of the dead kid and his sad friends. 'Cause it sounds edgy, right? Maybe even better than a "Heil Hitler."

Of course, making a disparaging remark about a dead kid isn't edgy at all. I mean, they're dead, so they can't even fight back. It's totally lame.

So.

I have a hope for Campbell Hall. I hope that Hart, the memory of that special, sweet, funny Hart, can help lift Campbell Hall up from the American culture of schoolyard bullying and elevate it to a sanctuary of genuine caring and kindness. High school is hard enough as it is; why add to people's misery by being crappy to each other? Right?

Why not choose kindness? Kindness is edgy. It's bad-assed to be kind. And what better way to honor the memory of Hart than to engage in random acts of kindness?

Imagine how amazing it would be if there were a high school where no one got put down because of their sexuality, their race, their gender, their economic background. Where there were no stigmas attached to mental health! People struggling with depression or anxiety are met by kindness and compassion from their peers. What if word got out that Campbell Hall was bucking the national trend and had become a true sanctuary school? How cool would that be?! How edgy and bad-assed would that be?

You know, Hart's last name is Campbell. This school kinda belongs to him—at least that's how I look at it. This is Hart Campbell's Campbell Hall. And I hope that a culture of kindness and compassion and inane absurdist humor will be my son's legacy. And we're willing to pony up cash to make it happen. Hart loved making money and he would regularly swindle his aunt Betsy out of her hard-earned money on a crazy bet or dare. So in honor of Hart's deep abiding love of the cash monies, we, and his aunt Betsy, are going to establish a Kindness Award at Campbell Hall.

Here's how it's going to work. There will be a suggestion box on the high school court. And every time someone goes out of their way to do you an act of kindness, or if you witness an act of kindness, you are all encouraged to fill out a brief description: who did it, what they did, and who did they do it for; sign it, and drop it in the box. And no ballot stuffing, or Hart's ghost will hunt you down and haunt you. At the end of the year, the deans will go through the suggestion boxes and tally them all up and give the Hart Campbell Kindness Award to the most deserving high school student—which will come with a four-hundred-dollar check. Two hundred for your charity of choice, and another two hundred for you to pocket and squander as you see fit.

We believe Hart would approve. He really loved Campbell Hall. Aside from the homework and tests and chapel, of course—the boy was no saint, after all. And the reason he loved it here at Campbell Hall was because of all of you: students and staff and faculty. So thank you.

And thank you all for listening. I look forward to giving one of you a four-hundred-dollar check in May.

GRIEF RESOURCES

Alive Alone: A national nonprofit organization that offers compassionate support for families whose children are all deceased. www.alivealone.org

American Foundation for Suicide Prevention: In addition to working to prevent suicide, AFSP provides support for those who have lost someone to suicide, and it lists U.S. and international suicide bereavement support groups as a public service to loss survivors. https://afsp.org

City and County Grief Support Resources: If you do an internet search for your city and/or your county and "grief support services," a city or county government page should appear with a ".gov" suffix. This page will provide local Department of Mental Health resources, including local grief groups, support organizations, and grief resources.

The Compassionate Friends: A national nonprofit organization with more than five hundred local chapters in all fifty states. Provides grief support groups and online support for bereaved parents, siblings, and grandparents. www.compassionatefriends.org

Didi Hirsch Mental Health Services: An organization that offers suicide prevention services, mental health counseling, and substance use treatment. Outpatient and residential. Based in Southern California, but nationally recognized. https://didihirsch.org

Dougy Center: Provides grief support in a safe place where children, teens, young adults, and their families can share their experiences before and after a death. They offer support and training locally, nationally, and internationally to individuals and organizations seeking to assist children who are grieving. www.dougy.org

G.R.A.S.P. (Grief Recovery After a Substance Passing): Offers understanding, compassion, and support for those who have lost someone they love through addiction and overdose. A national organization with grief recovery meetings in more than one hundred locations in North America. www.grasphelp.org

Military One Source: An organization that provides financial benefits, long-term support networks, and free counseling options to surviving families of deceased service members. www.militaryonesource.mil/family-relationships/gold-star-surviving-family

MISS Foundation: An international organization that provides support for family members who are experiencing the loss of a child. It trains Compassionate Bereavement Care® providers who are located all over the world, creating a network of support specialists. They offer online support groups as well as face-to-face support groups. They also run a Traumatic Grief Care Farm (Selah Carefarm) near Sedona, Arizona. www.missfoundation.org

Modern Loss: A website that includes essays about all kinds of loss. Offers candid conversation and community on the long arc of loss and resilience. Beginners welcome. www.modernloss.com

Mothers Against Drunk Driving (MADD): The national nonprofit organization offers Victim Assistance and Victim Advocates, as well as grief groups for victims and survivors of drunk driving crashes. www.madd.org

The National Suicide Prevention Lifeline: 800-273-8255
People who are deaf or hard of hearing can text the letters "HEARME" to 839863.

Our House: A Los Angeles–based nonprofit organization that provides grief support services, education, resources, and hope. They offer adult, teen, and children grief support groups, as well as resources. www.our house-grief.org

Parents of Murdered Children: A national organization that offers local grief group meetings, as well as resources and support to parents whose children have been murdered. https//pomc.org

Survivors of Homicide: This nonprofit organization offers free counseling, support groups, and advocacy. Based in Connecticut, but open to anyone. www.survivorsofhomicide.com

T.A.P.S. (Tragedy Assistance Program for Survivors): A nonprofit organization that offers compassionate care to all those grieving the death of a military loved one. TAPS provides a survivor helpline (800-959-8277), grief counseling, casework, suicide loss support, and educational assistance. www.taps.org

Warmlines: Similar to hotlines, they provide people with someone to talk to BEFORE they are in crisis. A warmline is a peer-run listening line staffed by people in mental health recovery themselves. There are warmlines in almost every state. For a directory of warmlines, visit: www.warm line.org

ACKNOWLEDGMENTS

I owe a tremendous debt of gratitude to all the friends and family who helped Gail and me through our time of greatest pain and loneliness: our Ikar community, all the people who showed up at morning minyan service week after week, our rabbis, all of Hart and Ruby's friends and families from the Hollywood Schoolhouse, Campbell Hall, Marlborough, Pilgrim School, and Fusion Academy, the people who brought dinners as part of our Meal Train, my Friday-night poker buddies, my Monday-evening Dungeons & Dragons crew, our loving neighbors, the Compassionate Friends, our Our House cohort, our loving and supportive families—in particular my sisters-in-law, Nina and Betsy, who moved in with us to help with the earliest, scariest days and who continue to be there for us every day. Together, all these people were the planks that kept us aloft as we foundered in the sea of our grief. Thank you all for being there for us, even though it was hard and scary.

Thank you to Christopher, Geoff, John, Lisa, Betsy, Nina, Cathy, Raffaella, Freddie, Max, and Cori for being the best uncles, aunts, and cousins to Ruby and Hart. Thank you to Joan, Malcolm, Roz, and Howard for being wonderful, loving grandparents. Ruby and Hart adored you all.

Thank you to Sharon Brous for guiding Gail and me through the Jewish path of mourning and for being there with us, fearlessly holding our hands through each of the most excruciating steps of our journey. I also want to thank you for being my consultant and sounding board on all things Jewish in the book. And for being a dear friend.

Thank you to Dr. Jonathan Grayson for helping Ruby through her OCD and depression, and for helping Gail and me in those early dark days. Thank you to Dr. Asher Keren-Zvi for helping me navigate the complex feelings of grief. You both helped shape my understanding of loss and gave me tools and words with which to examine my own complicated emotions.

An extra thank-you to my sister-in-law, Betsy Lerner, for all of your exceptional literary wisdom and guidance. You were invaluable in helping me shape my initial misguided effort into a coherent book proposal, and then offered such incredibly helpful and detailed feedback on subsequent drafts. From the title to final lines of the book, you were instrumental in shaping all of it. Thank you for being there for me in grief and in writing.

Other early and invaluable readers include my brother-in-law John Donatich, who gave crucial big-picture advice; my friend Christopher Noxon, who challenged me to be more nuanced; my agent, Amy Hughes, who guided me through the whole process with tremendous care and compassion; and my editor, Sara Carder, who took a chance on a first-time writer and brought my book into the world with such love and kindness. I am forever grateful.

I want to express my deep gratitude and appreciation to the many mourners who shared their stories and wisdom with me and permitted me to include their words in my book. It meant so much to me that you were willing to talk about your grief and loss with such openheartedness and generosity: Gretchen Boudreau, James Dutcher, Ruby Dutcher, Robert Getman, Stuart Gibbs, Irwin Grossman, Sharon Grossman, Lisa Laajala, Shirley Marquez, Jennifer Meraz, James Meraz, Christopher Noxon, Steve Richman, Eric Robertson, Lindsey Shockley, and Mike Stutz.

I also want to honor those they have lost—beautiful people who tragically left this earth too soon: Dana Boudreau, Carolyn Wendt Dutcher, David Getman, Suzanne Patmore Gibbs, Russell Grossman, Hunter

Morgan Hertel, Jonhairo Contreras, Luke Gabriel Meraz, Charles Noxon, Linda Richman, Michael Richman, Rebecca Richman, Ellie Robertson, Casey Shockley, and Sally Stutz. May the memories of your beautiful lives bring light, joy, and kindness into the world.

I want to thank my fierce and magnificent wife, Gail Lerner. Thank you for being my life partner, in darkness as well as joy. Thank you for being the best mother to our children and the best wife I could ever hope for. I am so sorry we are on this terrible journey, but I can't imagine going on it without you at my side. Thank you for helping me write this book every step of the way. All the ideas in here were hashed out together with you on our long walks in the desert, and for that I am so grateful. Thank you for allowing me to publicly share our intimate path through grief. Thank you for sharing your beautiful, open heart with me.

Finally, my deepest gratitude goes to my brilliant, inspiring, joyful, loving, and kind children, Ruby Arden Campbell and Hart Madison Campbell. Thank you for sharing your sweet short lives with me. I think about you and miss you and ache for you both every day. I love you beyond measure. But not beyond words. I will try my best to keep finding the words to express my love for you two precious sweethearts.

ABOUT THE AUTHOR

Colin Campbell is a writer and director for theater and film. He was nominated for an Academy Award for *Seraglio*, a short film he wrote and directed with his lovely and talented wife, Gail Lerner. He has taught theater and/or filmmaking at Chapman University, Loyola Marymount University, Cal Poly Pomona University, and to incarcerated youth through The Unusual Suspects. Campbell is currently developing a one-person show titled *Grief: A One Man Shit-Show*. He lives in Los Angeles and sometimes Joshua Tree.